Journeying

BOOKS BY CLAUDIO MAGRIS

IN ENGLISH TRANSLATION

Journeying
Blameless
Blindly
Danube
A Different Sea
Inferences from a Sabre
Microcosms
Voices

Journeying

L'infinito viaggiare

CLAUDIO MAGRIS

TRANSLATED FROM THE ITALIAN

BY ANNE MILANO APPEL

YALE UNIVERSITY PRESS ■ NEW HAVEN & LONDON

A MARGELLOS
WORLD REPUBLIC OF LETTERS BOOK

English translation copyright © 2018 by Anne Milano Appel.
Originally published as *L'infinito viaggiare.* © 2005 Arnoldo Mondadori Editore S.p.A., Milano.

Set in Electra and Nobel types by Tseng Information Systems.
Printed in the United States of America.

Library of Congress Control Number: 2017952564
ISBN 978-0-300-21851-0 (hardcover : alk. paper)

A catalogue record for this book is available from the British Library.

This paper meets the requirements of ANSI/NISO Z39.48-1992 (Permanence of Paper).

10 9 8 7 6 5 4 3 2 1

To Marisa and the companions of my journey
whom I have loved, and who have already arrived

CONTENTS

Preface 3

In Don Quixote's Footsteps 24

Marionettes in Madrid 31

The Bibliophage 36

At the "Mentitoio" 37

A Father, a Son 40

Spoon River in Cantabria 42

Don Serafin's First Flight 47

In London, at School 53

The Fortunate Isles 60

The Prussian Road to Peace 67

The Old Prussia Puts On a Show 71

The Wall 77

On Lotte's Tomb 82

In Freiburg the Day of German Unity Is Remote 83

The Dying Forest 87

Ludwig's Castles in the Air 93

Among the Sorbs of Lusatia 105

The Anonymous Viennese 116

Schoenberg's Table 121

The Rabbi's Dance 127

Musical Automatons in Zagreb   133

Istrian Spring   139

Cici and *Ciribiri*   145

In Bisiacaria   153

A Fateful Hyphen   163

On the Charles Bridge   169

The Country Without a Name   176

The Tragedy and the Nightmare   182

Poland Turns the Page   187

On Raskolnikov's Landing   193

The Birch Whistle   198

A Hippopotamus in Lund   201

The Woodland Cemetery   206

The Fjord   210

Parish of the North   214

Water and Desert   220

Is China Near?   236

The Borders of Vietnam   245

The Great South   254

Note   261

Translator's Notes   263

JOURNEYING

PREFACE

1. Prefaces are always dubious; useless if the book they are introducing doesn't require one, or a sign of the book's inadequacy if it does need one, they are also likely to spoil the reading—somewhat like explaining a joke or revealing the punchline. Even so, a prologue is perhaps appropriate to a collection of travel writings, since travel—in the world and on the page—is in itself a continuous preamble, a prelude to something that is always still to come and always just around the corner: the departure, the stops, the return, packing and unpacking the suitcases, recording in a notebook the landscape which takes flight as you move through it, which disintegrates and is then recomposed like a film sequence with its fade-ins and fade-outs—or like a face that changes over time.

A preface is kind of a suitcase, a kitbag, and it's part of the journey: at the start, when you put in the few predictably indispensable things, always forgetting something essential; along the way, as you collect whatever you want to bring home; upon your return, when you open the bag and can't find the things that had seemed most important, while objects you don't even remember putting in jump out at you. The same thing happens with writing: something that seemed fundamental as you were going through it and experiencing it has vanished, it's no longer there on paper, whereas something that you had barely noticed in life—during the journey of life—assumes a commanding form and stands out as essential.

The journey always starts over again, it always has to start over again, like life, and every annotation is a prologue; if the passage through the world is transformed into writing, it is prolonged as it moves from reality to paper—making notes, revising them, partially deleting them, rewriting them, shifting them around, varying their arrangement. A montage of words and images, captured from a train window or when walking down a street and turning the corner. Only with death, Karl Rahner, the great theologian on the path to spiritual evolution, reminds us, does our *status viatoris*, our existential condition as a traveler, cease. Travel therefore has to do with death, as Charles Baudelaire or Carlo Emilio Gadda well knew, but it is also a deferral of death: a way of putting off the arrival, the encounter with the essential, as long as possible, just as a preface postpones the actual reading, the moment of the final assessment and verdict. Traveling not to arrive but for the sake of traveling, to arrive as late as possible, possibly never to arrive.

2. The journey therefore as persuasion. Perhaps it is primarily in my travels that I came to know "persuasion," in the sense given to this word by Carlo Michelstaedter: the quest for that self-sufficient life, free and fulfilled, which Enrico, the protagonist in my novel *Un altro mare* (A Different Sea), pursues with self-destructive, futile tenacity. Persuasion: the possession of one's life here and now, the ability to experience the moment, every moment, not just the privileged, exceptional ones, without sacrificing it to the future, without annihilating it in projects and plans, without considering it simply a moment to pass over quickly in order to move on to something else. Almost always in life there are too many reasons to hope for time to pass as quickly as possible, for the present to promptly become the future, for tomorrow to come soon, because we are eagerly awaiting the doctor's response, the start of a vacation, the completion of a book, the result of some action or initiative, and so we live not to live but to have already lived, to move closer to death, to die.

Pressing, hectic travel, more and more frantically imposed by work necessarily transformed into a spectacle—especially on the intellectual, that manager of himself and of the Spirit, an exaggerated caricature of the corporate manager—is the negation of "persuasion," of pausing, of wandering; rather it more closely resembles the premature ejaculation that Joseph Roth, repeating a rumor about Napoleon in his novel *The Hundred Days*, attributes to the *empereur*, who doesn't so much want to make love as to have already done it, hastily getting it over with. A lecturer's travels, between one airport or hotel and another, is not dissimilar to this beleaguered orgasm.

But when I journeyed through the countless towns of the Danube or its surrounding microcosms, setting out in a certain direction, always open to impulsive digressions, stops, and detours, I lived "persuaded," as at sea; I lived immersed in the present, in that suspension of time that occurs when you abandon yourself to its gentle current and to whatever life brings—like an open bottle under water, filled with the flow of things, Goethe said, traveling in Italy.[1] On that kind of journey, places become both waystations and abodes along life's path, momentary stops and roots that allow us to feel at home in the world. There is the voyage beyond the Pillars of Hercules and lesser journeys like Pickwick's to the source of the Hampstead Ponds[2]—or the one from room to room in your home, no less adventurous an expedition or less abounding in delights and perils. The seafaring captains of Fiume[3] and Trieste who crossed the oceans mockingly called those who only traveled short distances between Trieste and Istria or between Fiume and the nearby islands of the Quarnero *capitan de cadin*, captain of the washbowl, though even in that gulf the bora causes storms that lead to shipwreck.

In the chapters of this book we will go to the antipodes, as well as to the microcosms of Bisiach or the nanocosms of Ciceria, and the traveler's tempo hopes to resemble the pace of Laurence Sterne. Traveling while at the same time constantly feeling both unfamiliar and at home, though aware of not having a home, of not owning one. The traveler is always a vagabond, a foreigner, a guest; he sleeps in rooms that will lodge strangers before and after him, he does not own the pillow on which he rests his head or the roof that shelters him. And so he understands that you can never really own a house, a niche carved out in the infinite universe, but merely stop there for a night or for a lifetime, respectfully and gratefully. There is good reason why a journey is primarily a return and teaches us to dwell more unreservedly, more poetically in our own home. Man dwells on this earth poetically, a verse by Hölderlin reads, but only if he knows, as he says in another poem, that the potential for salvation lies where there is danger.[4]

Traveling, a stranger among strangers, one compellingly learns to be Nobody, one realizes distinctly that one is Nobody. It is that which — in a much-loved place that has almost physically become a part of or an extension of ourselves — allows us to say, echoing Don Quixote, here I know who I am.[5]

3. "Where are you headed?" is the question in Novalis's great novel *Henry of Ofterdingen*. "Back home as always" is the reply.[6] Novalis's work is one of the illustrious books in which the journey appears as an odyssey or metaphor for the journey through life. Every odyssey poses a question regarding the prospect of traveling through the world, gaining solid experience, and thereby shaping one's character; the question of whether Odysseus — especially the modern one — ultimately returns home with his identity confirmed, having discovered or verified a meaning in life, despite the most tragic and absurd adventures, or whether he merely realizes the impossibility of shaping that identity, whether he loses himself and the meaning of his life along the way, splintering rather than coalescing over the course of his journey.

In the classical version of the subject, Odysseus, though lost in the dizzying whirl of things, ends up finding himself by facing up to this turmoil; making his way through the world — traveling around the world — he discovers his own truth, a truth that at first is only potential and latent in him, which he transforms into reality by confronting the world. Novalis's hero travels through distances in space and time, but in order to return home, to find himself through the journey; in *The Principle of Hope*, Ernst Bloch says that *Heimat*, homeland, the birthplace that everyone nostalgically believes lies in childhood, is instead found at the end of the journey.[7] The journey is circular; a person leaves home, travels the world and returns home, though to a home quite different from the one from which the traveler set out; thanks to the departure, to the separation, it has acquired significance. Odysseus returns to Ithaca, but Ithaca would not be what it is if he had not left it to go to the Trojan War, if he had not broken his visceral, immediate bonds with it, to later be able to rediscover it with greater authenticity.

The *Bildungsroman*, a novel of development that addresses a central issue of modernity, that is, whether or not and how an individual can realize his own identity within the increasingly complex and "prosaic" workings of society, is almost always—from Goethe's *Wilhelm Meister* to Novalis's *Henry of Ofterdingen*—a novel of peregrination as well, of a journey. Soon enough something in the relationship between the individual and the totality that surrounds him cracks; in the machinery of modern society, the journey also becomes an escape, a violent severing of limits and ties. The journey uncovers the precarious nature not only of the world but also of the traveler, the lability of the individual "I," whose identity and unity begin to break up—as Nietzsche discerns with brutal clarity—and who becomes a different man, "ultra man"; this in accordance with the most authentic meaning of the term *Übermensch*, which does not signify a superman, a normal individual more gifted than others, but a new anthropological stage, beyond classic individuality.

At that point the journey becomes an avenue of no return, leading to the discovery that there is no, can be no, and must be no return. In place of the circular, traditional, classic, Oedipean conventional journey of Joyce, whose Ulysses returns home, we have the linear, Nietzschean journey of Robert Musil's characters, a journey that moves in an ever forward direction, toward an infinite evil, like a straight line lurching into space. *Itaca e oltre* (Ithaca and Beyond), as the title of a book of mine reads: the two existential, transcendental modes of travel. In the second kind, the subject, the "I," the traveler, pushes himself eternally forward; he does not bring himself, all of himself, with him as he proceeds, but destroys his previous identity and discards himself each time. *Lâchez tout*, leave everything, set out on the roads, André Breton wrote in 1922 urging *dépaysement*.[8]

The "I" in the pages that follow sometimes, indeed frequently, walks on the brink of this dissolution, watching the traces of his life vanish behind him, but he's a guerrilla fighter who tries to resist the fragmentation and bring his whole life with him—loyal to it all, in spite of everything—like a turtle moving along carrying its house on its back. Losing himself in the world and abandoning himself to the world, the subject disintegrates, but ultimately also recognizes and finds himself again, as the Borges parable that I chose as the epigraph for *Microcosms* tells us: "A man determines upon the task of portraying the world. As the years pass, he peoples a space with pictures of provinces, kingdoms, mountains, bays, ships, islands, fishes, dwellings, instruments, stars, horses and people. Shortly before he dies, he discovers that the patient labyrinth of lines traces the image of his own face."[9]

4. There is no journey without crossing borders—political, linguistic, social, cultural, psychological, even the invisible lines that separate neighborhoods in the same city, the barriers between people, the twists and turns that in our inner recesses obstruct our own way. Going beyond borders, being fond of them even—since they define a particular reality, an individuality, and give it form, thereby saving it from indistinction—but not idolizing them, not making them into idols that demand blood sacrifices. Knowing that they are flexible, temporary, and perishable, like the human body, and therefore worthy of being loved; mortal in the sense of being subject to death,

like travelers, not a motive and cause for death, as they have been and many times are.

Traveling entails not only crossing to the other side of the border but also discovering that one is always on the other side as well. In *Verde acqua*, Marisa Madieri, retracing the story of the Italians' exodus from Fiume after the Second World War at the time of the Slavic revolt that forced them to leave, discovers her family's partially Slavic origins just at the moment when she is oppressed by the Slavs for being Italian—that is, she discovers that she is part of the world she feels threatened by, which is, to some extent at least, also her own.

When I was a child and went walking on the Karst, in Trieste, the border that I saw, very close by, was insuperable—at least, until the split between Tito and Stalin and the normalization of relations between Italy and Yugoslavia—because it was the Iron Curtain, dividing the world in two. Beyond that border lay both the unknown and the known. The unknown because it was there that the inaccessible, unfamiliar, threatening domain of Stalin began, the world of the East, so often exotic, feared and scorned. The known because those lands annexed by Yugoslavia at the end of the war had belonged to Italy; I had been there many times, they were a part of my life. The same world was both mysterious and familiar; when I went back there initially, it was a journey into the known and the unknown at the same time. Every journey involves a similar experience, more or less: someone or something that seemed close and well known proves to be foreign and indecipherable, or an individual, a landscape, a culture that we considered different and alien is shown to be kindred and related. To the people on one shore the inhabitants on the opposite shore often seem barbaric, dangerous, and full of prejudice against those who live on the other side. But if we begin to go back and forth across a bridge, mingling with the people going over it and crossing from one shore to the other until we no longer know which side or which country we're in, we will again find goodwill toward us and pleasure in the world. "Where is the border?" José Saramago asks the fish on the boundary between Spain and Portugal who in the same river swim now in the Duero, now in the Douro, depending on whether they dart near one bank or the other.[10]

5. The call of the known or the unknown? Don Quixote's quest is meant to be a discovery, verification, and reaffirmation of what is known, of the truth read in books about chivalry, of the immutable codes of love and loyalty, of Dulcinea's beauty and the giants' strength. The Ashkenazi Jews of eastern Europe, too, leave the ghetto or the shtetl, their wretched but familiar village regulated by the Book, to venture out to the West and enter History, thinking they will find a world governed by the Tablets of the Law; indeed they interpret everything, even the most disconcerting things, events most antithetical to their vision, according to the parameters of the Law.

But "Once you leave you're out in the open; it rains and snows. It snows history," as Yakov Bok, the luckless handyman in search of fortune in Bernard Malamud's *The Fixer*, says.[11] Don Quixote of La Mancha and the Jew from the East come face to face with the unknown, with the violence, brutality, and vulgarity of a world unfamiliar to them, though they try not to admit it; yet their loyal attachment to a known order is the very thing that causes them to experience the disorder of the world in which they venture more acutely. The traveler is an anarchistic conservative; a conservative who discovers chaos in the world because he measures the world with an absolute standard that exposes its frailty, transience, ambiguity, and paltriness. As Kafka was well aware, without a profound sense of the law you cannot experience its vertiginous absence in life. When Don Quixote comes out of the cave of Montesinos and recounts all the wondrous, magical things he's seen, Sancho objects, saying he thinks his master has been fed a bunch of "rigmarole." To which the Don replies, "All that might be."[12]

Utopia and disillusionment. Many things are lost when travel-

ing: certainties, values, feelings, expectations fallen by the wayside—
the road is harsh, but it's also a good teacher. Other things, other
values and feelings are encountered, gathered along the way. Like
traveling, writing also involves disassembling, rearranging, putting
back together; one moves through reality as in a theater of prose, shifting the curtains, opening new passages, getting lost in blind alleys and
blocked by fake doors painted on the wall.

Reality, so often impenetrable, suddenly gives way, crumbles;
the traveler, Cees Noteboom says, feels "the draft blowing through
the cracks in the structure of causality."[13] What's real proves to be
probabilistic, indeterministic, subject to sudden quantum break-
downs which cause some of its elements to vanish, swallowed up,
sucked into spatiotemporal vortices, whirlpools of the mortality of all
things but also of the unforeseeable emergence of new life.

Traveling is a Musilian experience, committed to the sense of
possibility rather than to the reality principle.[14] One discovers, as in
an archaeological dig, different strata of reality, concrete possibilities
which were not materially realized but which existed and survived
as shards forgotten in the rush of time, in deposits even now within
reach, in still fluctuating states. Traveling entails coming to terms
with reality but also with its alternatives, its gaps; with History and
with a different history or other histories precluded and deterred by
it, but not entirely stamped out.

Since the *Odyssey*, travel and literature have appeared closely
related: an analogous exploration, deconstruction, and recognition
of the world and of the "I." Writing continues the relocation, it packs
and unpacks, rearranges things, shifts plenums and voids, discovers—
invents? finds?—elements that escaped the list, and even the perception of what's real, almost as though putting them under a magnifying
glass. My *Danube* traveler also speaks of tears in the stage curtain of
everyday living, through which he hopes at least a breath or gust of
real life, concealed behind the backdrop of reality, will find its way
in.[15] The transcendency of all travel, though it founders in the flesh,

in the dust, in the immediacy of time running out which, to a greater or lesser degree, always upsets one's expectations. Just think about the arrogant assurance of "No surprises" given years ago by *Der Spiegel* when its best-seller column promised to feature only books that everyone was expected to be talking about.

Live, travel, write. Perhaps the most authentic narrative today is one which recounts not through pure invention and fiction, but through a direct description of facts, of things, of those insane, staggering transformations which, as Ryszard Kapuściński says, prevent us from grasping the world in its entirety and summing it up, allowing only fragments to be snatched, like a reporter in the heat of battle. He himself, moreover, creates a very lively literature by plunging into reality, depicting it with rigorous precision, seizing like a hunting dog its most fleeting, revealing details, and assembling it all in a picture that is faithful and at the same time reinvented: a portrait of the world and of a journey through the world. Perhaps journey is the expression par excellence for the type of literature, the "nonfiction" novel, exemplified by Truman Capote.

6. Traveling in space is a journey both through time and against time. The layered, condensed complexity of a place sometimes emerges violently, like seeds splitting the shell. We are condensed time, Marisa Madieri once said. A place, as well as an individual, is condensed time, plural time. Not only its present but also the labyrinth of diverse times and eras are interwoven to constitute a landscape; similarly, creases and wrinkles, expressions etched by joy or sorrow not only mark a face but *are* the face of a person whose age or state of mind is never of that one moment, but is rather a composite of all the ages and states of mind of his lifetime. Landscape as face, humankind in the landscape like a wave in the sea; landscape — as in Andrea Zanzotto's poetry — is a layering of geography and history. More than just nature and architecture, gulfs, woods, and houses, grassy or rocky paths, it is also and primarily communities, people,

actions, customs, prejudices, passions, foods, flags, faiths. The forest of the modern wayfarer is the city, with its deserts and its oases, its chorality and its solitude, its skyscrapers or suburban motels, its streets laid out in a straight line, stretching toward infinity. The observer with eyes and senses open is perhaps the most authentic traveler; his gaze penetrates and dismantles the urban scene like an insurrection, as Luca Doninelli does to a sacral and convulsed Milan in his powerful *Il crollo delle aspettative*, the collapse of expectations. Landscape is transition; it is also an approach, like a style of writing. Everyone travels through a place at his own tempo. Some swiftly, some idly. A city—a page—can be navigated in a thousand ways: attentively, slowly, syncopatedly, hastily, offhandedly, synthetically, analytically, distractedly.

The writing-journey is an archaeology of landscape; like an archaeologist, the traveler—the writer—moves down through the various layers of reality, reading signs concealed beneath other signs, gathering as many lives and stories as possible and rescuing them from the river of time, from the annihilating surge of oblivion, as though building a flimsy Noah's Ark of paper, all the while ironically aware of its precariousness. Landscape is also a cemetery, an ossuary that has become fertilizer and nourishment, the burial mounds that in Verdun seem like hills, though created by bombs and dead bodies.

Moving back and forth in space, not following fixed routes, and relying on detours rather than on a straight line, for a brief moment the traveler is able to suspend time, holding it in check for a while, like a juggler tossing his balls in the air and keeping them poised for a split second, even knowing that, sooner or later, they will all fall on his head.

7. Traveling is immoral, the Viennese philosopher Otto Weininger said as he traveled.[16] It's heartless, says Elias Canetti.[17] The vanity of escape is immoral, well known to Horace, who cautioned not to try to evade suffering and sorrow by spurring on one's horse since dark

Care, his poem says, sits astride the horse right behind the rider who hopes to elude it.[18] The strong Self, according to Weininger, soon cut short by cohabitation with the Absolute, must stay home and confront anguish and despair rather than attempt to be distracted or diverted from it, and should not turn away from reality and struggle; metaphysics is resident, it does not seek evasions or holidays. Perhaps at times the "I" who stays home is a semblance of the traveler, a simulacrum similar to that of Helen which, according to one version of the myth, followed Paris to Troy while the real Helen remained elsewhere, in Egypt, throughout the long years of the war.

Weininger denounced the temptation of irresponsibility in travel; the traveler is a spectator, he is not deeply involved in the reality he passes through, he is not guilty of the abominations, of the infamies and atrocities of the country he visits. He did not make those iniquitous laws and has no need to reproach himself for not having opposed them. If the roof were to collapse one night and he were fortunate enough not to be buried under the rubble, all he'd have to do is pick up his suitcase and move on a little farther. Traveling makes you feel relaxed because, aside from some disaster, an earthquake or a plane crash, nothing can really touch you; you're not putting your life on the line.

Traveling is also benign tedium, protective irrelevance. The most perilous, demanding, seductive ventures take place at home; that's where your life is played out, the ability or inability to love and to create, to know and bestow happiness, to grow courageously or shrink in fear; it's there that you're at risk. The home is not an idyll; it is the scene of concrete existence and therefore exposed to conflict, to misunderstanding, to error, to oppression and aridity, to failure. For this reason it is life's essential space, with its good and its bad; the setting for the most intense, at times devastating passion—toward the companion of one's days, toward the children—and passion's grip is remorseless. Traveling around the world makes it possible to enjoy a respite from domestic intensity, to unwind in pleasant, easy-going comfort, to let oneself go along passively—immorally, according to Weininger—with the flow of things.

There is another immorality in traveling: a closed mind toward the diversity of the world. The Mitteleuropean traveler is easily an Odysseus in a dressing gown, as Giorgio Bergamini wrote, one who prefers to navigate between an armchair and a library, on the oceanic blue of an atlas page rather than on the ocean's waves; a man for whom infinity is only the mathematical sign for it.[19] A person who travels on paper becomes imperceptibly unaccustomed to life, charting his passions on a line graph of life, on the statistical curves of its phenomena; he becomes a man without qualities for whom, as Musil writes, canned vegetables become the true essence of fresh vegetables.[20]

Even as he travels through the world, the traveler retains a tendency to button up his overcoat and turn up his collar, as if erecting a defense between himself and other things. Fortunately Danubian travelers also love the sea, and perhaps, like those in my *Danube*, they cross the great plains of Mitteleuropa under heavy skies mainly to reach the sea. It is on the shores of the "untried" sea, as Camoes called it, that one encounters the broad breath of life, which leads to momentous questions concerning destiny and the meaning of good and evil; the sea brings you face to face with ambiguity, it invites you to challenge it—on the immortal sea, Conrad writes, one attains forgiveness for one's sinful soul.[21] At the sea you disrobe, you strip off your stifling defenses and open yourself up to what lies ahead. This is another form of deliverance for the traveler, who on the city's pavements or in the mountains feels as though he's on the shaky deck of a ship tossed about by surging waves, a precarious if salvific ark.

The heartlessness of travel, Canetti warns: the traveler observes the world with curiosity and is somewhat inclined to accept what he sees, even evil and injustice, to note and be aware of them rather than oppose and reject them. Travel to totalitarian countries, for example, is always a bit guilty, implying a complicity with or at least neutrality toward the atrocities and infamies concealed behind the Potemkin villages that offer lodging.[22] Yet little by little, the traveler discovers — can't help but discover — the world's brotherhood and common destiny, and is made to feel that the entire world is his home; this feeling alone is what authenticates his love for the home he left behind, a love which otherwise would be blind devotion, appalling and regressive.

As in the case of Joseph von Eichendorff's good-for-nothing vagabond,[23] a love of wandering and a love of hearth and home coincide, because in that home one also loves the vast unknown world, while in the world, even in its most diverse forms, one glimpses the familiarity of the hearth. Dante said that he had learned to love Florence by drinking the water of the Arno but that man's country is the world, just as for fish it is the sea — each of the two waters, on its own, is insufficient and tainted.[24] Traveling teaches disorientation, the feeling of forever being a stranger in life, even in one's own country, though being a stranger among strangers is perhaps the only way to be truly brothers. For this reason the destination of the journey is people; you don't go to Spain or to Germany but rather among the Spaniards or among the Germans. "Read travel literature," Kant told a theologian, though he never set foot out of Königsberg.[25]

8. Sometimes places speak, sometimes they're silent, they have their epiphanies and their inscrutabilities. Like all encounters, those with places — and with the people who live there — are also adventurous, full of promises and risks. Some places, Venice or Prague, speak to even the most distracted, unaware traveler by the very fact of their appearance and the life that unfolds there. Others rely on an indirect eloquence, seducing only visitors who know what occurred amid those trees or in those streets: the room where Kafka died, in Kierling, speaks volumes, but only to those who know that Kafka lived his final hours within those walls and who view even the cracks on the walls in that light. Other places close up in opaque secrecy and the encounter fails; like any venture, a journey too is open to defeat

and sterility. This occurs when the traveler—out of ignorance, pride, apathy—cannot find the key to enter that world: the vocabulary and grammar needed to understand the language and decipher the culture. The status viatoris that religious thought attributes to human beings also implies a certain fragility: the alternation between the glory and the fall, the capacity for salvation along with the risk of failure and guilt.

There are places that enchant us because they seem radically different, and others that fascinate us because at first sight they seem familiar, almost like our motherland. Getting to know something is often, platonically, recognition; it is the appearance of something which until that moment was perhaps unknown yet is accepted as our own. To see a place one must see it again. The known and the familiar, continually rediscovered and enriched, are the premise of the encounter, of the seduction and adventure; the twentieth or hundredth time you talk to a friend or make love with the one you love is infinitely more intense than the first. This applies to places as well; the most spellbinding journey is a return, an odyssey, and the places along the customary route, the everyday microcosms navigated for so many years, are an Odyssean challenge. "Why are you riding through these lands?" the standard-bearer asks the marquis who is traveling beside him in Rilke's well-known ballad. "So I can return," the other replies.[26]

9. The reflections in the preceding passage are meager consolation. I can understand why some places remained silent for me through my own fault, closure, or aridity, and why I therefore, obviously, did not write about them. But what about the ones which fascinated and excited me, in which I recognized myself and which I thoroughly, albeit briefly, experienced—why didn't they ever make it onto the page, what shortcoming on my part obstructed their way? The Algonquin forest, Canada—with its incredible colors, the red autumn leaves that suddenly, in the rainy grayness, made you think the sun had reappeared—was an intense day of my life, as were the surround-

ing areas of Vancouver, where the search for traces of Emily Pauline Johnson—known as Tekahionwake, the Mohawk princess who portrayed her people, writing in English—coincided with a fundamental turning point in my life: my first trip with J. and the beginning of my journey through life with her. In Ushuaia, in Tierra del Fuego, I experienced a strong sense of the end of the world, which I nonetheless described only at the mouth of the Derwent at Hobart Town, in Tasmania; just as the unforgettable sensation experienced in the Borgesian barrio of Palermo,[27] in Buenos Aires, remained without a trace, along with an awareness of my own insignificance and banality one night in the same city, faced with a manifestation of poverty and suffering that I could not answer to. The groans and fractures of 1988 Moscow, whose details—seemingly insignificant yet revelatory of the imminent collapse—my sons Francesco and Paolo grasped much more readily than I, caught me unprepared to decode and sort out.

Leafing through these pages, I am especially struck by the absence of the United States, which I visited often in recent years and to which I travel more and more frequently, based on increasingly solid associations related to friendship and work, teaching and literary appearances. New York primarily, but also San Francisco, Chicago, Princeton, Bloomington, Bard College, and many other places that are, some more, some less, at the center of the world. In this case, it was perhaps an excess of accountability that stopped my pen, an insurmountable ambivalence toward the nation on which, for better or worse, the fate of the world depends, hence the feeling of not being able to talk about it. In any case, this disparity between living and writing is always sad, even for one who assumes writing as his own poetics; another example of how traveling can instruct one in humble self-irony.

10. Drawing on the distinction made by the great Argentine writer Ernesto Sábato, these travel accounts are probably more representative of diurnal than nocturnal writing. In the diurnal mode,

the author, whether depicting a reality external to him or creating a fiction, in some way expresses a sense of the world that he personally shares; he articulates his own feelings and his values; he fights the "good fight," as Saint Paul said, for the things he believes in and against those he considers evil. Diurnal writing attempts to understand the world, to explain its phenomena, to view individual destinies, even pitiful ones, against the backdrop of the whole of reality and its meaning. It is writing that strives to make sense of things; to place each and every experience, no matter how painful, in a totality that encompasses it and that, because it does, is able to frame it in a broader context.

The other type of writing, nocturnal writing, confronts the most unsettling truths that one would not dare admit openly, that one is perhaps not even conscious of, or that the author actually—as Sábato says—rejects and finds "loathsome and despicable." It is writing that often astounds the author himself because it can reveal what he doesn't always know he is and feels: emotions or epiphanies that escape the dictates of conscience and sometimes exceed what conscience would permit, contradicting the author's intentions and principles, and plunging him into a dark world. A world very different from the one he loves and in which he would prefer to act and live, but one in which it is necessary to descend every now and then to confront the Medusa head with its writhing snakes, at a moment when he is unable to make her more presentable. It is writing that, without his having planned it, finds itself head to head with the horrific face of a life barbarously unaware of moral values, of good and evil, of justice and compassion; writing that is at times an alienating, creative encounter with one's double, or at least with an unknown part of oneself, who speaks in another voice, whom the author must allow to speak even when he would rather that voice said other things and when he feels his moral convictions "betrayed," to cite Sábato again, by what it says.

In these pages dépaysement, prevalent in my other books, is held in check, contained or eluded by a diurnal, perhaps defensive approach. But the journey itself always introduces a nocturnal component into writing, snapshots of the unexpected and sometimes troubling faces of reality that disturb the traveler's moral hierarchies, epiphanies of the negative. Whether one gives in or not, it's tempting to let oneself go . . .

11. The journeys assembled in this book were completed—experienced and written—between 1981 and 2004. Many pages are therefore a number of years old and show it, as well they should; for that matter a face should also show its age, treated well if possible, with some damage legitimately mitigated, though not to mislead. Replacing a tooth which has been extracted is one thing, a facelift with Dorian Gray–like ambitions is pathetic. The meaning of our life lies in its journey in time, in history; the flourishing but also the ripening and withering of what the Bible calls "the flesh."

A page too has its age, and derives meaning from it as well; writing before the Second World War is not the same thing as writing that came after it. Not even the pages of great literature, which transcend their age for centuries and millennia, can erase their years; they show their date of birth, although thanks to their greatness they go on showing it forever.

Travel writing, as such, is particularly imbued with temporality; its pages are woven through with caducity since they are the account and depiction of a particular moment, a reality that has quickly fled. Unlike other books I've written describing my travel experiences while transforming them, such as *Microcosms* or *Danube*, this volume is composed of pages related to the time the trip took place, when I crossed a border or a country that perhaps no longer exists, when I glimpsed a gesture or an expression on a face, heard a cry. In *Danube* and *Microcosms* the journey, the people and things I saw, the stories gathered along the way are re-created and retold; they become the story of a character, largely fictional. They are no longer a part of the journey; they're in a different dimension, a different time,

moments fused and composed, a literary time which does not corre-
spond to that of verb tense or even that of History.

The time of the pages that follow, by contrast, is unequivocally
that of the moment in which they were experienced and written. The
course of subsequent events has at times confirmed and at times dis-
proven their impressions, hopes, judgments, and predictions. From
one chapter to another, radical changes took place, momentous and
personal. There are journeys made before and after the fall of communism. There are journeys through the world which, for me, are
viewed primarily through the eyes of Marisa, and journeys through
a world so profoundly changed, for me, which were more difficult
to appreciate, after her death. Journeys made with friends—Alberto
Cavallari, Stefano Jacomuzzi, Paolo Bozzi—who taught me to see
the way, to observe things, and journeys made after they departed,
leaving me so much more alone along the world's byways; journeys
made with J., with whom I ventured out on those roads again. If this
book is able to capture some likeness of the world, I owe it to the
people I've loved, my sons first of all, who traveled its roads with me
and taught me—teach me—to see it.

Like the journey itself, its journal also travels through time.
Some chapters about Berlin were written at the time when the Wall
existed and might have seemed destined to last a long time, others
after its collapse; some pieces speak of the Soviet Union in the present
tense or record signs or groans of its collapse; others remain doubtful over some uncertainty that has meanwhile been resolved—for
example, the pages depicting the atmosphere in Prague in the days
when one wondered what the name of the country would be: the
Czechoslovakian Republic, Czecho-Slovakia, or Czech and Slovak.
A country which shortly thereafter resolved the problem by ceasing
to exist, or, rather, by splitting into two different states.

As I see it, this is precisely the contribution that travel writing can
make to an understanding of History, that is, of our lives, individual
and collective. History does not consist only of what has occurred,

much less of absurd, far-fetched alternatives, but also of possibilities, as Musil would say, of the potentiality that is markedly latent in a particular situation, of what, at any given moment, was or is possible. The hopes of a generation in a specific historical period are part of the history of that time, and they too have therefore contributed to making us who we are, even if the course of events later overlooked them or proved them wrong. That hyphen that could have or should have (or should not have, according to some) united Czechs and Slovaks by differentiating them, and differentiated them by uniting them, no longer exists, at least for now, but the moment when it symbolized a possible goal is a real moment in European history.

Similarly the pages written on the eve of, during the course of, or immediately following the dissolution of the Communist world can enable us to understand, not so much the views and hopes of the traveler, which count for little, but the complexity of the situation experienced at that moment in time, the range of all the forces then in play, even those which soon turned out to be—at least temporarily—the losing parties. To experience and see firsthand what was considered possible or what was hoped for in a given situation—an outcome different from what later developed—helps us more fully comprehend what happened, which can only be understood if one does not assume that it was necessarily the only outcome possible from the beginning. Some chapters, for example, focus on the menacing nationalisms and micronationalisms that flared up during those years when they were still in an uncertain state of turmoil, when it was not yet inevitable that they would explode in such disastrous proportions. For better or worse, life and history have marched on beyond these pages; to cite one example: following our meeting with Karlo Stajner, an old man by then—whose imprisonment in Stalin's gulag is recounted along with his indomitable fidelity to his ideals and his incredible humanity—he went on to endure the oppression of the Tudjman regime and other struggles of existence until the final days of his long life.

The traveler remains constant even to opportunities he has missed or lost; he does not correct the past or himself with hindsight but tries to bring as many things forward—perceptions, circumstances, assumptions, plans—into a future which is just as precarious as the past and destined to soon be overtaken. The journey is an occurrence in the indicative, but also in the subjunctive. Each journey clearly has its tempo, its rhythm, its pace, and its lulls. Some slower, more relaxed wanderings open the way to a multiple, epic time, which also encompasses the past, and—like the chapters about the Cici or about the Bisiachi, or the initial Don Quixotian journey—approach the orchestration of *Microcosms*. Other chapters instead plunge headlong into the brief breath of an instant, into the flash of an experience that is immediately resolved or dissolved in itself. At times these pages are also a quarry of materials, experiences, and epiphanies that will later be reworked and metabolized in narrative texts. Certain motifs, episodes, and figures, sometimes even the initial intuition or central, seminal idea for a book—for *Danube, A Different Sea, Microcosms, Il Conde*—have their source in a preliminary inspiration recorded in these pages, in a revelation, a providential spark that flared up almost by chance and was noted in the travel diary.

Literature, as we said, is in some way like relocating. Curiously, the places in this journal are a little different, at least in part, from those that make up the primary landscape of my other books, those not about travel; here Spain and Scandinavia in effect prevail over Mitteleuropa. On occasion it's as if the traveler had reemerged from the black hole of his own persona and was almost surprised at the direction in which his steps have led him, revealing beloved homelands of the heart that he himself was previously unaware of. "Le voyage," as a crazy Parisian said, "pour connaître ma géographie," a journey to discover my geography.[28]

June 30, 2005

IN DON QUIXOTE'S FOOTSTEPS

1. Tielmes, almost at the gates of Madrid, is not yet in La Mancha and is not, strictly speaking, part of the "Ruta de Don Quijote," the route of the Knight of the Sorrowful Countenance. Our group of friends journeying idly in his footsteps starts out from this little town partly because one of the greatest authorities and scholars of the ingenious hidalgo and his travels lives here: Manuel Fernández Nieto.[1] His library is a Cervantian universe, though his seventeenth-century cellar, with its huge earthenware amphorae and fine, damp, musty smell, is no less alluring. Years ago a mummified dog was found in this basement. A cellar, a no less regal tomb than a pyramid, as befits *Don Quixote*, the book in which the sublime and the absurd, the sacred and the bawdy, belief in man and mockery of him, faith and chaos coexist like two sides of a coin. This is one reason why Dostoyevsky thought that Cervantes's book on its own would be enough to justify mankind's odyssey in the eyes of God.[2] He was right, because the smelly sheep's-milk cheese running down the face of the heroic, scorned, ridiculous Don Quixote resembles the blood and sweat of Christ.

Tielmes is lively, displaying the vitality that characterizes Spain, a country which in recent years has perhaps been renewed and transformed more than any other, with incredible creativity. In the midst of this poised energy, a closed, seedy-looking bar stands out by contrast, and like an allegory in baroque theater, it bears a sign that reads "Bar Moderno." Today the Modern, with its faith in progress and in the possibility of directing the course of history, seems like a dusty old museum piece. We act and live in a postmodern Middle Ages, global and sophisticated, which technologically transforms the world at a staggering pace yet does not feel it can give it meaning. Don Quixote, a knight-errant who thinks he's from olden times, is the Modern hero par excellence; his quest is to conquer the world but primarily to substantiate its significance, to find a staunch value that transcends it. Today modernity seems as rusty as his weapons and the roll-down shutter of this bar, but at times the rust shines like an enchanted sword, sparking reflections of El Dorados, flashes of poetry and meaning.

2. It is not at all certain that the indeterminate place in La Mancha from which Don Quixote started out is, as tradition has it, Argamasilla de Alba. Perhaps the departure point should remain uncertain, like the direction in which the hidalgo set off, not choosing a route but letting his noble, scruffy horse Rocinante pick one at random. The plain of La Mancha—flat, virtually unchanging beneath a gossamer sky, the horizon its only real boundary—is a fitting landscape for letting life take you where it will, since like the desert it seems to offer endless avenues of possibility.

A stroll also eludes the precise control of a plan and purpose, because you cannot know if and for what you will deviate from the intended path at the first intersection you come to. All the fundamental things—love, joy, pain—happen by chance or by grace, once you drop the reins and let life carry you along, like a walking stick in the hands of a wayfarer. If unexpected gifts follow as a result of encountering whatever happens, we gladly give ourselves up to life, trusting in its magnanimity and ready to believe that it can provide what we need better than we can. Yet for some, life brings nothing at all, or merely the disgrace of misfortune, which can only be countered—as a great passage in Antonio Muñoz Molina's novel *Beatus Ille* reads—by sad irony.[3] When that happens you begin to fear the foolish unpredictability of life; the horror and dismay that grip the heart cause you to clutch Rocinante's reins more firmly, to direct the way with maniacal precision, to keep life in your grasp to the point of crushing it if it doesn't behave, not taking a step without consulting detailed maps, drawn to protect against the chaos of things that inspires such fear. You then wander through the corridors of Kafka rather than the plains of Cervantes.

Don Quixote is not afraid; he exposes himself to the uncertainty of life, which brings him adversities, beatings, dirty tricks, and humiliations. He has no faith in life, which doesn't know what it's doing, but relies on books instead, which tell not about life but about what gives it meaning, its insignia. He fights for these insignia and is nearly always ridiculously beaten because good nearly always loses and evil wins. But he never doubts those insignia, not even when he's unhorsed. Argamasilla is the home of bachelor-at-arms Samson Carrasco, the aspiring knight who unseats him, but Don Quixote unsaddled asserts that his weakness does not compromise the truth of what he believes in.

3. The plain of La Mancha, an open expanse, a good externality of the world. The truth does not reside *in interiore homine*, in man, in the stifling autarchy of interiority, but rather in measuring it against other people, against things, colors, smells, events, foods, physiological functions, the sweat and calluses of hands. Don Quixote without Sancho Panza — even grander than he — would be a mannequin, and his books of chivalry, without those cheeses, sausages, and manure, would be worthy of being discarded. Something which remains solely internal easily sours, turns cloudy and spoils; it becomes a failing or delirium; even passion can get mired in the heart's sludge or be distorted into sterile daydreams unless it's shared with others, an open affair. Solitary interiority easily misplaces the notion of good and evil, as in dreams, where you can do anything without feeling guilty. Interiority must be turned inside out like a glove, reversed to interact with the world, just as Don Quixote's chivalrous ideals mingle with the promiscuity of reality, thereby becoming even loftier. It is only

because Don Quixote thinks he sees Mambrino's helmet in a prosaic barber's basin that the legendary helmet acquires its enchanted
poetry.

4. El Toboso is first and foremost a spectrum of sheer color: the
dazzling white of the houses, the deep indigo of the sky and of the borders painted on the walls; even the wind seems to have the clarity of a
luminous tint. The town features the Cervantine Museum, to which,
among other things, heads of states and governments from all over
the world customarily send prized translations of *Don Quixote* in the
languages of their countries, complete with dedication. On view in
display cases, exquisite editions and translations from every continent
flaunt celebrated signatures penned on the title pages. Among them
is an Italian edition with Mussolini's signature, dated July 31, 1930:
a sprawling, energetic signature, maybe a little megalomaniacal, but
with a generous stroke. They all send copies of *Don Quixote*, except
for two individuals. Hitler sends a weighty edition of the *Nibelungs*,
with a tiny signature that can barely be read, a twisted squiggle, letters
in a fetal position. He is, however, outdone in garish vulgarity by Gad-
dafi, who sends his *Green Book*, a discourse on revolution. Both reveal the arrogant insecurity of a boss who threatens, "You don't know
who you're dealing with," while the greatness of Don Quixote, as
Unamuno wrote, lies entirely in the humble confidence with which
he says, "I know who I am!"

5. Campo de Criptana. Poets are always concrete, even in their
wildest fantasies. The four large windmills that can be glimpsed on a
hill in the distance really do look like giants. Don Quixote's madness
is always, in some way, both realistic and visionary; certainly much
more so than the myopia of those who see only the facade of things
and mistake it for a single, immutable reality. It is the Don Quixotes
of the world who realize that reality can crumble and change; the so-
called practical men, proudly immune to dreaming, always believed

the Berlin Wall was destined to persist, right up until the day it fell. There were once forty windmills in Campo de Criptana; now there are about ten, standing against the white of the village, the blue of the sky, the brown of the earth. A cold, clear sky, continental winter; yet in the air there's that freedom and dryness of the South that so enchanted Nietzsche.

6. The cave of Montesinos, the underworld cavern in which Don Quixote descends among ravens and crows no less fearsome than the monsters of Avernus and where he, like Sancho, thinks that the marvels and magical wonders — which he actually saw — may merely be "rigmarole," as all esoteric mysteries and initiation rituals generally are.[4] The real mystery lies in the surroundings, in the undulating, slightly hilly landscape, in the ravines that fascinated Azorin in his quixotic journey of 1905, in the waters of the nearby lakes of Ruidera, in the glancing light of sunset which lends the trunks of oaks and pines a poignant gentleness. The soil is red, like that of Istria. As we saunter along, Mercedes Monmany, to whom we owe some very discriminating pages of literary criticism and brilliant essays on various literatures, proposes the invention of a new discipline, comparative landscape.

7. Villanueva de los Infantes, with its magnificent neoclassical main square, the plaza Mayor, is home to the House of the "Knight of the Green Gaban," with whom Don Quixote — having just challenged the lion who, instead of attacking him, yawned and turned his backside to him — judiciously discusses poetry and his own wisdom and folly.[5] Also in Villanueva is the convent of Santo Domingo, where the writer Francisco de Quevedo died on September 8, 1645; affixed to the wall of his cell is a sonnet he had composed two months before his death, on the final "negra y fria," the black, cold hour.[6] Great Spanish poetry of the seventeenth century, like the baroque period in general, is obsessed with death; as a sonnet by Luis de Góngora

tells us, "you and all of these together turn / To earth, smoke, dust, shadow, nothing."⁷ But not even death extinguishes passion: body and soul and bones will turn to dust, Quevedo writes, but dust in love; and the supreme Lope de Vega, a devotee of stormy passion who is, of course, represented in the theatrical museum of the nearby splendid Almagro, says of his dead lover that, though she has dissolved into dust, she's still beautiful, and continues to wage war on him, not letting him live, while she rests in peace.⁸

Most of life revolves around the role that death plays in it, depending on whether death is dismissed, feared, courted, or viewed as part of living. When Don Quixote dies, Sancho is sad, but life goes on unperturbedly, his niece eats, the housekeeper makes a toast; in the end even Sancho is serene, as befits the faithful squire of a fearless knight. But dying can assume more melancholy forms than the final headlong tumble. One of our group, Maria José, looking at the fields, cites the *aterradora* chilling verse of a flamenco: "Who knows what happened / to that fine grass, / which was green and then withered."

Even the House of the Inquisition, in Villanueva, suggests a death of another kind. On the old doorway, surmounted by an architrave with a shield depicting a crucifix, skull and crossbones, a sign informs us that the building is for sale.

8. In Almagro the Madonna is venerated as "Nuestra Señora de las Nieves," Our Lady of the Snows. Bullfighting too is promoted, and the plaza de Toros borders the sanctuary, which looks right out onto the bullring. When the ritual slaughtering of the bull is celebrated, a window of the church is opened and the statue of the Virgin is turned so that she may watch what is happening and preside, so to speak, over the ceremony.

9. Almagro, Chinchón, Tembleque, Ocaña, and many other charming towns are laid out around magnificent squares. Columns, arches, balconies; beauty and sociability, a sense of community

within a town. It is the square that makes a city, large or small; the exteriors count even more than museums abounding in masterpieces. Near Ocaña is Fuente Grande, "great spring," a grandiose, magnificent washhouse built between 1574 and 1578. A sort of Renaissance temple in honor of water: arcades, bridges, pillars, canals, but above all a splendor built not for feasts or naumachiae, the mock naval battles that brightened courtly amusements, but to rinse and water the horses.

We return. The night is cold, windy. The chill that is felt to a greater or lesser degree at the end of a long or short trip, when the bond that has fraternally connected a group of people dissolves; the friendship endures, but that particular constellation and its atmosphere will not be repeated. The disaggregation of a moment, of a unique formation in any case — like the shape of clouds, says J., whose laughing eyes know no fear though acquainted with melancholy. "How many landscapes turn away from you, in your sorrow," reads a poem by César Antonio Molina, a very fine, omnivorous essayist and intense poet who is now taking us back to Madrid; "oh, if they only knew that you exist, that you love them . . ."⁹

March 4, 2001

MARIONETTES IN MADRID

The Sunday crowd in Retiro Park has a dreamy, peaceful look, the relaxed vitality of people strolling aimlessly, enjoying the hours that lazily slip away like an ice-cream cone absently being licked. The evening will soon cloak the symmetry of the French garden, the waters of the pond, and the tall stone statues, conventional yet full of mystery in their stereotypical monumentality. It is a moment of pause, of indolent suspension, in the life of a country that is undergoing a radical and tumultuous transformation, a fervid, all-too-rapid growth. Today's Spain is an exemplary illustration of what is happening in Europe, a place where the process that in recent years has changed and is changing the world and its views is particularly evident.

Centuries-old traditions and barriers and the struggles to overthrow them are crumbling like rubble tackled by a bulldozer and immediately cleared away; long-standing cultural parameters and criteria are shown to be totally inadequate before such rapid, widespread change, which balks at ideological conventions. Shackles and taboos are toppling together with values and certainties; freedom and emancipation proliferate, accessible to ever broader circles, alongside pockets of persistent backwardness; combined with a euphoria of progress and development is a sense of dismay at an accelerated loss of historical memory. Economic enterprise creates opportunities previously unknown for individual autonomy and dignity, but the rampant yuppie seems to have left no room for either Don Quixote or Sancho Panza.

If our postmodern period is a cocktail of progress and disenchantment, Spain today is a stimulating and disturbing distillate of it; a pressing revitalization is liberating it, removing many shackles, and seems to want to get rid of not just the past, by disrupting historical continuity, but also of recent things. In this sense, Spain is now a theater of the world, a throbbing heart of the West and its future. The mixture of a recalcitrant, archaic past being cleared away with an ephemeral, vital present currently make Spain a demanding, insistent country, in which the traveler, like Don Quixote, often has his expectations belied by reality, as he meets the mobile prose of a marked secularization and certainly not the enchantment and immutable certainties of chivalric legend.

The nature of the world, according to the inscription on the commemorative plaque facing the Prado, also includes irony, and the irony is that of contemporary history, which discloses ever broader horizons but also elides and erases relentlessly. Spain, with its Civil War, has been a symbol of great ideological conflict, of political choices—such as the one between fascism and antifascism—based on ideals experienced as absolute values, on global visions of the world, on the struggle between good and evil. Today you sometimes get the impression that the war might never have taken place or might have ended differently, and that, in such case, things might not now be so very different from what they are. Of course, the feeling of history being unreal—when instead it is made up of flesh, blood, and tears, of concrete individuals and concrete convictions for which they fought, lived, and died—is an intellectual and moral temptation, the deceptive seduction of social gears and mechanisms, which tend to distract us from questioning their significance and erode our confidence in being able to change them. The odyssey of disenchantment, our daily journey through reality, lies entirely in the ability to resist the Sirens' call of disenchantment, to hear their song without plugging up our ears, recognizing that which is true in it, those aspects of our historic period it describes and reveals, though not passively surrendering to its allure, not believing that that truth is definitive and complete, that the ultimate questions and things no longer exist.

Moreover, it is precisely at times of global transformation — when reality is dismantled and reassembled like stage sets for a new performance — that, amid the cloud of dust raised by the reinstallation, the larger issues concerning the meaning and meaninglessness of life, the indestructible metaphysics printed in our genetic code, are revived. The knights-errant were never so intrepid and real as when Don Quixote mistook the windmills for giants; Mambrino's helmet never shone with such splendor as when the hidalgo of La Mancha perceived it in a barber's basin. It is not those who wax nostalgic for olden times and confuse the eternal with the past, or those who retreat to pathetic, arid seclusion, archaic and aristocratic, but those who humbly consent to mingle with promiscuous, everyday turmoil, with the changing of all things, with customs and hierarchies that are relative who are loyal to valor, having learned to recognize and respect the dignity of all people even when it appears in ways and forms that they are unfamiliar with and which may even disgust or disturb them.

The battleground of the good fight, which the apostle exhorts, is not an idyllic refuge untouched by history, its violence and its circus, but the place at the front lines vulnerable to the future. The countries most alive, those most rife with danger and salvation, resemble the world foretold by Goethe in his great *Faust, Part II*, which Benedetto Croce did not like because he thought it was unpoetic and affected: a world, albeit artificial and precious, disrupted by violent transformations, at times as false as a stroll down a runway, but eternally the setting for humankind and our destiny, for the wager between the Lord and Mephistopheles, for the bout for salvation.

If Madrid is a metropolis, or a stage of the "great world," as Faust put it, tonight in Retiro Park a more modest but charming puppet theater is on view. Outdoors, in front of an audience composed mainly though not solely of children, three marionettes are performing a concert: one plays the flute, another the violin, a third the piano. The music, an eighteenth-century sonata, comes from a record or cassette hidden behind the curtains; the three musicians, manipulated by extraordinary puppeteers, perform all the movements in perfect sync with the sounds they appear to produce. The marionettes, a little over a foot and a half tall, are wearing white powdered wigs, dark red jackets with silver buttons, and shoes with buckles; a small sword hangs at their side. Their faces are marked by prominent features: a large rapacious nose and thick black eyebrows, a greedy mouth twisted into a grotesque, painful grimace, eyes aimlessly turned sideways. The pianist shakes his head with imperious jerks, the flutist, when he moves the instrument from his lips, looks anxiously at the others; the violinist, head tilted and eyes half-closed, is completely rapt, lost in an impenetrable solitude in which the mystery of things, of inanimate and unfathomable objects, seems to mingle with the mystery of the heart and that of the music. You can't see the wires that move the marionettes; it's as though the three puppeteers—who loom over them and, in front of everyone, pull those wires—did not exist. No one pays any attention to them, eyes fixed on the three musicians, on the melancholy and sorrow with which they, like the characters in *The Tales of Hoffmann*, convey the music's spell.

Hoffmann's characters, racked by a passion for music, generally play it poorly, with strident dissonances and often even the wrong tempo, like the attorney Musevius, who in the quartet almost always finishes a little too early or a little too late; theirs is an infelicitous love for the art, unrequited. By contrast, the music that the recording transmits beneath these trees is an excellent performance, yet the three musicians—by their gestures and by their faces, which seem to come to life and even change expression—display a deep, yearning sorrow, as if those notes awakened in the heart a longing for all that is missing, as well as an awareness of not being able to express it, despite everything, of not being able to touch another heart. Their gestures and movements, with that modicum of mechanical woodenness that not even the puppeteers' skill can avoid, become the rigidity of decorum and dignity, the pathos of conduct that seeks to contain and conceal the chaotic confusion of feelings.

The audience watches and listens, spellbound, as a big man with a huge, spread-out red beard that comes down to his belt wanders among them, like Pinocchio's Fire Eater, to collect the price of the show. Perhaps tonight some of those children will learn forever that in every love for art there is at least a hint of nostalgia, of passion that is not entirely reciprocated, and that this lack is proof of its truth; love, it has been said, is everything that you don't have. Evening descends pleasurably, the three musicians bow and disappear into the little theater, along with a black cat that follows them, curious. Beyond the park, the lights of the metropolis can be seen, but youngsters, indifferent to the theater of the great world, chase each other along the paths, more fascinated by the marionettes than by the puppeteers of our destinies, not all that impressed by the wooden musicians either, and willing to skip the lesson on melancholy.

March 26, 1989

THE BIBLIOPHAGE

I am at the National Library of Madrid, with its rich collections, its facilities where books and manuscripts are cared for and restored with ultra-modern techniques and age-old patience, its computerized Book Museum, which is disseminated through its writing and printing workshops, and the public that attends its literary sessions, a public that—as usual in Spain—is one of the most vibrant and exciting in the world, among the most gratifying for a writer.

They tell me that during the Spanish Civil War, the library was damaged, and a man—I'm not sure whether it was to escape wartime violence in general or someone in particular who was trying to kill him—hid among the books abandoned in the unsafe rooms, remaining there for several months. I can picture him slinking out at night to get food, like a predatory animal whose lair lies among incunabula and glass display cases, then coming back to cook and eat it, surrounded by the volumes. It is difficult to guess whether he read those books, if living with them in those circumstances taught him to be passionate or indifferent to reading; perhaps he viewed those illustrious tomes merely as objects, walls that concealed and protected him from the elements, a potential, reassuring fuel, should the need present itself.

The story about that man brings to mind what a friendly restorer in the library's workroom—he was dipping some prints from Goya's *Tauromachia* series in an aqueous solution—told me about certain insects that devour books and for that reason are called "bibliophages," bookworms.

March 19, 1996

AT THE "MENTITOIO"

Madrid. In the splendid district which includes the homes of the great poets of Spain's Golden Age—Lope de Vega, Cervantes, Quevedo—a plaque on calle León commemorates a place, a kind of club (today we would say a "space") where nineteenth-century merchants, intellectuals, writers, politicians, journalists, and businessmen met. In those rooms they discussed politics and art, struck deals, speculated on business ventures or literary magazines, and formed and disbanded groups of all kinds, from cultural avant-gardism to those of economic or ideological interest. Mostly they talked and talked.

That place, as the plaque records, has a name, the "Mentidero de representantes": the place where people talk without too much regard for truth, a *mentitoio*, a place where one lies. By universal, frank admission, formalized even in the sign, conversation, entertainment, and in particular negotiations and social discussion are associated with an untruth (*mentira*), and the shrine in which the sociocultural rites take place is by definition the place where one goes to lie.

Of course the fact of not concealing the falsehood but rather recognizing and proclaiming it may have an exorcizing function, and can be a ploy to give ourselves a license of sincerity by denouncing the untruth; if we all know we're lying—and acknowledge it—we are under the illusion that there is no deception, since no one is led to trust another's good faith. In actuality, the little game does not in the least atone for the lie, just as ostentatious vulgarity—which is practically cited in falsetto in snob circles—is certainly not redeemed but aggravated by the pretense of making fun of it; a swear word spoken coyly by someone who thinks that he is so refined and above such coarseness that he can afford to say something crude is more vulgar than a swear word that can honestly slip out of someone's mouth when he bashes a finger.

The plaque on calle León does not, however, seem to be sternly moralistic, nor does it seem to urge against empty, illusory worldliness or commend a strict, ascetic retreat into deep, silent interiority, in which the echo of frivolous exterior vanities is not heard, but in which the soul communes with itself and with God. Most likely the smiling authors of the plaque — and before them, the even more smiling local inventors of that name — were well aware that cavernous interior solitude does not guarantee the truth any more than mundane chatter. Often you think you're talking to yourself or to God when instead you are only talking to the abject, pretentious ghosts of your own fears or idols and mistaking the echo of your own delirium for the voice of truth; in a salon it is at least easier to notice that you are being fatuous and banal like the others around you, whereas in a soliloquy you are likely to be convinced that you are hearing an absolute truth and becoming its prophet and slave.

The plaque might be intended to remind us that the Mentidero de representantes, that place of social representation, is a theater and that, as the great baroque poets who lived in those streets could teach us, the whole world is a stage on which what happens can refer to a truth that transcends it — depending on religious belief — and that in any case should not be taken literally or too seriously. Those who lie, the name of the club tells us, are primarily "representantes," who claim to represent something (no matter whether it be a firm, an ideology, an institution), and therefore come to speak — creating an illusion, claiming to speak — not for themselves but for someone or something else. And even when they think they are speaking for themselves, it makes little difference, because it's as though they were their own double or stand-in, an actor playing a part with that name who fills in for the real person, like stuntmen, who in a movie perform the most dangerous scenes, falling from their horse in place of the star.

Modernity has made this representative function increasingly universal and at the same time impossible, just as it has made it impossible to write poems glorifying the king or the president of the republic. It always feels uncomfortable when we are a replacement for someone and have to speak on behalf of a school, a party, a church, a government, or an association, whether philatelic, veterans, or philosophical; at the same time we realize that we are nearly always standing in for someone else, that we are hardly ever able to speak in our own name, and indeed that we have forgotten what the voice of that vague, allegedly real "I" sounds like which expresses itself less and less in our own words and mainly in official words suited to the occasion, in discussions and roundtables, at conferences or public talks.

We all more or less find ourselves in that mentidero, in that "place of lies." We try to get by as best we can, navigating among the lies that float and burst without causing a stir, like soap bubbles. At times the chatter buzzing around us is good mundane medicine; it's like an undertow, a murmur that covers the sound of time passing and blunts the awareness of pain and emptiness. As the great poets of the theater of the world who lived in that area knew, the truth can be painful, like a throbbing nerve that must be dulled. The truth, said another great baroque Spanish writer, Gracián, can be dangerous, because it is a bloodletting of the heart.[1]

November 25, 1998

A FATHER, A SON

In the gallery of the monastery of Pedralbes, in Barcelona — one of the great monuments of Catalan Gothic — which houses a section of the Thyssen-Bornemisza Collection, a father and son duo are among the sparse number of visitors. The elder is a trim gentleman around seventy-five, small in stature, with a serene air; he's leading the son by the hand, the younger man evidently suffering from Down syndrome or, as it is improperly referred to, mongolism.

Ahead of me, the two stop in front of every painting as the father, still holding his son's hand, explains each one: Fra Angelico's *The Madonna of Humility*, a favorite theme of the mendicant orders; the shadow from which the *Portrait of Antonio Anselmi* by Titian emerges;[1] the canary that escapes from his cage in the *Portrait of a Lady* by Pietro Longhi. The son listens, nods his head, murmurs something every so often; he might be forty or fifty years old, but for the most part he displays the indeterminate age of a faded child. The father talks, listens, answers. He's probably been doing this for a lifetime and doesn't seem either tired or troubled by it; rather he seems pleased to be teaching his son to love the Masters.

When they come to the *Portrait of Mariana of Austria, Queen of Spain*, he stoops to read the artist's name, then abruptly straightens up and, turning to his son, says in a somewhat excited tone of voice: "Velázquez!" And he sweeps off his hat, raising it as high as he can. His son's condition, the cross that a deplorable injustice saddled him with, has not bowed the man's shoulders, has not bent or made him bitter, has not robbed him of the joy of recognizing greatness, paying tribute to it, and sharing it with the one person for whom he most likely lives, his son. Often pain breaks people down and poisons them, understandably driving them to reject what others—to whom fate has been more prodigal with its gifts—have managed to create to attain glory in the world. An affliction such as a disability, which confines one to the shadows, makes it especially difficult to rejoice and delight in the brilliance achieved by someone else. The father's respectful, joyful act of doffing his hat is a regal gesture, as is, even more so, the obvious pleasure with which the elderly man shares his enthusiasm with his son. Their paternal and filial love ensures that those two individuals suffice for one another, just as love suffices. That man, who unknowingly became a kind of mentor for me, is one to whom we should all tip our hats.

March 19, 1996

SPOON RIVER IN CANTABRIA

I don't know if the *Beata coorte* (Blessed Cohort) still exists, if it is in print and available. It was a series of brief, sometimes very brief, biographies of saints who had been part of the Jesuit order that would easily find its way into the hands of a young boy in the via del Ronco district, in Trieste, where the Jesuit parish of Sacro Cuore was a lively, exciting center, an epic fraternal place where lasting, picaresque friendships were formed, as in the classroom, and where you learned to regard the great cold world intrepidly, with humility but also with an air of swagger.

The biographies that made up the *Beata coorte* were often quick, essential, such that one of the reverend fathers, still my friend to this day, liked to call them *vitellae*, to lend them a classical dignity and playful lightness. That brevity was indeed a lesson in literature, the ability to trim away the verbosity of existence, like a good barber snips and tosses into the trash the long, thick hair covering the neck, and to accentuate values and meaning, as in an epitaph: it was the art of selecting and omitting, essential to every narrator. Those vitellae — even those of saints belonging to other orders and published mainly by the Salesians, less selective and less competitive than the compilers of the *Beata coorte* — were, in their own way, a *Spoon River*. Perhaps the brevity was not just a stylistic choice but was related to sanctity, which is not a humbling renunciation but a determined ability to prune the tempting, oppressive weeds (the world's "pompous regalia") that entangle us on all sides; to shake off the frills, fetters, and shackles and throw them in the refuse bin, reducing life to essentials and being free to live, like Joseph Roth's holy drinker.

To be candid, those biographical sketches also included some mediocre trash, edifying naïveté, sententious piety, warped, prudish reticence toward sex. But overall, despite such flaws, the vitellae aroused interest in lives actually lived and made it clear that sainthood resembles childhood (before children, realizing that they are different from adults, start performing, *being* children) and old age, conditions in which a person simply is, behaving and acting freely without worrying about how others look at him or her, or maybe — not yet or no longer observant of the rules — not even knowing that anyone is watching. As a result, those modest biographies suggested an indulgent, cheerful indifference to the hierarchies and glories of the world; they taught us to enjoy life rather than wasting it on the anxious concern to affirm it above that of others; they made clear, once and for all, that every king is a poor, third-rate strolling player who in the end takes off his cardboard crown, and that all the newspapers celebrating his success end up in the latrine.

Maybe that's why it is easier to find saints at the margins or at the lowest levels of society, among individuals at times overcome by hard work and struggle, unable to get completely in tune with the world's ways, to fit in, even only internally, with society's hierarchies. The holy drinker could hardly be a corporate CEO or the winner of a Nobel Prize for literature because he has not directed his life toward that goal, he hasn't aimed for any goal except, at most, how he will procure that day's meal. It is not surprising that the last "beata coorte" I happened to come across — an entirely secular and profane beata coorte, though also abounding in halos — is a series of brief biographies, low-quality and plebeian, common and rambling, reconstructed and assembled by a loving, accurate biographer with the care and precision that historians and philologists give to world-renowned figures and great poets, to heads adorned with crown and laurel.

At first glance, halos are certainly not seen on the heads of the eccentric characters assembled by the poet Rafael Gutiérrez-

Colomer, but rather crumpled caps, at most, or if they are women, skillfully balanced crates of fish or baskets of laundry. The book that I came across by chance, whose first edition was published some years ago, is a gallery of popular figures of Santander and is titled *Tipos populares santanderinos*; I bought it at a bookstore in the city, not far from the area of Puerto Chico, the port that is the background of most of those stories and those lives, of their unassuming, spirited day-to-day epic. Those humble and indestructible characters embody the maritime vitality of their city, its vigorous trade and aptitude for dogged independence, overlooking the Cantabrian sea on which the Spanish navy was born, the Mare Tenebrosum, dark ocean, where according to the ancients the world ended. It is among these shores, these quays, and these boats that the characters whom Rafael Gutiérrez-Colomer resolutely saved from oblivion go about their lives.

With compassion and precision, he has reconstructed their meager, obscure existences, delving into his own recollections and into old newspapers, talking to witnesses equally unknown and obscure, but truthful and reliable, gathering recollections and memories, echoes of that local epic and its forgotten deeds. For each of his heroes, who lived on the fringes of life and—like the saints—were often unable to adapt to the world's strict rules, he acquired a photograph as well, resorting—when he did not find one—to the help of a draftsman, Indalecio Sobrino, who, based on the descriptions of friends and witnesses, sketched the portraits, affectionate caricatures at times touched by a shadow of sadness.

The result was a humble, plebeian *Decameron*, a calendar or almanac of unorthodox, vagrant saints. The gallery is quite varied. There are colorful, pathetic characters whose misfortune or bizarreness elevates them to a pedestal that is sublime in its way. For example, Bohemio, the old, charming, impoverished womanizer, fallen on hard times, who ends up a beggar and who, when a friend restores him to a tidy, comfortable life, can't help returning to the shadows,

retaining the only wealth he has, the magnificent long hair and bib-
lical beard that allow him to earn some money as a photographers'
model, until in a home for the poor they shave him, robbing him of
his only means of survival. Or Don Adolfito, "el loco del violin," as
skinny as Don Quixote, whom a doomed love causes to take leave
of an illustrious family and his senses and who earns a living by playing the violin in the streets. There are also those who are able to react
better to the pains of love, like the mayor of a small village who fines
a girl guilty of having refused him five pesetas, charging her with in-
sulting a public official.

There are oddballs like Arcilla, who spoke in verse, proclaimed
himself world champion of mental boxing and the earth's defense
counsel, and wanted to change the name "America," unjustly derived
from Amerigo Vespucci, who had usurped the credit from Columbus. There is the glory of those who rescued people from drowning;
the shoe shiner's nose for sniffing out crime sites; the fraudulent im-
pudence of "Gabardina" with his cinematography school that was
mixed up with initiation into arts of other, more pleasurable genres;
the mishaps of Fresno, who had set up an agency for wet nurses and
maids but was so disorganized that his wet nurses were dry while his
buxom little maids were overflowing with milk; the science of Lucas
the astronomer, who climbed trees to study the stars more closely,
and also sounded the alarm when he sighted the police.

Sometimes these wretched lives cross paths with History, like
that of the prankster Dr. Cambrillon, author of all kinds of satirical
formulas, who one evening in the early days of the Spanish Civil War
was picked up by several armed men while on the way to his usual
café. But tragedy and death have no need of historical apocalypses;
they swoop down each day, silent and habitual, by way of illness, hunger, work accidents, storms at sea, fate. The majority of these individuals in fact live a simple story of drudgery and its rare respites of joy and
pleasure, hard work, and a few hours at the tavern or café.

These lives are lit by concerted fraternity, but are also obscured in a darkness all the more bleak as it is banal, as in the story of "Bota," a shoemaker plagued his entire life by the unwitting cruelty of generations of children from a nearby school. At other times cruelty and kindness become entangled as in the story of the fake wedding of a poor disabled girl, deceived but also made happy by that pretense she believes is real.

A regal place, in this coorte, is occupied by women, robust, generous fishmongers, deft of hand and tongue, ready to bear life's burden like the baskets of fish on their heads, but also to slap life in the face when it becomes tyrannical, like a too intrusive suitor: Cruza, La Chata, La Teta, so called for her magnanimous breasts.

Though prematurely wilted from toiling away, arms used to carrying heavy loads and hands accustomed to washing, scrubbing or cleaning fish, all of these women, in the faded photographs that immortalize them, display an imperious and maternal vitality, a generous opulence, the tender, imperious sensuality of bodies passing through the world undaunted. It must have been quite a feat to be the consorts, more or less legitimate, of those queens. The brief biographies allow us a glimpse of their battered erotic glory, but above all document incidents of kindness and charitable solidarity, as befits those free, complete women, who in their own way are a worthy part of a beata coorte.

September 24, 1989

DON SERAFIN'S FIRST FLIGHT

The Canary Islands, the *Gaceta*, gazette, of Santa Cruz de Tenerife reported a few days ago, are a Danubian problem. With that ironic metaphor, printed in conspicuous type, the island's newspaper meant to point out that the uncertain, composite border identity, much talked about in regard to central and Eastern Europe, is a problem — reality or myth, merit or deficiency — felt with equal intensity at the opposite confines of Europe, at the southern and western extremities, in the archipelago that, well before becoming an obligatory tourist destination, had good reasons to lay claim to being recognized as the fabled lands longed for by the ancients, the Fortunate Islands, the Elysian Fields, Atlantis, the Hesperides.

Thousands of miles away from the Old Continent, close to Africa, the Canaries were shaped over the centuries by many different peoples, who left their traces and legacies, like the various strata of the walls of Troy; the aborigines — the tall, fair-skinned, red-haired Guanches and other Semitic- or African-type groups, the Phoenicians, the Greeks, the Egyptians, the Marseillaise, the Carthaginians, the Romans, the Arabs, the Genoese, the Castilians, the Galicians, the Portuguese, the Mallorcan, the Andalusians, the Basques, the British, the French, the Barbary corsairs, the Dutch . . . In his voluminous and fascinating *Historia de Canarias* (History of the Canaries), combining a meticulous gathering of material and fanciful digression, the eighteenth-century scholar Joseph de Viera y Clavijo mentions, besides the visits made by Christopher Columbus, the arrivals of Heracles and Solomon's fleets as well. Echoes of this manifold, layered history have remained even in the dialect, a friend tells me, terms derived from different languages and assimilated into the islanders' Spanish.

But the Canaries have an advantage over the Danubian mosaic, maybe that extra edge that, in spite of everything, Latin countries often prove to have: freedom from an obsessive fixation on their own identity, an easy distinction that cannot be superseded by an insular complex. In these islands, which, especially in their interior, offer an intense, diverse beauty, at times stark and harsh, at other times tangled and embracing, you feel as if you're in Europe, despite the new, surprising landscape. You don't remember that just a short distance away lies Africa, the desert, another world; only an occasional inscription on the walls, showing solidarity with the Polisario Front, the movement demanding Sahara's independence from Morocco, recalls for a moment a political world far removed from ours.

You feel at home, as though in Europe, in one of the liveliest rooms of the common European home. Here too separatism exists, which with its extreme visceral reactions, often renders many claims for autonomy oppressive. But a few lone graffiti, "Europe go home" or "Españoles fuera," are merely pathetic and underscore the absurdity of particularisms carried to excess, like the latter one against the Spanish, written in Spanish and probably by a Spaniard.

The driver, as the car passes in front of that inscription, taps his forehead. The autonomist movement is irrelevant, both politically and numerically; the people I meet—intellectuals active in the cultural policy of the Autonomous Government such as Juan-Manuel García Ramos or Carlos Díaz-Bertrana Marrero, poets, writers, and scholars like Domingo-Luis Hernández, Arturo Maccanti, and José Antonio Otero—justifiably love their islands and introduce me to its literature, but without any particularistic insistence, talking about Saba and Joyce more than about the Canary surrealist movement. I find an openness to the world, a cosmopolitan ease that I am familiar with from the white harbors of Istria and Dalmatia. Islands and coasts are often less insulated, less shut up within themselves, than places located in the heart of the mainland; the sea often precludes stifling isolation.

Traveling only in my head isn't enough for me because I am interested in people and things, colors and seasons; nevertheless it's hard for me to travel without paper, without books to hold up before the world like a mirror to see if they confirm or contradict one another. There are two types of books a traveler can bring along: those written by authors who express the genius loci, which the traveler reads to better understand the unfamiliar reality in which he is venturing forth, and those written by authors who, like him, came there from afar, knowing little about the place, which the traveler reads to see how other people viewed those places for the first time.

On this occasion I have with me *La fiera navigante* (The Seafaring Trade Show) by Livio Garzanti, a Bildungsroman that recaptures, from a time that seemed remote and inaccessible, the anxious, desolate hope of our immediate postwar period, and unfolds in a picaresque ocean voyage which—like the navigators who sailed to the West Indies—stops at the Canary Islands, in Las Palmas. It is fitting that the story of a life that opens up to the world, as the novel's protagonist's does, should take place, as every odyssey does, at sea. The young man, troubled by the grave triviality of existence, steeped in intellectualism, tenderness, sensuality, and disillusionment, and snared, in his sensitivity, by the irrelevance and bitterness of things, discovers in the Canarian sea in which he swims an epic feminine quality that restores a bit of childhood and a sound indulgence for the world's frigidity.

The sea, in Spanish, is masculine, as in Italian, but the people of the coast who encounter it concretely, physically, call it *la mar,* feminine. Maybe it is thanks in part to that article that the sea resists nihilism, the unreality that seems to deprive us of the tangibility of things, objects, and perceptible experience, the continuity of life and its transmission. The sea's epic nature is also and particularly terrible, shipwrecks and storms, hardships and distance, but it is never abstract, fictitious. Perhaps for this reason it may be a symbol of harmony, despite its devastating fury, so that even in a movie of palatable consumption such as *The Abyss* by James Cameron our contemporary anguished imagination is able to believe that rising from the ocean's dark depths are not monsters but benevolent creatures who come to our aid — "colorful butterflies," Giovanni Grazzini calls them in his *Cinema '89*, as if to suggest that grace and gentleness, the harmonious appearance of good, have sought refuge at the bottom of the sea.

Canary Islands literature is permeated by a sense of the sea, by an Atlantic whisper; not just the memory of ancient seafaring venturers, from Saint Brendan with his eighth untraceable island to Christopher Columbus, or of battles with Drake or Nelson, who left his arm there, but the sea as backdrop and general feeling of life, which transforms and assimilates even what comes from the mainland. In the Canarian *Romancero* the caballeros become *marineros*. Naturally, there are also many forests in Canary Islands poetry, like the famous one in Doramas lauded by Cairasco de Figueroa, the Renaissance translator of the *Gerusalemme liberata* (Jerusalem Delivered). But this shady, enchanting forest is celebrated by the poet in an addition which was unduly introduced in the translation of the fifth canto of Tasso's poem, in a description of the Canaries as the Fortunate Islands . . .

Famous for their beaches, often ruined by some of the worst construction speculation, the Canaries reveal an extraordinary beauty, especially in a landscape as diverse as that of a continent, sometimes rugged, sometimes lush, in the colors of the plants, particularly the blue of the jacaranda and the red of the Gabon tulip tree, and in the magnificent volcanic craters of Mount Teide. In Gran Canaria, the Roque Bentayga was worshipped as a sanctuary by the island's original inhabitants; looking at this massive metaphysical peak, you think about the monolith in *2001: A Space Odyssey* and come to understand the relationship between the divinity and the mountains. In Icod, on Tenerife, there is an ancient dragon. The *Dracaena draco* is the tree par excellence of the Canaries, a mythical symbol of the islands, an object and site of worship and veneration. The one in Icod is very old, centuries old according to some, and millenarian according to others; it rises, but mainly it spreads out and expands, in danger of toppling over due to too much vigor, to an excess of vitality, to being too outstretched in the world. Cracks split open like wrinkles on its trunk and branches, and features sprout—venerable beards and bushy eyebrows, knobs of calloused hands and chinks of demonic eyes. That tree is a plurality; it is a great many trees, it is a mountain carved by ravines and rivers, it is a face transformed into many faces, a tangle, it is the grimace and the ironic smile of metamorphosis.

Standing before the dragon tree you feel the seduction of old age, luxuriant with time and endless stories, Dionysian in the proliferation of its dissolution; the dragon's age, as well as the death it heralds, has a majestic grandeur but above all a disturbing erotic vitality, an endless transformation and regeneration.

Canarian literature is rich and diverse, from the *romances* that preserve the oral tradition, with a vibrancy equal only to that of certain Sephardic communities of North Africa or Eastern Europe, to fiction and poetry open to the most vivid contemporary experiences. I am reading, among other things, Alonso Quesada's 1919 *Chronicles of the City and of the Night*, a satirical, grotesque representation of the cosmopolitan ambiance of Las Palmas, with its eccentric characters, especially the English. Little by little, Quesada's irony drains reality, turns it inside out like a glove, and reveals its emptiness, its void, an intangible lack that makes all life seem like the unreal basin of night. Quesada's writing recalls Ramón Gómez de la Serna, though also Pessoa at times, his featureless plurality, his nothing inside of nothing. As the title of an epigrammatic chapter of Quesada says, an individual sits on a bench, takes a walk, or reads books to convince himself that he exists, but he does not exist. He smiles, the melancholy, mocking smile of Nobody.

José Antonio Otero tells me that in Santa Cruz de Tenerife he met an elderly farmer from Las Palmas, Don Serafín, with his coarse coat and country dweller's hat. It was the first time Don Serafín had been to Tenerife; it was the first time he'd taken a plane, to travel from Gran Canaria, the neighboring island where he lives. He'd come to say good-bye. He'd been diagnosed with an advanced, incurable illness and decided that before dying he had to say good-bye to a couple of friends in Tenerife. And so he saw Tenerife as well, for the first time. He told his story quietly to Otero, drinking the coffee he bought him. That evening, for the second and last time in his life, he would take the plane and return home.

April 21, 1990

IN LONDON, AT SCHOOL

1. The red marks on the notebook that is returned to me on Monday morning are few, and the overall grade, at the bottom of the page, is a gratifying "good" that fills me with rightful pride despite the trace of envy for the "very good" that my classmate, a Dutch girl, got. It had been a long time since I'd done any assignments, either in the classroom or at home, quite a while since I had notebooks to keep or grades to get. However, in that small classroom whose windows face the flood of people and things streaming down Oxford Street like an allegory of Time, eyes meeting for a second and quickly lowered, I am back in school, subject to judgment — a specific type of judgment, based on verbs conjugated correctly or incorrectly, not left up to the magnanimity or misgivings of the reviewers.

I cannot choose the theme, as I choose the topic of a newspaper article or a book I'm going to write; the teacher is the one who decides what I must write about, and today my imagination, my intelligence, and my pen are all dedicated — by unappealable decree of Carol, our class captain — to the analysis and description of the job of milkman, the advantages and hardships that it involves and above all the physical and moral qualities that it demands. Quite apart from the difficulties of English, the result is far more uncertain than what happens in my customary activity; getting a failing grade on my theme or translation from the class is more likely than having a book rejected by a publisher or an article by the *Corriere*.

So for five and sometimes seven hours a day (not counting homework, of course), I am here at school. When at home I'd announced my intention to take some time off from university teaching to attend an intensive English-language course in London and Oxford, one of my sons had interpreted it as a Faustian desire to be rejuvenated while the other had instead viewed it as an obscure desire to be humiliated, to get rapped on the knuckles or at least be scolded for some syntactical error or flawed pronunciation. The imperious certainty of grammar, which leaves little room for hermeneutical speculation, suggests giving little credence to scoffing or disparaging lucubrations. The milkman has to get up hours before dawn and brave bad weather, but in recompense he's free all afternoon and he has occasion to meet a variety of people, to be treated with tact and sensitivity, that's life, or at least the wisdom of life, expressed in an English ever more worthy of that "good."

2. Last night I went to Blackfriars Bridge, the place where Roberto Calvi was found hanged. History is no less ironic and ludicrous than school, even though it is so much crueler; today that place has become a destination for Italian tourists, one of the sights to visit in London. It's not surprising, seeing that many Americans return on organized tours to places in Vietnam where they fought, killed, lost loved ones, saw, inflicted, and experienced atrocious acts of violence; for that matter the Tower of London, clearly teeming with visitors, is also a place of mourning, pain, and barbarism. History is a slaughterhouse, and on any tourist journey or educational visit to places steeped in history there is the tasteless, cruel vulgarity of those who enjoy the suffering of others as though it were a spectacle.

The darkness, the flowing water, the hybrid panorama — mingling the disreputable squalor of the desolate shore and the profile of the City's buildings, in which the administrators of Reality reside — is a scene all too symbolic of the tragedy that took place in this port. I wonder what the last thoughts of the man who met his end here were, the last thing he laid eyes on, the last pub he perhaps went into and drank a beer. Under the bridge, at rest like eternal darkness, are all those years of obscurity and delirium that led to that death, those tangled webs so mysterious as to make us want to forget. I think with gratitude of Alberto Cavallari, who in those years guided and saved, in the shadows, the ruined boat of the *Corriere* struck by the chaos, and I think that in those three years, on that drifting ship, I grew interiorly. Flowing in the water with which back then, for lack of money, we had to dilute the ink in order to print the *Corriere* was also the blood of tragedies like the one that happened here, a few steps from where I stand.

3. Apart from the hours of so-called "individual tuition," there are six or seven of us in a class. The others are more or less my sons' age and I look at them—the girls, I mean—the way a father looks at his daughters, that is, according to Italo Svevo's teaching, the way a father looks at other people's daughters. Like an animal who has escaped from the zoo, who instantly, even years later, rediscovers the scents and signs of the forest and the ability to fit into their law, I quickly align with class life and the mechanisms that rule it: figuring out the teachers' demands, foibles, and weaknesses, making sure that it is always another who stands out and takes the lead, so as to follow in that person's wake and work a little less hard, making everybody laugh and at times prompting that genuine humor based on nothing at all, a great gift of the gods which life, so miserly, dispenses with glorious nonchalance at school. In a few weeks it will all end, but for now it is as if the essential bonds, for each of us, were those that constitute our shared existence: answering the questions, competing in quizzes or games, suggesting, copying, consuming dreary sandwiches during the short breaks. The youngest, an Argentine young man, will turn eighteen in a few days, but a common lot makes us equal, just as during military service when I—a university lecturer, author of books and head of a family—was nevertheless just a simple private, never even promoted to corporal, sharing duty with my fellow soldiers.

Schola magistra vitae. Here too, in fact, there are victories and defeats, glory and captivity. And so I experience triumph over the words I encounter, which I not only unravel brilliantly but am also able to invent and put together, and suffer defeat in the language lab, because I almost always press the wrong key. Then too, there are also misunderstandings: in the description of preparations for a party, I make a mistake because the correct answer with regard to appropriate drinks was not a sparkling white, as I suggested, but Coca-Cola. Another time I spoil the fun because the teacher gives us a sheet of paper with the story of the death that awaits the Vizier in Samarkand; it is incomplete, however, and we are supposed to reconstruct the ending by asking the right questions. But I already know the story, which is indeed an old fetish of mine, and I give it away immediately.

4. In the *Guinness Book of World Records*, which assembles the most absurd "record bests" of all kinds, I read that on June 8, 1980, an Indian woman, Mrs. Shakuntala Devi, mentally multiplied 7,686,369,774,870 by 2,465,099,745,779, achieving the correct result, 1,894,766,811,795,426,773,730, in twenty-eight seconds. That's not to say that the lady deserves more admiration than the Cuban cow, Urbe Bianco, who produces 28.9 gallons of milk per day. I wonder if multiplication has been of use to her in love, in friendship, in gazing at colors, in growing old. Any work, not just that meaningless figure, even a literary masterpiece, can be equally senseless if it is merely a performance, albeit exceptional. A great work, like that calculation, is nothing in itself; it becomes something only as a result of the significance it assumes in our lives, of whether it is integrated and transubstantiated into life. If not, we're better off with the parrot (another record) who knew more than eight hundred words.

5. Nevertheless, perhaps the thirty-one-year age difference between me and Jens, the Danish young man, does count. Most likely the air-raid siren, sounded from a recording in the underground rooms, or better yet cells, of the War Cabinet, now a museum, does not arouse in him what it stirs up in me from buried, though con-

served, depths, because I, unlike him, have heard that siren before.
In these cells, in which Churchill presided over the government during the Second World War, you can sense, enduringly, the greatness
of that hour, the indestructible force of the resistance to the Leviathan. Looking at all the things that have been left in place since then,
tables, telephones, old typewriters, maps dotted with markers, the
bedrooms—those of the generals, even in a crisis, are partially car-
peted, the prime minister's even has wall-to-wall carpeting—you get
the impression that in there, or down there, difficult times were experienced, not sad days though, but fiery, filled with meaning as well
as day-to-day tranquillity; there is the telephone with which Churchill spoke to Roosevelt and even the chamber pot that Churchill
himself used, equally essential.

Of course, here too there are many shadowy areas; just a short
time ago a book came out in England denouncing the racist isolation
surrounding black American soldiers sent to England to fight and die
in order to defend civilization from Nazi racism. It is in part thanks
to them that in these trenchlike rooms civilization, though stained,
was saved. Next to an old Remington typewriter stands a bottle of Pol
Roger, Churchill's favorite Champagne, which he never did without
even in the most dreadful moments. Perhaps such verve is necessary
to withstand evil, the ability to take pleasure and not let the Medusa
spoil that joie de vivre, not allow anything to ruin the taste for Champagne. In his bedroom, on the wall in front of him, Churchill had
a large map depicting the military situation, but—unlike in all the
other rooms—he also had thick drapes, which he drew in front of
that wall so that in bed he wouldn't see that map. Maybe one of the
reasons he won was because after a full day of fighting he was able to
draw those curtains and for a few hours not think about the terrible
things that awaited him, about the fate of the world.

6. In Westminster, on a sarcophagus, there is a memorial inscription: "Dubius sed non improbus vixi, incertus morior, non perturba-

tus. Humanum est Nescire et Errare . . . Ens Entium miserere mei."
It is a fine statement of the complementary nature of doubt and faith:
as if it were our destiny—and perhaps our dignity—to doubt and fully
accept, without fear, the uncertainty, over which arches the heavens
of a God who is invoked, apart from any conjecture regarding Him.

The Thatcher administration attempts to launch moral cam-
paigns, seeks an alliance—rejected however—with the church, touts
values. But it is Thatcher's policy itself, even moderate newspapers
observe, that has triggered global economism, that radically utilitar-
ian conception that elevates money as the sole ideal and promotes a
social transformation that dismisses all values, especially traditional
ones, and any strict morality. Social conservatism destroys moral preservation. Thatcher's most fearsome adversaries are in the House of
Lords.

7. At Canterbury, in the old Anglican Church of Saint Dun-
stan, a plaque issued in 1946 lists the twenty-five categories of people
whom a man and a woman respectively cannot marry for reasons of
kinship. A father, for example, cannot marry his mother, his daughter,
his sister. But the list goes on and, thanks to the Saxon possessive, becomes quite humorous. Among those prohibited are the mother's
father's wife, the wife's mother's mother, the daughter's son's mother,
the daughter of the son of the daughter, and so on. In the end the
problem recedes and all that remains is a pure play on words, the satisfaction of classifying and recording that serves to conceal the absurdity of life.

8. The course is almost over. Today we practiced verbs that express the most diverse animal sounds, to bellow, to chirp, to squeak,
and a smiling Japanese man, who did not remember "to trumpet,"
tried to imitate an elephant, throwing back his head, and for a moment I read in his eyes his surprise at not seeing his trunk as he looked
up. The imminent end gives a sense of cheerful excitement, the

pathos of saying good-bye, as when, in the last days of military service, we sang: "Saluteremo i tenentini / comandanti di plotoni / tutti gran rompicoglioni / non li rivedrò mai più" — Say so long to petty lieutenants / commanders of platoons / all of them pains in the ass / we won't see them again soon.

Still, during these weeks I rediscovered how much more interesting it is to learn than to teach, to study irregular verbs than participate in or attend debates. In *Moby-Dick* Melville talks about an Usher in a school who loved grammar because it reminded him of his mortal nature. A bit of time has gone by while we recited verb tenses. And now that we are about to scatter like the crew of the *Narcissus*, perhaps we too, like the sailors in Conrad's novel, have redeemed our sinful souls somewhat, even if only by toiling over grammar and not, like that ship's crew, "on the immortal sea."

April 1, 1988

THE FORTUNATE ISLES

The boat that lands in Tresco crosses a brief stretch of sea, yet the passenger who steps foot on the island has the impression of having made a much longer journey, from one latitude to another, from northern Europe to the South Seas; a few hours earlier — or twenty minutes, if he chooses a helicopter — he left behind him the western tip of Britain, in Cornwall, and now finds himself in the midst of tropical vegetation, agaves and palm trees, Australian eucalyptus, South African violet-blue irises and lilies, orchids, purplish clumps of Mesembryanthemum, the scarlet Echium that stands erect like a defiant erotic crest.

Tresco is one of the more than three hundred islands that form the archipelago of Scilly in the Atlantic Ocean, twenty-six miles west of Land's End, where Cornwall stops: it is one of the six inhabited islands, the largest of which is Saint Mary's, where ferries and ships from Britain arrive. On the side exposed to the ocean, its waves and its storms, the Scilly Isles — as well as Tresco — are rugged and barren, but on the interior side, facing Saint Mary's, it too is mild and lush; the Gulf Stream and the genius of Augustus Smith and his nephew and successor Thomas Algernon Smith-Dorrien-Smith — who in the previous century fostered the island's incredible growth and that of its horticulture — created a paradise, an island of Alcina, a garden of Armida.

Augustus Smith became Lord Proprietor of the Scilly Isles in 1834; he promoted the building of schools and lighthouses as well as the Abbey of Tresco with its gardens, in whose development Algernon Smith-Dorrien played a part, transplanting flowers and plants from all over the world and creating a thriving industry. But the origin of this Eden of the Scillies—though the isles were extremely poor for many centuries—is much older.

The first precious bulbs of exotic flowers were brought there in the twelfth century by the Benedictines, those Christian Odysseuses who intrepidly ventured far afield and put down roots in unknown lands, teaching a love of truth and knowledge as well as *stabilitas loci*, the intense, serene love for one's homeland that enables a person to spend his entire life in a remote corner yet feel settled in the world, with no desire to leave and escape. In Tresco the site of the old priory is still visible.

But like every paradise, the search for which goes back farther and farther until it vanishes in a remote nontemporality, that of the Scilly Isles also harks back to still more ancient origins. These were the Cassiterides of the Phoenicians, rich in tin and jealously kept concealed from the routes of other navigators; they were primarily, according to legendary tradition, the Fortunate Islands, one of the possible locations of the Elysian Fields, of the Hesperides, of the Blessed Isles, lush with flowers and plants, where perpetual summer reigned and heroic adventurers, having crossed the waters, discovered the land of eternal youth, of immortality.

The Scillies, Tresco in particular, deserve to be identified with the Fortunate Islands, the Hesperides, the Eden that Robert Louis Stevenson or Gauguin sought in the South Seas, timeless life, eternal sea, joy with no original sin and no history. The enchantment is perfect, unchanging; the dry, crisp clarity, the triumph of vitality in all its forms and colors, the diversity of plants and birds, gulls and herons, cormorants and petrels, mallards and sandpipers, curlews and starlings. While we eat something at a table under the trees, many of these birds, as in a fairy tale, come to eat out of our hand and from our plates: the sparrows, more confident and greediest of all, snatch a morsel out of the others' beaks and from our fingers.

But every Eden, land of immortality, is also a land of death, the place beyond the water where the feverish, familiar insignificance of life stops. The Fortunate Isles are also a province of the dead, of a sun that never sets but that shines on a different life, perfect and for that reason foreign to the life which men lead. The Scillies, like Cornwall, are connected to the Celtic legend of Lyonesse — or, in Cornish, the dialect or language of Cornwall, Lethowsow — the country sunk beneath the waves which vanished from the earth, and to the legend of Arthur, the late king whose grave many places lay claim to, though it is said that he never died; the enchanted Arthurian world is a magical spell, aquatic and melancholic, crepuscular and lunar, life that retreats to the irreality of fable and death.

The sea inexplicably has a double face. On the open shore, but also among the rocks and islets, it is the sea of storms and hurricanes, of the more than three hundred shipwrecks that occurred in the Scillies since the seventeenth century, with the loss of so many lives: it is a place of adventure and challenge, of trial, of struggle. On the sheltered side it is a place of delight, of great enticement and great abandon, of an unconditional yes to life, surrendering to the waves or lying on the sand, in harmony with pure, absolute being devoid of activity and resolve, with the slow, empty revolving of hours that is perhaps the freest, most intense and most blissful sensation in the world. Perhaps it is also the memory of amniotic waters, of the original ocean from which our species comes, and of what we knew at the beginning of our individual existence.

During these days, at least, the Scilly Isles — as well as many of the bays of Cornwall, Sennen, Botallack, Carbis Bay — disprove a sea passage of Raffaele La Capria that I love, the one in *Armonia perduta* (Harmony Lost) in which he contrasts the monotonous metallic gray of the ocean to the diaphanous, luminous blue of the Mediterranean, the sea of gods and guises, not of the formless Leviathan. Today the ocean around the Scillies is limpid and transparent, turquoise depths with patches of cobalt, the tenuousness of the edge pale blue with snow-white foam and an inexpressible intensity of indigo. But this

enchantment is also ambiguous, dual; it holds both the inexhausti-
bility of life and the lure of death. For that matter even in the *Odyssey*, Calypso's blue and purple sea casts a fatal spell, like the Sirens'
song. In every seafaring exhilaration there is melancholy, there is the
indolent oblivion of the lotus-eaters, which Tennyson, the poet of the
death of Arthur, fascinated by these islands, saw in the sea, an oblivion that is like sinking into the waters, into sleep.

The sea is absolute, intense to the point of becoming painful at
times. Among the colors of the water and the quartz sand that lends
it a white phosphorescent sheen, everything that is inconsequential,
incidental, relative falls away: there is the urge to grasp the essence
of life, free ourselves of all the trappings of existence that prevent us
from living, strip off the mechanisms of empty rhetoric the way you
strip off your clothes. One layer after another is peeled away from a
false life in order to reach the real one, bliss, and you get the feeling you're approaching a nucleus so essential, so pure as to resemble
nonbeing. Love for the sea is also a love of death, said Thomas Mann,
reminded of Shakespeare's expression of farewell, Prospero's words:
"and my ending is despair."[1] But the feeling arises because the sea
allows us to glimpse for a moment—and even enjoy, touch, possess—
that enticement, that contentment, that fullness that we would like
to have always.

The inhabitants of the Scillies have had little time over the centuries for these maritime metaphysics. The ocean for them meant
fishing, arduous and provident; it was war that brought enemy ships,
Spanish or Dutch; above all it brought danger, tempests, and winds,
hurricanes described in epic, terse reports, numerous shipwrecks. To
be truthful, the latter were not viewed unfavorably by the islanders;
it is said that they prayed to the Lord, not so that He would actually
cause ships to sink, but that if it were God's will that some shipwrecks
occur, they at least do so in the Scilly Isles, so the islanders could
seize their cargo.

Though guidebooks and histories of the island categorically deny that at night the locals tied a lantern to the tail of a donkey or cow on the shore to deceive ships and lure them onto the rocks, a story is told of a minister who once interrupted his sermon from the pulpit to announce news he'd just been given of a vessel shipwrecked on the reef. Some time later, after the sermon, he stepped down from the pulpit and when he got to the door of the church, said that another ship had run aground, but that he hadn't announced it sooner because it was only fair that they all leave together, even-steven, to run and grab the goods.

In addition to shipwrecks, smuggling is also a goldmine of stories, traditions, and anecdotes; a gallery of spirited, bizarre figures, from the Rev. John Troutbeck, author of a 1794 learned volume on the Scillies and equally zealous smuggler, forced to leave the island, to the famous John Carter, called "the King of Prussia," active in Cornwall, who also gave his name to a bay.

An amiable insouciance reigns among the saints as well, like the Irish Saint Warna, who might also be *Santa Juana*, a Spanish ship wrecked on the rocks and thus doubly revered by the islanders. Celtic Christianity is a great chapter of history that especially in Cornwall and also in the Scillies is mixed up with myth and fairy tale, saints and giants who play spiteful tricks on one another but also flirt, saints who are friends of fountains and especially of miraculous fish, enterprising saints, like Saint Brychan, who arrived by sea with three wives, several concubines, twenty-four sons, and twenty-five daughters, all in the end canonized.

The Scillies have had and have their own literature, of which they are proud; small bookshops and kiosks display novels with titles such as *Hell Bay*, by Sam Llewellyn, or *Storm Islands*, by Ann Quinton, and numerous poems celebrate waves and seashells. A more robust verse animates the spirited, ironic epitaphs of those who drowned, fanciful old legends of magic and clairvoyance, ghost sailors, witches, and mermaids, who, like the one whose image is found in the Church of Saint Senara in Zennor, Cornwall, lure the pious cleric into the breakers as he sings his psalms.

The poet of the Scillies is Robert Maybee (1810–1891), an illiterate oral bard who sang of ancient customs, wars and storms, ballads steeped in epic intimacy with the sea, death and the Almighty. Today the best-known poetic voice is Mary Wilson, wife of Harold Wilson, the former Labour prime minister who lives in the Scilly Isles; her lyrics celebrate the blue and purple sea, churches set amid golden daffodils, the sound of the surf, and make her the ideal figure of an official hometown poet, virtually the "poet of the city," a title for which Thomas Mann envied, with irony and nostalgia, the old, accomplished Emanuel Geibel, whose statue adorns the park in Lübeck. All of this literature is, of course, in English; unlike the other Celtic languages, Cornish has all but disappeared, despite recent linguistic and literary attempts to revive it. The only consolation lies in fragments of medieval mystery plays, in which God speaks Cornish and the devil English.

In the Scilly Isles, as in all of Cornwall, archaic vestiges from the time of the Druids can be found, large boulders marking tombs and burial chambers, enigmatic megaliths, mysterious signs of primordial beginnings. The Merry Maids, near Penzance, in Cornwall, are a circle of nineteen huge stones, perhaps an ancient sacrificial area or some such, where each year the Gorsedd takes place, a gathering of bards who seek to revive the memory of the Celtic heritage. Among these stones one certainly senses a respect for the murky, vanished past, for the forebears who are to this day common ancestors, of humanity and of civilization. But that reverence, that sense of mystery, have to do with the simplicity of life that passes and ceases to exist, the stones and the cows grazing peacefully among them with their secret of animal life.

We can and we must have *pietas* for the Druids and certainly even more for the victims of their rituals, because they were poor devils like us and were certainly worse off than we are. The ways of Celtic tradition become vulgar at times, however, in esoteric initiation rites, in a false neo-paganism, in complacent superstition. The cult of the arcane, of magic, and of origins is always a sophisticated garishness, like all irrationalistic affectation. So much more profound than any sibylline ritual is the old Cornish saying about the three most beautiful things in the world: "A woman with a child, a boat with unfurled sails, and a cornfield swaying in the wind."

July 9, 1989

THE PRUSSIAN ROAD TO PEACE

In 1849, Frederick William IV of Prussia refused the imperial German crown that was offered to him by the National Assembly in Frankfurt; he rejected it, after much hesitation, because he thought it unseemly that a sovereign should be legitimized by a parliament, but also because he feared that his realm, Prussia, might be swallowed up in the greater entity of Germany: "The colors black-red-gold, namely, those of the German empire," he had said a few months earlier, "must not overpower the glorious black and white of my cockade," that of Prussia. In the same period Bismarck also had an ironic riposte for a deputy who preached the idea of a national Germany: "So you too have been bitten by the Germanic tarantula?"

German history's centuries-old quandary is the conflicting relationship between the particularistic patriotism of individual states, which made up the mosaic of the splintered empire, and the drive to unify the nation. The defenders and proponents of the latter were, in past centuries, primarily writers and poets, often at odds with the politicians, princes, and ministers who pursued the interests of their own kingdoms or city-states. Günter Grass vehemently reminded us of it a few nights ago in a debate that took place in the Hebbel Theater in Berlin as part of the events that accompanied Berlin's thirty exhibitions on Prussia.

Discussing the Prussian legacy with Klaus von Bismarck, great-grandson of the Iron Chancellor and director of the Goethe-Institut, and with the publisher and essayist Wolf Jobst Siedler, Grass referred to the progressive inspiration of national sentiment professed by great poets of the past adverse to chauvinism and fraternally open to the world—think of Gotthold Lessing—and asserted a similar ethico-political role for contemporary German writers, in his view particularly essential today. Beyond the merits and demerits of the old Prussia, for Grass there is a moral duty that the writer must perform with Prussian rigor, applying the lesson of an ethical style based on suprapersonal dedication to a categorical imperative. This duty—Grass said, speaking just days after the violent street clashes that had marked U.S. Secretary of State Alexander Haig's visit to Berlin—was the struggle for the sentiment of German national unity and for peace.

These two ambitions seem to Grass to be inseparable facets of a single problem. East and West Germany appear to be two worlds increasingly more distant and alien to each other whose mutual estrangement is cultivated and compounded by the political power of both parties, more concerned with preserving their own domains and their own system of alliances than about the country, like the eighteenth-century princes who sold their soldiers to foreign powers. East Germany seems to ludicrously exaggerate the worst Prussianism, despotism, to the point of parody, while the government of Bonn—which Grass sees as being more and more dominated by a materialistic ideology of immediate gratification—for him expresses the vindictive revenge of the old Catholic states of the southwest against the Prussian hegemony that had unified the country.

There is a lapse in *memoria patriae*, observed Siedler, who favors a growing sentimental disinterest: in the West a train accident in Marseille is bigger news than one in Halle, few young people have a clear idea about Dresden and not even the year of Prussian celebrations induces the federal citizens—millions of whom have fled from the East—to sacrifice the exciting Mediterranean beaches to spend their vacations, undoubtedly with some discomfort and inconvenience, in the waters, heaths, and villages of the old Brandenburg March, so rich in natural allure and early German history.

Unless we want to see the rebirth of a perverse, aggressive nationalism, Grass thundered, wreathed in smoke from the cigar clamped beneath his drooping mustache, an open, progressive response must be given to this real need for a feeling of a common fatherland. He proposed the creation of a common cultural foundation for both Germanys which, renouncing any unachievable—and in his view risky—political unification, would preserve or reawaken a spiritual unity that would rise above governmental divisions.

It is the old German dream of the "republic of scholars," of a national culture as opposed to a state that denies it in obedience to a logic based on power; a nation that—in the aspirations of eighteenth- and nineteenth-century patriots—was to transcend territorial boundaries to become the custodian of a cosmopolitan spirit, forsaking political unity to be the spokesman for supranational values. Grass identifies these values with the struggle for peace, against Russian and American power politics, which in his view rekindle the threat of war while also keeping the heart of central Europe under those nations' vassalage and solidifying central Europe's divisions. The struggle for a German cultural nation would thereby be a struggle for humanity, since, by awakening forces against the large states' desire for power, it would curb the aggressive mechanism.

His fellow debaters countered Grass with a pragmatic's skepticism, and he reproached their myopia as pragmatics who do not improve the world because they are convinced of the impossibility of improving it. His utopia certainly appears ingenuous, at a time when the logic of destruction is regaining momentum among the great powers and may already be driving them toward some *foedus sceleris* that might entail sacrificing a nation that wants to be itself to the lust of a state in exchange for allowing the other a free hand in some other part of the world. But the awareness of things as they are cannot allow us to forget the need for things as they should be. Nonetheless, to be sound, Grass's utopia should not have the bold certainty rightly challenged by Klaus von Bismarck: it must be aware of its paltry frailty and fight, knowing that it will be promptly defeated, but knowing that defeats also change the world.

This could well be the ethical Prussian style evoked by Grass, although he himself violates it when, with the nonchalance not uncommon in literary figures, he tenders superficial judgments on the economic situation or overestimates the importance of what is happening in the cultural community, under the illusion that a meeting between writers of East and West is indeed a step toward an opening of the world, whereas it might simply be a corporate ceremony, an international association's tradition. Poetry that rebels against power must squarely face up to its own fragility, which consigns it to immediate defeat but does not diminish its good fight; like the seed in the gospel, it too must be able to sacrifice itself and die in order to bear fruit.

September 24, 1981

THE OLD PRUSSIA PUTS ON A SHOW

The epithet *prussien*, Bismarck said in a speech given before the Chamber on May 25, 1871, is very nearly an insult. The inexorable chancellor was referring to France and the "contrived intrigues" of its government, which had helped make that term odious among the French; elsewhere as well the term is often surrounded by an aura of suspicion or aversion, amid numerous doubts and misunderstandings.

Awash in pathos, the word seems above all a sign of contradiction, a term for which history and common opinion suggest antithetical definitions. On the staircase in the Martin-Gropius-Bau, which leads up to the largest of the thirty Prussian exhibitions unveiled in recent months in Berlin — *Prussia: Attempt at a Balance* — billowing white flags display in large letters some of these conflicting interpretations. Alongside Churchill's dismissive phrase, pointing to Prussia as the origin of all evil, are the words of Frederick II that extol the religious tolerance of a country where every man was free to go to heaven in whatever way he pleased. The paragraph of the law by which in 1947 the Allies dissolved the Prussian state hangs from above like a heraldic crest, while the flow of visitors slightly stirs the banner which bears the concerns of Theodor Fontane — one of the greatest writers, most sadly enamored of old Prussia — about his homeland, which to him did not seem like a country that had an army, but rather like an army that had a country.

Fontane's words are the most meaningful, because, unlike the others, they are not born of ignorant hostility or self-serving tribute, but rather of a critical love, of a passion that — like every true passion — engenders a sharper, more uncompromising gaze toward that which is loved: Fontane, the imperturbable, late-century narrator who published his first novel at age sixty and his masterpieces when nearly eighty, is a stoical bard of the old Brandenburg March, moved by its traditions and its ethos while at the same time conscious of its waning and the vulgarization of its world. His criticism of Prussia, floating in the air over the heads of the crowd visiting the exhibition, stems from an interior Prussianism, a profound attachment to that austere, suprapersonal style of life, that ethical militancy that had been the foundation of Prussian civilization.

The more truthful balance of the legacy of that civilization is found in the writers who loved it most, who absorbed its moral rigor, making it an absolute measure by which to judge every historical reality and therefore that of Prussia as well. As a result of appearing degenerate and unfaithful to its own ideal model, Prussia is often harshly criticized, especially at a time when, by unifying Germany and establishing a great modern state, Frederick's old Prussia and its grand style break up amid the babel of industrialization and contemporary standardization. It is not surprising that Klaus von Bismarck, great-grandson of the founder of the empire, stated a few days ago in a debate in Berlin that Prussia did not die in the postwar period—when it was officially obliterated, territorially dismembered, and politically broken up—but rather in 1871, when it radially transformed into the German empire that it itself had created.

In the history of poetry, Prussianism is mainly a broad category of the ethical conflict between diverse duties and times of duty, a symbol of the clash between an absolute principle and the ambiguity of life. Prussian is the inner conflict of the prince in Heinrich von Kleist's *Prince of Homburg,* who wins a battle by disobeying the commander's orders and is suspended between his subjective truth and the general one which transcends it; Prussian is the affable, melancholy steadfastness with which the Junker Dubslav von Stechlin, in Fontane's novel, remains in place in his world, even while noticing its decline and seeing the need for that decline and the progress that it may lead to; Prussian is the battle for justice, stemming from faith in the law and its rulings, that inspires *The Case of Sergeant Grischa*, the socialist and pacifist novel by Arnold Zweig.

Prussian tradition offered writers, who in some way identified with it, a context in which to frame the conflict between a moral law, perceived as absolute, and the multiplicity of existence, in an impetus to go beyond the individual to a higher value to which that individual must submit. Current opinion, often misinformed where Germany is concerned, tends to see only the worst aspect of this transcendence — which undoubtedly exists as well — viewing it as total subordination of the individual to the state, or rather the ruling class, which claims to coincide with the state. In this sense Prussianism is equated with a prostrate deference to higher orders and is seen as an anteroom leading to National Socialist discipline. But in addition to Hegel's Prussia in its most conservative aspect, which posits the state as absolute, there is the Prussia of Kant, whose categorical imperative — also originating in the fervid climate of intellectual inquiry, religious tolerance and state-building that characterized the Prussia of the Enlightenment — is a universal law that rises above any political order. The anti-Hitler conspiracy of July 20, 1944, also derives from this Prussian ethos.

Those who now confuse Prussia with Germany in general, even now with its Nazi perversion, forget the great differences among the various German states and the political cohesion that made Prussia, during the Weimar Republic, the *Land* characterized by the most solid democratic loyalty and greatest socialist receptiveness, in accordance with a tradition that made West Berlin, even in the postwar period, one of the least conservative cities of West Germany. The waning of Prussia, namely, its absorption into Germany — despite the federal structure, which existed de facto until 1934 — was often seen as a parable of the end of the world of tradition, assimilated into mass society and its collective phenomenology, such as racist nationalism, which has little in common with the feudal patriotism of the Junkers. The Prussian heritage, much discussed in recent weeks in Berlin, is the rigor of a conservative morality, which perceives its own end—at times mindful of the need for this end and at other times trying to suppress the discomfort of such awareness.

The thirty exhibitions, especially the central one, are meant not to take sides but to bring to life Prussia in all its diversity and contradictions. From room to room, among the many ears of corn that evoke the agrarian character of the country and the base of its economy, the visitor retraces the historic path from the ancient March to the Hohenzollern monarchy through portraits of sovereigns and imperial edicts, maps of provinces and charts of historical battles, everyday objects and symbols of power, documents of the old working-class autonomy and the Berlin paving stones with which the revolutionaries raised the barricades in 1848, forcing the monarch to issue a hypocritical proclamation addressing them as "my dear Berliners." Other exhibitions among the thirty focus on particular aspects or periods: one documents the life and culture of Jews in Berlin during the great period of the Enlightenment; one is devoted to Hegel and one dedicated to E. T. A. Hoffmann, who had been branded by the former as an example of pathological disorder;[1] one illustrates the age of Biedermeier and one aligns, in impeccable symmetry, the military uniforms or regiments of tin soldiers, in whose colorful geometries Hoffmann and Hegel, imagination and logic, seem to come together in a daring attempt to impose order on the world's chaos.

There is the controversial, aggressive exhibition on Borussia, or rather on the fanatical self-aggrandizement of Prussia, in a mixture of spine-chilling death drive, fascination with spiked helmets and skeletons, and consumeristic kitsch, meant to show that all magnificence, even that of the Prussian eagle, ends up in the trash bin of Time and, in the modern age, in the degradation of commercials, in the gossip of glossy magazines or ads for Bismarck herring.

The Musée sentimental de Prusse illustrates the details or refuse of history: the rusty, reddish old knife used to cut the 1,005-ells-long sausage presented to Prince-Elector Johann Sigismund on New

Year's Day 1601, poignant photographs of military orphanages visited at Christmas by some benevolent, distant authorities, the chamber pot of the Kaiser, anatomical models used in the legendary medical faculties of the nineteenth-century university, the great historical words of the chancellor or emperor which ended up adorning coffee cups, the radiography of the prince of Homburg's silver leg, the uniform of the fraudulent Captain of Köpenick.[2]

There is the neoclassical Berlin of the architect Karl Friedrich Schinkel, who wanted to cultivate beauty, the Berlin of the slums and the gay, popular one of the taverns, whose spirited humor was captured by the satirist Adolf Glasbrenner and whose proletarian physiognomy was depicted by the talented illustrator Heinrich Zille.

Three key moments, of course, get the lion's share of attention: Frederick's Prussia; the one—perhaps the greatest—dominated by the generals and reformers of 1812, the year of the anti-Napoleonic wars of liberation, which tried to establish a vigorous, enlightened state, shortly stifled by the restoration; and Bismarck's Prussia. A large statue of Wilhelm I is suspended in space, in the vault of a vast hall whose floor is intentionally overcrowded with objects, steam engines, photographs, guns, chassis. The hall reproduces the Prussian pavilion at the Exposition Universelle, the International Exposition of 1867 in Paris, which shows how Prussia wanted to appear to the world. This excessive self-exhibition combines the fixity of an aquarium—in which things appear to be relegated to a very slow, almost eternal decomposition—with the chaos of a battlefield, albeit a battle among pompous, useless objects.

We are still in the age of Bismarck, but hovering in this room is a foretaste of the theatrical, lavish, funereal kitsch in the rooms to come, the realm of the belligerent, showy, upward-twirled mustache of Wilhelm II, which replaced the drooping, austere whiskers of the great chancellor. In these last halls, among oleographs impartially depicting the Kaiser as helmsman of the empire and August Bebel as helmsman of socialism, Prussia seems truly at an end. World history has become a carnival of itself, a cyclorama or a diorama like the famous Kaiserpanorama, opened in 1883 by entrepreneur August Fuhrmann near the boulevard Unter den Linden.

In the automatism of the contemporary world, in which even tragic events become a spectacle of themselves and in which life seems to become its own advertisement, there is no longer any room for the old Prussia, for the feudal idyll of Brandenburg evoked in the exhibition dedicated to Fontane or for the genius of Clausewitz, who had imposed intellectual order and stylistic significance even on the chaos of war. Prussianism will become the symbol of nostalgia for meaning and style in the contemporary babel of the formless and absurd: it will be the mask of Erich von Stroheim in *Grand Illusion*,[3] the defensive pathos of his conduct that unites a decorous inner life of intense, profound, almost anarchic, feeling and loyalty to an objective standard, to a moral uniform, seeking in this combination a barrier against barbarism and carnage, against the indistinct.

The barrier is insufficient, as the film itself showed, because its subjective nobility is based on an anachronistic aristocraticness and an objective social injustice. Today nostalgia is rediscovering Prussia, even in the German Democratic Republic, where the monuments of Frederick II and Baron von Stein were recently returned to their place in the center of East Berlin, and where Prussia's cultural legacy is being widely discussed and reassessed, no longer considered synonymous with reactionary. What is the focus of this nostalgia? Not the iron jewels, displayed in a case at one of the exhibitions, or the claws of the Prussian eagle, but a clear desire for style and form, which the age of Nashville unexpectedly misses;[4] it is a capacity for discretion, the virtue most dear to Fontane, who did not like the new Prussia, had no illusions about the Prussia of former times, which he loved, and deplored the fact that Bismarck was talented but devoid of magnanimity.

September 30, 1981

THE WALL

On the Berlin Wall last year someone printed in big black letters the well-known words of Friedrich Hölderlin, with which the great German poet accused his countrymen of being a divided, torn people par excellence: in Germany, the inscription reads, you see workers and priests, masters and servants, old and young people, but you don't see human beings, individuals who are whole and complete. German culture has been great for the lucid intensity with which it denounced the split between the individual and society, the alienating process that levels humans into a one-dimensional role, forcing them to be only a cog in society's gearwheel and preventing them from fully developing their personality, thus reducing society to a group of amputated beings.

Classicism and German Romanticism — with Goethe, Schiller, Hölderlin — spring from the awareness of this disability and from the dream of healing it. For its poets and philosophers, Germany becomes an exemplary clinical case of this political malady or a proving ground for history, its disasters and its hopes: the country in which such impairment is most evident and produces both the loftiest plans for total redemption and the most pathological, lethal reactions to the distress.

Fascism was the most raging, self-destructive response to the difficulties of modern society, a virulent disease mistaken for medicine, which exacerbated the split and disintegration it was meant to heal. Germany divided in two by the Nazi apocalypse is the visible sign of this laceration that cuts through history and Europe: the borders that separate the two German states are the edges of an open wound, a scar that has not healed, that disfigures not only Germany but Europe, because a divided Germany prevents any genuine European unity. Berlin—divided in half, occupied by four powers, and carved by a grotesque wall—is the burning image of an unnaturally blocked history.

In Berlin the provisional aspect has crystallized into an absurd eternity, into the grimace of a repeated tic. It has been forty-two years since the end of the Second World War: a period twice as long as fascism, almost four times that of Nazism, an era equivalent to that, in the history of France, during which the monarchy fell, the Revolution triumphed and failed, Napoleon conquered and lost Europe, the Bourbons returned and were driven out again. Today the planes of Lufthansa, the West German airline, cannot land in Berlin; American, British, French, and Russian soldiers born twenty years after the end of the war stand guard as if having just arrived yesterday at the ruins of the Third Reich.

Meanwhile the political geography of entire continents is being transformed, age-old gods are falling, customs and values are changing, radical anthropological adaptations can be seen, laboratories and apprentice wizards promise or threaten new living species, ape-men, as many identical creatures as you like, produced by cloning, the extinction of *Homo sapiens*, the return of the dinosaur. Berlin's permanently provisional statute, which prolongs 1945 indefinitely, shows that the only eternity now available is the perpetual blockage of that which is fleeting and random, a jammed engine that continues to screech, the needle of a record player that scratches incessantly because we forgot to press a button.

The festivities in Berlin, to which 1987 is dedicated, are a grandiose, conscious mise-en-scène of the paradoxical situation of a city that is one and multiple, center and periphery of Germany and of Europe, senile and adolescent, artificial and brilliant mirror of our reality or, better yet, of our irreality. With its rich program of events, whose list alone fills lengthy catalogues, Berlin is celebrating its 750 years of history, rather few, in fact, worthy of the city that Konrad Adenauer, proud of the Roman origins of Cologne, regarded with dislike, and that Walther Rathenau, who conversely loved it, described as "the metropolis of the parvenu." But Berlin's allure lies precisely in this relative poverty of history; Berlin is a metropolis, and a metropolis does not know stability and tradition, the reverent continuity of the past; rather it is the very instantaneous breath of the new, the constant transformation that continually swallows and erases every image of reality, just as a jukebox eats and forgets one record after another and the glitter of neon advertising has no memory of the day before.

The exhibitions, tours, and performances certainly do not neglect the history of Frederick II's Berlin, the nineteenth-century city with the idyllic romance of its sedate houses and the tranquil waters of the Spree, the Prussian Berlin and the staunchly socialist one. Nevertheless it is significant that the great architects of German history—Frederick II, Bismarck, Adenauer—did not love this city, perhaps because what reigned in Berlin, as Bismarck observed contemptuously in 1881, was always "progress," that is, becoming, metamorphosis, the flow of life that sweeps away all stability and permanence. Since the end of the century, the greatest poets have seen in Berlin, in its metropolitan throbbing, in its landscape in which nature and artifice transcolor one another, the very image of modern poetry, of its uprooted, drifting flux that reveals a love of form, of structure, through the seduction of the chaotic and formless.

For the great lyric poetry of Gottfried Benn, for the unforgettable novel *Berlin Alexanderplatz* by Alfred Döblin,[1] for many other masterpieces, Berlin is the face of art, of a complex and at the same time poignant art, as experimental art often is, whose mixture of artifice and ingenuity, sentimental pathos and programmatic intellectualism, aggressive protest and helpless abandon is reminiscent of adolescence. But the greatest praise of Berlin appeared in April 1941, in a Jewish newspaper printed illegally in the Nazi-occupied Warsaw Ghetto, in an article that spoke with passionate longing of a dark, secret, underground Berlin, buried under Hitler's posters, flags, and parades; an invisible Berlin, but one that the author said he still felt was alive, dormant and hidden, a karstic river that would one day emerge. On that day the clandestine journalist would also regain, as he himself said, the right to live.

Rebuilt after 1945 and devoid of historical buildings, which are located mostly in the eastern sector, West Berlin today is a new city, Americanized, a window and showcase of the West, but unlike other neon cities, which convey the prosaic squalor of the industrial or postindustrial era, Berlin also expresses a secret fascination, the lure of ephemerality inherent in rapid production and consumption, a nostalgia, an aura of disenchantment, which the metropolis has in common with youth.

Berlin's 750th birthday is celebrated throughout the year in both East and West, with separate and distinct initiatives—primarily the wish of the Eastern government—which are nevertheless linked, in a spirit that shows how real and deep the need is for ever closer relations between the two Germanys in any case.

The East tends to offer a more solid, cohesive, traditional picture of Berlin's history, in accordance with the conservative classicism of Communist ideology in Germany; in the West, the uncertainty, the mobility, the disturbing provisional aspect of this history are emphasized—the anti-Communist conservatives are uncomfortable because they would like to see in the West a conformist, edifying authoritarianism like the one they accuse communism of.

The intended center of the celebrations is the Martin-Gropius-Bau, but events proliferate and branch out into the streets and squares, all Berlin virtually becomes a demonstration and exhibition of itself, with neighborhood parties and festivities, tours and processions, shows and debates, a rich range of programs revealing the intellectual creativity of a city for which—as for many cities in crisis—culture has become an essential element of life and work, a primary productive activity, and a real reason for being.

The Berlin that is celebrated, with an impassioned but also ironic, self-critical eye, is an extremely diverse and contradictory city, a city economically troubled and supported by subsidies from Bonn but full of ever new initiatives; a city whose resident population is aging—and whose elderly are perhaps accountable for the 82,121 dogs, companions of solitary walks—but one to which young people come from many different parts of the world, feeling at home in that seismographic station of precariousness.

The programs evoke eras and circumstances, Nazi terror and the Bauhaus; they highlight the two official Berlins but also many other concurrent, intermingled cities: Jewish Berlin, the Turkish one composed of numerous immigrant workers who by now have become Berliners—their children study the Qur'an but their mother tongue is German—the multinational, multicultural melting pot that, despite the stalled political and economic situation, goes on fusing and amalgamating the most disparate components in the liberating metropolitan hybrid.

Literature also has a role, and a significant one, in this year's celebration. Readings of texts, discussions, dialogues with the public. I too find myself at one of these events, at the Hebbel Theater, with my *Danube*. Often literature-as-performance (the author reading a passage in the original text, an actor who then reads it in translation, the presenter commenting on it) is an uncomfortable rite, a ceremony that like many social customs has no real justification, but in which you take part so as not to remain excluded from the liturgy. But in Berlin, literature is at home, you feel it in the air, it is palpable and indispensable, an everyday activity, like walking, drinking, or sleeping, a physiological necessity. In Berlin, Heinrich Mann said in 1921, one lives the future ahead of time; it may be that today we are living, beforehand, the absence and improbability of a future. Whatever it may be, it cannot help but concern all Europe, not just its western half. That is why it pays to live in Berlin, because, as Uwe Johnson said, "here we see what is happening."

July 26, 1987

ON LOTTE'S TOMB

On the way back to Italy from Berlin, I stop in Hannover. Garten-friedhof on Marienstrasse is where Lotte is buried—Goethe's Lotte, from *Werther*, one of the most beautiful love stories of all time, the second best seller, after *Robinson Crusoe*, of world literature. As the name tells us, the cemetery is a small park; among the graves, beneath the chestnuts and oak trees, children run around, mothers chat, a man is lying on the grass sunbathing without a shirt. This relaxed ease does not annul death; it brings those who are buried familiarly close.

Lotte's grave marker is a kind of squat, low tower, with curv-ing friezes that suggest plants and seashells; the inscription reads, "Here lies Charlotte Sophie Henriette Kestner née Buff," followed by the dates of birth and death and, on the back, the words "Widow of Hofrat Johann Christian Kestner." Death pays no attention to pas-sions, indiscretions, disturbances of the heart and returns each indi-vidual to the objective order to which he or she belongs, to marriage, to caste. In real life Lotte—the actual Lotte, the one who rests here below—was the wife of the Hofrat, the mother of his children; she shared his life. Given all that, a Buddenbrook would say, the fact that she may have in some way been the inspiration for a character in an immortal novel is of little relevance, hardly more than curiosity or idle gossip.

June 11, 1989

IN FREIBURG THE DAY OF
GERMAN UNITY IS REMOTE

Freiburg. A police van is stationed near Freiburg's Gothic town hall, a few hours before midnight, which will mark the beginning of the new, united Germany.[1] But the big night in Berlin, its television images broadcast around the world, is far removed from nightfall here, which a short time ago engulfed the hills of the Black Forest and now envelops the reddish bell tower of the cathedral, guardian for centuries—like the woods surrounding it, among which Heidegger liked to wander and lose himself—of one of the hearts of old Germany, of its secret intimacy and mysterious forebodings. When I ask the policeman if and where any special event for the unification might take place on this historic evening that will be among the dates to be memorized in school, the officer is surprised and bewildered; he says he doesn't know and that he doesn't think there will be anything special.

I'd gotten the same answer that afternoon from the proprietor at the Hotel Deutscher Kaiser, as she was carrying beer to guests playing cards beneath deer antlers and old portraits of Wilhelm II— returning much later, I found them all still animated by the games and the resulting squabbles, happy to be able to play a little longer thanks to extended open hours on this exceptional night. "I don't know, I don't think so," the proprietor had said, "but look in the paper, under the events listing, or ask in the city" (whose center is a fifteen-minute walk from the hotel).

The "city" seems a little more lively than usual, but not much more than on a normal weekend evening; a sign on the door of the

Cha-Cha-Cha discotheque announces that it will remain open later than the usual wee hours in honor of German unity, but the young people with shaved heads or tinted hair thronging to get in are talking about anything but that. Cafés, pubs, restaurants, taverns are jammed with people chatting or clamoring with no mention of the momentous date, no one is watching television in the bars, and no one on the street stops in front of store windows, like that of Radiobastian on Kaiser-Josef-Strasse, where TV sets are tuned to the crowds at the Brandenburg Gate, the streets and squares of Berlin, panel discussions and debates. On a screen you see Günter Grass speaking, contentious and torrential, his mouth opens aggressively under the showy mustache, but no sound comes from beyond the window glass, like watching an old silent film.

In the two days surrounding October 3 that I spend in Freiburg, in various places in the Black Forest or in other towns and villages in the German countryside, reunification reaches me somewhat like that television broadcast behind the glass, muted in the irreality that surrounds those who are faint of hearing. In Kaiserstuhl, they tell me, people are too busy with the harvest; in Friedrichshall, near Heilbronn, a young man mutters that the authorities sugarcoat things as usual, and we'll have to tighten our belts more than we think; in Schauinsland the pretty, talkative clerk at an inn overlooking the black and russet woods tells me about a waitress who came from the German Democratic Republic who was fired because she did not want to work, while a mechanic, he too an East German, is very good, but he's worried all the same that too many people from his area of the country might possibly come. As for flags on private homes, I saw only one.

In Freiburg, on the night of October 2, one of the most conspicuous signs of unification was the timid announcement of a "counter-celebration," albeit very restrained, on Habsburger-Strasse. Talking to people about German unity does not bring to mind similar experiences of journalistic reporting or impressions of other crucial moments in history or in recent German annals, but rather evokes memories of youthful times, pleasant though misguided attempts to strike up a conversation with fabulous German girls. I wonder, for a moment, if people's detachment from such an event is a legacy of the old Habsburg rule in Freiburg, of Austrian reluctance in the face of exceptional events and a consequent desire and preference not to be present when they happen, to be elsewhere.

But this low-key atmosphere should not fool us, it is not—or not only—a sign of indifference, a self-centeredness on the part of those afraid to give up a little prosperity, or an insensitivity to national unity and its great moments. "We're not unexcited about it," Pastor Ahrend says, "but we must not forget that many problems remain unresolved." A secondary school teacher tells me that the best way to celebrate unification is by silent, conscious reflection, without any orgiastic enthusiasm. Of course, in all of this there is also a dose of the old German particularism, now accentuated by resistance toward Berlin as the capital; a gentleman, a wine merchant, indignantly comments on news reported by the *Badische Zeitung*—Freiburg's progressive, well-written daily newspaper—about scumbags who, in exchange for handsome compensation, offer the television networks advance news of the time and place where acts of vandalism will take place in Berlin on the momentous night, or propose staging Nazi demonstrations in front of the TV cameras for a fee. "Only in Berlin can that happen."

Apart from these self-interests, people's attitudes reflect in their own way those assumed, especially in this area, by newspapers and other mass media. The media express joy over the fall of the totalitarian regime and for the country's unity, but avoid any jubilation, urging a dose of skepticism which is the salt of any joy that is not rhetorical; they recall the iniquities of the GDR regime, but encourage people to remember the infamies of Nazism, they talk about national values and about those that transcend them, they acclaim the liberation of the East Germans but also fully emphasize the hardships, the disorientation, the unemployment, the uncertainties, the lines waiting at the employment offices, generations of individuals cut off from prospects of a job.

Behind the indifference of people around here there may well be, as everywhere, self-interest and hostility toward strangers, but deep down there is also a sober, brusque, positive cordiality. The East Germans who come here, as one of them, a construction worker, tells me, are in the end welcomed with sincere simplicity. At a time when the world, faced with the new Germany, has so many fears, both founded and unfounded, this quiet, inconspicuous, provincial Germany—which does not display its muscle, is not fond of historical moments, and experiences unity as an event devoid of exhilaration and indeed rooted in the good prosaicness of reality—ultimately shows a reassuring, familiar face, enabling hope for a viable future.

October 4, 1990

THE DYING FOREST

In Goethe's *Faust, Part II*, the bard of the eternal generative force of nature seems to advance the ironic, sorrowful suspicion that modern society has supplanted or is about to supplant nature. In a mocking, grotesque masquerade, he depicts the triumph of the artificial over the authentic, of fashion over the seasons, of the manufactured over the natural; flowers no longer grow in obedience to the ancient laws of blooming and withering, but according to the needs and conventions of the market, which imperiously interferes in the natural cycle and alters it at will. Always ambiguous and sibylline, Goethe does not make clear whether this is a real, definitive defeat of Mother Nature or one of her demonic tricks; whether humans really are diverging and disrupting her or whether they are unconsciously playing along with her game, her charade, even while profaning her. Nature, which generates flowers as well as hurricanes that devastate them, may also create fake flowers and induce human intelligence — which invents the plow and presses the grape, turning it into wine — to manufacture synthetic materials, using substances created by the ancient mother.

It is difficult if not impossible to tell if an abnormal, disproportionate technological growth can destroy nature or whether it too, like earthquakes and Egypt's plagues, may be a manifestation of nature itself, of its vitality. The extinction of the dinosaurs does not dismay us and appears to perhaps be in harmony with some mysterious natural law that governs the birth and death of the species; for the dinosaurs, of course, it was a disaster. The cries of alarm over wounds that technological and industrial evolution has inflicted, and continues to inflict, on our ecological equilibrium are ridiculous if we fear that a petrochemical can kill the great Pan, but maybe they're not so ridiculous if we fear, more simply, for our survival and our well-being.

Likewise the death of the Schwarzwald's forest, and many other forests, may not disturb Brahma, Spinoza's God or the Great Whole, but if it continues to spread at its current pace, it will certainly have ruinous consequences over countless individuals, their existence, their history, their loves, their ghosts, their day-to-day life. The forest is dying, and its end, especially in the Black Forest, is cloaked in a tragic, heroic aura, like that of a king in an epic poem.

There is an entire literature in Germany on the death of the forest, especially the Schwarzwald, the Black Forest, virtually a cycle of songs and deeds about a fallen hero: *So stirbt der Wald* (So the Forest Is Dying), *Unser Wald darf nicht sterben* (Our Forest Must Not Die!), *Der Stress des Waldes* (The Stress of the Forest), *Stirbt der Wald?* (The Death of the Forest?), *Das Waldsterben* (Forest Dieback); the list of apprehensive, protesting, and alarming books that continue to come out, especially in Baden-Württemberg and in Freiburg, the old capital of Baden, could go on at length. Though in the *Chanson de Roland* the wounded hero leans against a pine tree, his last gaze turned toward dear France, his distant homeland, now the fatally wounded epic hero is the pine itself, which seems to be spreading its great shadow for only a little longer, sinking its roots into its motherland for nearly the last time.

The Black Forest, the beautiful German woodland bordering France and Switzerland, is a heart of old Germany, of its pensive, romantic intimacy, of the dreamy, poignant idyll of German inner life that breathes, shy and heartfelt, in the nostalgia of the Lieder. The Black Forest is a land of poets and philosophers, of pensive meditation and songs of wandering, a spirituality in harmony with the seasons and proud of its independence. In these black forests, in past centuries, a hushed Protestant devoutness flourished, which inspired the loftiest philosophy and the loftiest German poetry.

In the Black Forest were writers of "calendar stories," like the great Johann Peter Hebel, whose laconic, pithy tales contained, with the essentiality of the classics, epic wisdom and political savvy, the life of the individual positioned in human history and in the still greater saga of nature. Mark Twain, wandering through these forests, met the villagers and saw in them the heroines of Berthold Auerbach's *Tales of the Black Forest*; nature and art, the scent of wood and paper that poetry spoke of, were all one, in an indissoluble syntony. This idyll could, if necessary, defend itself; the Black Forest is a land of traditions protective of freedom and progress, and outspokenly courageous in defending them, even with weapons, against tyranny and reaction, as in 1848–1849.

The ailing, dying forest is a symbol of a disease that is also devastating the ecology of mind and heart, assaulting a cradle of German culture. The issues of the magazine *Merian* dedicated to the Schwarzwald seraphically celebrate the primeval forest, the sagas of the nymphs of the Mummelsee, the enchanted lake, and the unspoiled allure of the Belchen, the dazzling, hoary mountain, but in the same window of the bookshop other books show horrific photographs of devastated firs stripped of their needles, sparse, twisted forests on the banks of the lake and on the flanks of the mountain. The ads for vacation resorts continue to tout tranquillity and well-being, but for some time now they have ceased to boast about the "wealth of ozone in the forest air." The Black Forest, as documents distributed by the DNR, the German League for Nature and Environment, report, tops the charts of ecological deterioration, which moreover show as many as one-third of the forests seriously ruined throughout Germany. The king of the Schwarzwald, the silver fir that fascinated Turgenev, is the most recurrent victim, here as elsewhere, on a par with the pine, which is also losing its needles everywhere; if the current course continues at the same rate, statistics tell us that all the firs will die by 1990 and all the pines by 1992.

The death of firs and pines — as well as that of birches or oaks — is one moment paraded with sensational effect, the next concealed, the way our culture, anxious to repudiate death, conceals certain deaths in accordance with rules of human respect and good manners. Life, even abject, is seductive; tourists and hikers do not see the trees' gangrene. At the Triberg waterfall 17 percent, in a survey, respond that they have noticed some devastation, at the Mummelsee it is 34 percent; women, who according to Otto Weininger are always more content, deny much more often than men that the forest is dying or may die (37 percent, compared to 52 percent of the strong, pessimistic sex).

The mass media, by dwelling on the ecological disaster, end up inuring people to the demise; by dint of seeing signs, books, and photographs on the death of the forest, they no longer see the trees that are dying. But death is there, and even those accustomed to looking more at books than at plants can see it, despite the snow, when walking along the Titisee, on the slopes of the Belchen, along the so-called Black Forest High Road. The treetops are bare, the branches of the conifers have no needles; attacked by acid rain or snow the trees look like skeletons of bombed-out buildings.

It is no wonder that the University of Freiburg, which remained peaceful in '68, was instead contentious in the green protest. Until three years ago, Professor von Ditfurth, engaged in the eco-pacifist movement and the author of well-received books on the subject, tells me, the Greens were accused of being agents provocateurs from Moscow, reviled by the Christian Democrats and also, though somewhat less so, by the Socialists, and opposed by the unions, fearful that anti-industrial protests could eliminate jobs. Today the situation has changed: the losses are so evident that the authorities can no longer pretend not to see them, even though they alternately issue statements of commitment and press releases that play down the damage. The Greens themselves, however, have changed; they have abandoned rhetorical, adolescent approaches in order to engage in serious study of possible remedies, without a wholesale, puerile rejection of industrial progress.

The forest's death throes did not start recently, and the contentious volumes that confront it reproduce documents from past centuries which denounce ecological disasters that are not all that different, though of more limited proportions. Technology, mechanization are not malevolent inventions of the present day, as proclaimed by apocalyptic rhetoricians, who, however, are quick to make use of the car when they need it. In his poetry, Johann Peter Hebel, who died in 1826, evokes the death of the Belchen and his native landscape.

What is striking, in the current debate, is its earnestness and its calmness, a disinclination to point a finger at easy scapegoats and an extreme caution in identifying causes. A few days ago in Karlsruhe, a conference of experts stated that in addition to the more obvious factors of pollution due to industrial waste (primarily dioxin), many other factors remain to be ascertained, some of which might even be traced back to "natural" causes (insects, changes in temperature, and so on). Alongside the Green polemic against capitalist profit logic is the censure of equally serious disasters in the Eastern European countries (the German Democratic Republic, Czechoslovakia).

No ecological problems can find a solution that is national only, especially not in the Black Forest, which adjoins two other countries and suffers the consequences of what happens beyond its borders, such as in the petrochemical plants of Chalampé in Alsace; in 1983 Freiburg's newspaper, the *Badische Zeitung*, reported the contradictory and unintentionally hilarious statements by French authorities who frantically retracted their accounts every few days, waving around certificates of the forests' good health and then demise.

Is the forest dying? It is difficult to say because the causes and effects, losses and protective measures are being appraised years later. Of course, those focused on eternity respond that the earth itself will end one day, along with our galaxy and our transient universe. In these forests Martin Heidegger found luminous clearings, which seemed to him to be the amenable face of the all-embracing Being; he exchanged a few laconic words with the villagers, asking their advice on whether to accept invitations from other universities. His son, Colonel Hermann Heidegger, welcomes me to his home, it too in the forest, a few miles from Freiburg. He is a tall, gentle man, his gaze filled with kindness, and a face marked by profound integrity. He talks about his father, but he does not have much to tell me; the philosopher-shepherd of Being,[1] whose peaceful conceptual work and isolation his wife rigorously protected, was affectionate with his children, but must not have had much time for them, wholly intent as he was on meditating, at his desk or in his cabin in the Black Forest, on the world's global nihilism.

I ask the colonel whether his father, in his analysis of the forgetfulness of Being and the assault of technology, thought that it was a grave but nonetheless transitory crisis in our civilization, or a fatal malady, a termination.[2] "With regard to us, to our land," the colonel replies, "he thought the game was over, that our terrestrial ship was destined to sink." The shepherd of Being became the lieutenant of Nothing. Afterward, of course, there was the All, Being. But who knows if there would have been forests like the ones he loved, their luminous clearings that inspired his philosophizing. Heidegger loved the pathos of great epoch-making turning points, fatality. Perhaps it is not necessary to see metaphysics in factory smokestacks; the death of the forest, as Ditfurth says, is not necessarily destined.

March 15, 1986

LUDWIG'S CASTLES IN THE AIR

1. The most significant monument to Ludwig, the unfortunate, impossible monarch of Bavaria, is not one of his improbable, fantastic castles but a cross planted in the water on Lake Starnberg, near Monaco, where the king mysteriously drowned on June 13, 1886, along with the doctor who was his caretaker and warden, the determined, sinister Dr. Bernhard von Gudden. The cross, adorned with a fresh garland, does not represent, as a moralizing scenario set might suggest, the truth and simplicity of death as opposed to the gaudy, verbose kitsch staged by the king throughout his life; rather the cross represents the continuation and triumph of the kitsch, Ludwig's posthumous victory over the raison d'état that with abrupt brutality had put an end to his anachronistic and extravagant rule.

Today summer reigns over this curving, maternal shore; bodies enjoying the water uninhibitedly, the uncaring pleasure of slow, drawn-out hours, unconcerned with historical tragedies and the individual suffering of those who are not in sync with the flow of life, like the sovereign who died in this lake. But the ribbon on the wreath, hung on the cross "in memory of June 13, 1886," is addressed to Ludwig himself on behalf of "your loyal subjects." The politically impotent monarch, duped by Wagner, manipulated by Bismarck, and deposed by his own ministers with ridiculous ease, today has loyal subjects, clubs named after him, those nostalgic for the throne along with the regal majesty that he had viewed as a symbol of the poetry of life, of beauty as opposed to the drabness of quotidian prose, to the imminent rise of modernity and industrialization.

The wreath was solemnly laid two months ago, on the anniversary of his death, by the "King Ludwig Club," in a crowded, impressive ceremony, an outmoded spectacle like those the king loved to arrange in disdain for the history and events of his time, even though he held them in secluded solitude, only for himself or a chosen few, certainly not for the masses that he, an egocentric narcissist, despised, even when those masses were devotees and loyal followers.

Present at last June's ceremony, mixed in with the crowd, were the major political figures of Bavaria: Christian Socialists, Social Democrats, and Liberals—not in an official capacity, of course, because the government and opposition to the *Land* of Bavaria, which is part of the Federal Republic of Germany, may not profess monarchist and legitimist nostalgia for the crown of the Wittelsbach. But the Christian Socialist or even Socialist leaders could not afford to pass it up for fear of being punished electorally for having shown scant Bavarian patriotism, so dear to the republican parties as well as to those nostalgic for the monarchy.

Among the Ludwig enthusiasts, naturally there is also a minority of sophisticates fascinated by the farcicality and bad taste cultivated by the "fairy-tale king"; these latter-day admirers are the least loyal followers of Ludwig's world, given that their snobbery winks at the garishness precisely as such, whereas the solitary king loved the Disneyland that he built with a consuming passion, foolishly squandering state finances. In those castles or in those artificial scenes he sought beauty, the Platonic ideal of Beauty, something absolute, not the pleasure of bricolage.

But followers with a taste for camp, as it is called in America, would certainly not have been plentiful enough to throng the banks of Lake Starnberg two months ago. That crowd paid homage to Ludwig because they saw in him a symbol of the old Bavaria rooted in feudal and agrarian tradition, uncorrupted by modernization or prussianization, determined to defend—even against the leveling effect of a united German state—its age-old uniqueness, its ties to the land and to the seasons, a sanguine peasant and Catholic vitality.

This Bavarian lifeblood, with its sturdy peoples, also animates libertarian, dissenting political forces of the left, which reject, in the name of the same cultural and regional autonomism, any monarchical and feudal patina; in conjunction with the tribute to Ludwig there was to be a protest on behalf of the "other Bavaria" (with an opposite political label, but an analogous way of life), a demonstration that was prohibited by the authorities, for whom an anarchist, disruptive king such as Ludwig is still less dangerous than a populace roused by ideas and progressive sentiments.

Ludwig thus becomes—as is especially evident in this centennial commemoration—the symbol of a Bavarian independence movement, which asserts itself against official policy but also helps maintain the existing order and equilibrium, dominated by the CSU (Christian Social Union). The Wittelsbach are still popular in Munich today; young Prince Leopold—privately referred to as Poldi— a racecar driver and author of memoirs despite his young age, is a character in this Bavarian folklore who plays a political role. The novelist and playwright Georg Lohmeier, the life and soul of the King Ludwig Club and scornful critic of Prussian-industrial development, embodies this popular-conservative spirit, as does the dialect actor Gustl Bayerhammer, a member of the good-timers association Schlaraffe, that is, the idlers who inhabit Schlaraffenland, the Land of Cockaigne.

Even these pleasure-loving followers of Ludwig are a far cry from their cherished sovereign, who was not fond of the lusty pleasures of life but preferred a solitary, mortuary beauty; moreover Ludwig marked the end of Bavarian independence, which fell under the rule of Prussia and the unification of Germany that took place in 1871. He was the first king of Bavaria to become—as he himself said, with deep, painful humiliation—a vassal and prefect of the king of Prussia crowned German emperor.

On the other hand Ludwig was a victim of the raison d'état of the Wittelsbachs and of Bavaria, who eliminated him because he, being politically inept, conducted the kingship as if it were a priesthood or a political spectacle, an example being the quixotic recitation of sentimental poetry indifferent to any interest in power. A kingship dreamed of, lived, and enacted by Ludwig was a figment of power, that is, poetic fantasy, anarchic and socially useless, irreconcilable with reasons of state.

That is why Paul Verlaine was able to celebrate him as the king of poetry, of its haughty, sublime, aching futility, and why Ludwig was removed by his ministers and relatives. Moreover, he refused to listen to those who were closest to his anti-prussianism and his ideas of popular patriotic independence, well represented numerically in the Bavarian Parliament, because his absurd, anachronistic concept of absolute monarchy, which led him to worship and seek to imitate the Sun King, allowed him to be a puppet in the hands of his ministers, appointed by him, rather than accept advice from parliamentarians, elected by the people.

2. Ludwig was an architect of dreams, constructed literally like castles in the air—the castle of Neuschwanstein appears to be suspended on a mountain—counter to all the manifestations of the nineteenth century: rationalism, science, technology, industry, the bourgeoisie, the state, liberalism, nationalism, democracy, socialism. His mania for building, which the panel of psychiatrists engaged by the government classified as a symptom of paranoia, is an incessant outpouring of dreams, images that rise from the depths unrelated to any reality principle, bits and pieces of fantasy assembled with no concern for style or coherence, head in the clouds, ideas that occur to everyone, certainly to every teenager, and come to nothing, but that a king, having access to state coffers, can transform into stone.

Ludwig did not want his castles to be eternal; he once said that after his death they should be blown up to protect them from desecration by the crude outside world. A month and a half after he died,

Neuschwanstein Castle, in which he had been arrested and deposed, was opened to the public with an entry fee of three marks.

In 1984, the same castle was visited by 1,130,000 people, and this year there will certainly be many more. These August days when the depopulated cities offer peace and solitude, the crowds at the castles are impressive. To visit Linderhof Castle I have to wait my turn, in a procession of cars headed for the park, for three hours and forty-five minutes, then stand in line another two hours in front of the ticket booth; no parking is to be found for miles and miles around Neuschwanstein Castle.

The visits, exhibitions, and excursions for the centenary—from the residential buildings in Munich to the collections of picture postcards—constitute an imposing spectacle of mass tourism, a giant stage set, disproportionate, wrote Bruno Visentini, to the modest historical relief of the actor.

Herrenchiemsee Castle, on the lake of the same name, is located on an island that was purchased in 1873 with the illicit funds Bismarck received in exchange for the endorsement given to the assumption of the imperial crown by the king of Prussia. Ludwig loved that castle, one reason being that the water separating it from the mainland gave him the illusion of being inaccessible to reality. The castle is meant to be a Versailles, inspired by Ludwig's ardent love for Louis XIV, who to him seemed the embodiment of absolute monarchy and whom he dreamed of imitating.

In his pitiful *Secret Diary*, now published by Siegfried Obermeier with an obsequious commentary, Ludwig records with remorse and shame his onanistic and homosexual temptations and peccadillos, each time resolving not to sin again, placing his trust in God but especially in the Sun King, issuing decrees against sin and temptation, often in French. Nevertheless his Francophilia was so strong that—despite his scrupulous conscience, which looked with horror upon sexual temptations, especially his own—he idealized the insouciant libertinism of the French court, of Pompadour and Du Barry, whose portraits he kept in his castles as if they were those of pious benefactors.

His love for France was so ingrained that in 1870 he shuddered at the sight of the Prussian victory over the French and the "dishonor" of Versailles, occupied by Bismarck's troops. He even went so far as to spit on a bust of the Kaiser placed in Hohenschwangau Castle and to snub the Prussian crown prince, who was visiting Munich. The psychiatrists, in their certification, were quick to classify this love for France as another sign of dementia.

Ludwig went to Herrenchiemsee at night in a gondola, by torch-light, and there he retreated to the grand hall of mirrors, with more than eight hundred lighted candles. The castle today says little to us, and not just because of the crush of visitors that makes feudal soli-tude unlikely; it is similar to many others, a copy of Versailles but also of many other copies, it has the elegance but also the monotony of aristocracies, the same everywhere and apparently lacking the fan-tasy that makes the dwellings of other social classes, albeit modest abodes or row houses, much more individual. Much more poetic, on the island, are the wooden boat sheds, ducks swimming among the reeds with their ducklings, the oaks, maples, and birches that Ludwig loved, so much so that the doctors reproached his habit of greeting a tree that was dear to him, unaware perhaps of the deference for trees rooted in Bavarian tradition, which made woodcutters, when they felled one, respectfully doff their cap.

Linderhof Castle, completed in 1879, also reflects a penchant for France's *Grand siècle*, though it has a Moorish cloister as well, symbolic of the poetic, fabulous Orient. In the park is the famous artificial underground cave, the apogee of kitsch, constructed from landfill material, camouflaged in the landscape and adorned with fake stalactites and stalagmites.

The cave is a mind-boggling summation of all the evocations dear to Ludwig, brought together in a heterogeneous, bizarre pastiche, an imitation of the most diverse elements: Capri's Blue Grotto, the Mountain of Venus from *Tannhäuser*, the cliff from *Das Rheingold*, *Lohengrin*'s swans, a boat shaped like a seashell, in which the king was taken out on waters which were moved artificially by a mechanism hidden on the bottom and heated for the dancers who performed as Naiads in the ballets.

In this cave Ludwig, on a simulated dais between fake rocks, listened to musical performances or to the actor Josef Kainz, who was forced to recite endless poetic passages amid effects of colorful changing lights and artificial, intermittent waterfalls. The cave is one of the many mise-en-scènes of Ludwig's passion for Wagner and his music, also attested to by the six hundred letters and telegrams making up the quivering, excited correspondence between the two — an agitation felt by Ludwig and deftly acted by Wagner, nicknamed "Lolus" in Munich because he had fascinated Ludwig, leading the king to support him unreservedly by frittering away public funds, just as the beautiful dancer Lola Montez, decades earlier, had turned the head of Ludwig's grandfather, the gallant Ludwig I.

Wagner, as it is known, had no qualms about indulging the king in his passion, shamelessly conforming to the exalted style of the relationship that Ludwig chose, and for the needs of his art taking advantage of the inexperience of the young sovereign, who was totally unacquainted with life. Ludwig's tone, when he speaks of Wagner or with Wagner, is grotesquely emphatic, yet Ludwig, creator and lover of kitsch, demonstrated exceptional artistic intuition by recognizing the new revolutionary grandeur of Wagnerian music at a time when to many it still seemed like a strident, unacceptable breach of traditional taste.

Perhaps Ludwig, like Nietzsche probably, was even in love with Wagner, though he had not yet met him in person when at fifteen he listened to one of his works, *Lohengrin*, for the first time. He proved to be a keener judge than many others; certainly more perceptive than Kaiser Wilhelm, who in 1876, after having seen a performance of *Siegfried* and *Götterdämmerung*—masterpieces of the musician who among other things had become the bard of the German Empire—called the spectacle at the Bayreuth Festival "insufferable." Ludwig saw himself in the Swan Knight, who comes from mysterious distances and who in the end must disappear from reality. Though Wagner treated him with the domineering manner with which an artist propels his characters, Ludwig was magnanimous toward him, even when the maestro shamefully toyed with his honor, and even forgave him for his apologia in praise of the Prussian-German Empire.[1]

When he showered Wagner with favors and money, Ludwig said he thought it was the maestro who gave and he who received; apropos of gifts, Nietzsche also wondered who should do the thanking, the one who gave or the one who received. Naturally Ludwig was less magnanimous with his servants and lackeys, even with his favorites, on whom he alternated liberality, lenience, and small sadistic caprices, leading his secretary Friedrich von Ziegler to call him "our Little Ivan the Terrible."

3. Neuschwanstein is the most fantastic and dreamlike of Ludwig's castles, with its white, rounded towers soaring in the air, its eclecticism, and its rooms inspired by the German Middle Ages and the works of Wagner. The model was to be the castle of Wartburg, the mythical site of the Meistersingers' song contest and the heart of a medieval Germany that for Ludwig—along with the Sun King's court, in a fantastical hybrid contamination—was the landscape of poetry. When he visited Schloss Wartburg, Ludwig retreated alone to meditate in the hall of the singers, but when he rebuilt the castle in Neuschwanstein he was inspired not by the original but rather by the stage set designed for the Munich performance of *Tannhäuser.*

Ludwig himself spoke about "the dreams of adolescence," with whose vague elusiveness, oblivious to reality, he identified the poetry of the heart. Adolescent thirst for authenticity is almost always dewy with evocation, with calling forth, with déjà vu; it is stirred by copies and imitations, it sings its yearning in words and rhythms unknowingly taken from a cultural repertoire that may even be hackneyed.

In Neuschwanstein reproduction, imitation, triumphs; the castle replicates the stage design inspired by Wartburg; at its feet, restaurants, stands, cottages, souvenirs mimic its towers and arcades in a hundred ways. The castle itself seems known and familiar to us because we've already seen it in the copy made by Walt Disney as the castle of Sleeping Beauty. Nevertheless in this orgy of the fake, like the echo of an echo, glimmers the distant memory of a true poetry, the castle of Goethe's king of Thule or of the Romantic Lieder, the mystery of a lost childhood and happiness, which reverberates in the kitschy baubles piled up in profusion.

Absolute monarchy, for Ludwig, was the desire to regain and rebuild, by waving a magic wand, the lost paradises of fantasy, the dream — individual and historical — of the poetry of life. That monarchy was a caricature of Romantic poetry but also a caricatured continuation of it, of the need to transform the world and find the magic formula capable of inaugurating a reign of beauty, negated by historical evolution. The longing to poetically compel reality is a mirage of European literature, from Novalis to Rimbaud, and is also present in Munich tradition, from the Hellenizing buildings built by Ludwig's grandfather to transform Munich into Athens to the grand, radical aestheticism professed at the end of the century by Stefan George and his school of poetry.

Evocative from a distance, the pomp and splendor appear pedestrian and clumsy when viewed up close. Miramare Castle, built in Trieste by the more moderate and responsible Ludwig who was Maximilian of Habsburg, is more moving because it discreetly blends in with its natural surroundings and immediately reveals its untruthful fragility. Ludwig's castles claim to be a complete depiction yet suggest a sense of mediocrity, not grandeur.

Ludwig wanted to be a Sun King at a time when the role reserved for kings was to symbolize bourgeois respectability, as well as the petite bourgeoisie's concern for the family. Leopold I of Belgium recommended suitor Pedro of Portugal to his daughter Carlotta, later the wife of Maximilian of Habsburg, because "Portugal has a future, and since it has fewer people, there are, despite some minor revolts, security and prospects for the royal family."

It was in Neuschwanstein that Ludwig was deposed, not as a king but as a burdensome relative the family managed to have declared incapacitated. The psychiatrists who on June 8, 1886, declared him mentally unsound had never examined him, but as they told him on June 12 when they went to pick him up at Neuschwanstein, they had not felt it necessary.

Ludwig was certainly unbalanced, and there was a valid reason for removing him from the throne, namely the ruinous dissipation of state finances, which showed him to be irresponsibly indifferent to the fate of his subjects, but the psychiatric justification for the raison d'état is appalling: the medical certification, still respectfully referring to him with the title of Majesty, cites as symptoms of incurable insanity—apart from hereditary defects—his penchant for solitary walks and for trees, his admiration for France and for Wagnerian music, his contempt for his ministers, his fondness for the color blue (the romantic color of distance, but also of the Bavarian flag), his disgusting way of eating, stuffing down the food, staining himself with sauce, and other details reported by the servants. The disclosures of notes fished out of the trash basket or the toilet, Bismarck remarked scornfully, should never be sufficient to condemn a man to death.

The arrest in Neuschwanstein, if it can be called that, is heartbreaking. The king—now a shadow of the young man he once was, obese and coarsened by his cravings, lost and defenseless—is bewildered by the brutality with which his subjects with medical degrees deprive him of his ability to plan and decide; wavering between pride and dismay, he asks in vain how it is possible to issue an expert opinion without an examination, while admitting to insomnia and abuse of sleeping pills.

He is faced with a power more formidable than the monarchy: Science, which is never wrong, the psychiatrist who, like a medicine man or high priest, controls occult forces and embodies truth. Science is personified and administered by Dr. Gudden, an undisputed, dismissive authority; when his son-in-law Professor Grashey, whom he had placed in that post, tells him that in his opinion Ludwig may perhaps not be incurable, Gudden, the real Sun King of the situation, replies curtly, "We'll talk about that some other time."

Reading the accounts of this ordeal we can understand why, among the many literary works inspired by Ludwig, the one that stands out is the play *Delirium*, written in 1920 by a madman interned in a mental hospital—whose name, by an ironic twist of fate, was Ernst August Wagner—for having killed his wife, four children, and nine passersby in a delirium of persecution and grandeur. The mad murderer in the play identifies with Ludwig, with his megalomania, but analyzes, better than a psychiatrist, those titanic designs, his and the king's, as morbid manifestations of a sick personality. The madman who portrays himself and Ludwig as mad reveals, paradoxically, an understanding and compassion that Gudden, in his arrogance, might envy.

Life is ironic, however, and even scientists pay a price. Taken into custody, Ludwig had asked to stay at Neuschwanstein, but Gudden decided to have him sent to Berg Castle, on Lake Starnberg near Munich, in order to coordinate his day-to-day clinical activities in the capital and his daily observation of the king, a patient of considerable medical interest.

The arrangement seemed perfect, but one day later, on June 13, Gudden was dead, along with the sovereign, in the waters of the lake. The causes of that double death—now investigated in a recent volume by a magistrate, Wilhelm Wöbking—are obscure: a suicide

bid by Ludwig, dragging the doctor who tried to restrain him underwater, an escape attempt that the doctor tried to prevent, an arranged
murder.

Scratches were found on Gudden's stout neck along with marks
left by hands squeezing it; any hypothesis is a wild guess, but it would
not be all that strange if Ludwig, remembering that it is not fitting
for a king to perish without defending himself, had thought to settle
his score with the doctor. A century, however, reconciles differences:
the same crowd that hung the wreath for Ludwig on June 13 would
probably have been ready to lend a hand to the psychiatrist; after all,
he too was a Bavarian authority, when he tried to bar Ludwig's way
to freedom, whether on the other shore or in death, and to keep him
in a cage.

August 24–September 3, 1986

AMONG THE SORBS OF LUSATIA

1. The journey among the Sorbs—or Sorbians—of Lusatia begins in Dresden, even though the Saxon capital—at one time a splendid "Florence on the Elbe," demolished by Allied bombs in February 1945—is not part of the territory, which, in addition to a German majority, is inhabited by one of the smallest, least-known peoples of Europe, a Slavic people with its own distinct national and linguistic individuality, first mentioned in the histories in A.D. 631. But the name Dresden is derived from an ancient Sorbian word, indicating a settlement of people of the riverside forests. Michal Frencel, one of the first bards of his people's national consciousness, wrote proudly to Tsar Peter the Great, appealing to the great Slavic brotherhood, that Dresden had been built by the Sorbs—perhaps thinking of the obscure, patient work of his people, excluded for centuries from the controls and hierarchies of power and relegated to the humble labor that builds cities and empires but leaves little trace in the annals of history, just as hands that construct a house stone upon stone leave no imprint on the stones. It is also true that Frencel, like all nationalists, was prone to exaggerate, as when he wrote that the Slavic language was spoken even in China.

I am in Dresden for the first time since the fall of the Wall. It's been a number of years; nonetheless the scene is still scarred by ruins here and there, not just metaphorical. On the streets you come across works in progress every now and then, which though on the one hand are reminiscent of the interminable works in the Eastern Bloc countries during the period of "real socialism," on the other are an expression of vigorous renewal, imposed and superimposed on a still

stagnant world. Even now there are crumbling, abandoned buildings, shattered, paneless windows gaping in uninhabitable houses;
the mud-colored sandstone facades, blackened by smoke from the
chimneys, accentuate the sense of desolation, making all of life seem
like a gray drizzly day. Every so often I forget that I am in Germany,
I feel as if I am in an Eastern country of some years back; the resig-
nation toward malfunctions that in "the West" would lead to protest
is an indication of this.

There is certainly no lack of tumultuous signs of bustling reconstruction, of the inexorable capitalist energy that is transforming the country: elegant shops, new or renovated hotels, large de-
partment stores, nightclubs, offices—none of which, however, is part
of a coherent urban landscape—stand in strident contrast to rundown shops, to the still visible traces of former poverty and neglect,
to certain urban developments hastily thrown together, which relate
a Mitteleuropean-socialist melancholy to that of certain American
small towns.

On some streets you breathe an emptiness, you have an acute
feeling that something is missing; groups of young people with shaved
heads or tinted hair, holding bottles of beer, gather for a squalid party
on a sidewalk or in the lobby of a train station, moving in a metropolitan space that is also the scene of a social, existential, almost metaphysical vacuum—a vacuum of historical memory, of political vision,
of the Tablets of the Law. For a moment you feel a little frightened,
as if from that vacuum unthinkable disasters, violence, racism, tragedies might suddenly emerge—as if more than half a century of wars
and horrors have been forgotten, have not been able to teach anything, and it might all come back, repeat itself or assume other faces,
no less devastating.

On the one hand it is as if World War II had just ended, because you can see signs of it in the ruins that are only now about to
be removed; on the other hand it's as though the memory of it, still
present to us despite the reconstruction that has taken place over

many decades, has been lost and no longer acts as a warning against the evil, infamy, and anguish that are constantly lying in wait. Perhaps it would be better not to restore the Frauenkirche, as is being planned, whose ruins rise among the chaotic mass of rubble like a disemboweled body or a face with empty eye sockets. The church was destroyed in the atrocious bombing of February 13, 1945, one of the decimations of World War II; it seems as though the bombs fell yesterday and that the first rescue teams are just arriving: the horror of war and the delirium that willed it stand before your eyes, visible.

It would be better not to rebuild, not to fill the void of those lacerations that, unlike the other impalpable void, is full of things, of memories, of feelings, of teachings. Somewhat farther on you can see magnificent surviving buildings that tell us what the Dresden of one time must have been like. Depending on the quality of the stone, time and severe weather have blackened the statues that adorn the cupolas and facades; everywhere black angels, black cherubs and nymphs, black faces. Life is oxidation and all the grandeur that adorns and extols it—as in the wondrous baroque splendor of the Zwinger, the residence of Augustus the Strong of Saxony—mainly emphasizes friability, celebrating death.

2. The first encounter with the world of the Sorbs occurs in Bautzen—in Sorbian, Budysin—a turreted city that stands like a sentinel on the border with the Slavic world, in this case Czech and Polish; one of the many bastions of German civilization that can be seen, austere and melancholic like a Lutheran hymn, in the most diverse countries of East-central Europe, in the vast territory of conflict between Germans and Slavs. The Institute of Sorbian Folk Culture is near the station. Bautzen has numerous Sorbian institutions; it is in fact the capital of Upper Lusatia, where the majority of Sorbs, about forty thousand, live; the others, about twenty thousand, live in Lower Lusatia, whose capital is Cottbus-Chosebuz, and speak a distinct language, Lower Sorbian.

The Sorbs, who belong to the Western Slavic group, have lived in these lands for centuries, having come from the East with other peoples in the sixth century; subjugated by Charlemagne and later by Saxon emperors and their margraves, they have never formed an autonomous state. Throughout a long history which saw them, through shifting ups and downs and diverse conditions, under German domination, in particular Saxon and Prussian, they defended their identity tenaciously, almost always through passive, peaceful resistance, at times, albeit cautiously, looking to their Polish or Czech neighbors. They belong to those populations who in the nineteenth century were called—by Friedrich Engels as well—"nonhistoric peoples," that is, agrarian groups without a ruling class capable of managing a self-governing state. A small subordinate population is easily vulnerable to assimilation, especially if, like the Sorbs, it does not constitute a minority that can look to a mother-nation beyond its borders, but is a self-contained people, relying solely on itself: the Sorbs exist only in Lusatia. Indeed by becoming an apprentice of some trade guild, the Sorb tended to become Germanized; in the eighteenth century, Jan Hórcanski, preceptor and writer, observed that the Sorbs, in their social ascent, tended to deny their origin and to embrace German prejudices against their own people.

It is a situation common to all minorities. But in general the Sorbs are distinguished by an ability, rare in minorities, to live all in all in harmony with an identity often felt as dual. Rarely in their history does a desire for autonomy emerge; it occurred in 1918–1919, with a quickly failed plan for separatism or annexation with Czechoslovakia, and was repeated in 1945, with a similar failure and rather poor support on the part of the population. The "forgotten nation," as it has been called, has defended itself by being faithful to its traditions and customs, to its sense of group affiliation, rather than through political demands. Oppressed or dubiously cultivated, as in East Germany, depending on the period, the Sorbian nation seems to have survived thanks to the singular, almost paradoxical ability of many of its members to feel simultaneously Sorbian and German.

Though Sorbian literature — one of whose most notable current poets, Kito Lorenc, who writes in German as well, edited a rich bilingual anthology — resounds with laments and protests over the nation's humiliated condition and calls for, in the words of many authors, an awakening and defense of a national consciousness, in the tradition experienced by the people we see instead a binational symbiosis. One story says that in the village of Schleife-Slepo there are three innkeepers; the first is a Sorb who speaks German, the second a German who speaks German, and the third, the favorite, a German who speaks Sorbic. But even the language is cultivated as a familiar, cherished parlance rather than as an extreme political defense; at some conferences Sorbic is also necessary for certain community participants, with simultaneous translation into German. Though the Nazis evidently tended to deny the existence of a Sorbian nation and used the expression "Germans speaking Wend," the term "Wend" (which originally referred to the Illyrian peoples and was later extended and virtually transferred to Slavic groups) is used, especially in Lower Lusatia, by the Sorbs themselves, without the pejorative nuance that it had toward Slavs in German countries.

3. In Bautzen-Budysin bilingual signs are used for public buildings and street names; at one time they were common for shops as well. The Sorbian mark is immediately noticeable, but its preservation is dependent mainly on culture: in addition to the Institute and its scientific publications, there are a theater, a daily and a monthly newspaper, children's magazines, educational publications, a museum, publishing houses, clubs, radio broadcasts (television presence is scant); in Leipzig, at the university, is an Institute for Sorbian Studies. The umbrella organization which the various initiatives come under is the Domowina. As for schools, there are the so-called

"A" type, in which the majority, though not all, of the material is taught in Sorbic, and the "B" category, more numerous, in which Sorbic is studied but as a foreign language.

In theory Sorbs have the right to speak their own language in court, but in practice no one does; in fact, the Sorbs I talk with, who hold prominent positions in the life of their communities, remark that it would be a pointless insistence, since they know German very well. As he accompanies me to the theater by car, the director of the museum, which lovingly displays memorabilia and timeworn tokens of its people, sings an old folk song (from the collection of the great Jan Arnost Smoler, one of the fathers of national consciousness) recalling the last Sorbian victory against the Germans in the tenth century, but he too says that he would find it unbefitting to address the court in Sorbic—which moreover does not have its own regular interpreters but resorts, in rare cases, to individuals hired from time to time.

All of this contradicts the fundamental demand of every national minority group: that is, the ability to use its own language in dealings with authorities. But it is not a matter of surrender; in all likelihood the Sorbs not only speak German perfectly—a situation that occurs with other minorities as well—but they also, beyond any technical proficiency, see it as a mother tongue, whose use satisfies psychological and affective needs as well. It comes as no surprise that many writers (and the best of them), passionate bards of their world, also write in German or express their feelings and their fantasies in both languages, not viewed as conflicting. The tendency to tone down conflict, I am told many times in meetings with various community exponents, is persistent in Sorbian tradition; even the fall of the German Democratic Republic did not lead to terribly harsh clashes with the ousted leaders.

In this, the Sorbs, in many cases, have an edge, they have an identity that is richer, dual, and not lacerated. In that sense they could be a concrete intermediary between Germany and the Slavic world. In Bautzen, the German-Sorbian Folk Theater, where the manager Michael Lorenc welcomes me, puts on performances in both languages (generally ten to twelve shows in German and six in Sorbic, one of which is included in the main repertory and the rest presented in other stagings, thus enabling tours in villages populated by the minority). In the city the Sorbian presence is discreet but visible in cafés, bookstores, craft shops. Relations between the two communities are far-reaching, even though there is no lack of grumbling from the Germans, Dr. Jentsch at the Institute tells me, over subventions and grants to Sorbian cultural institutions that are considered disproportionate to the minority's numerical strength, while the Sorbs for their part fear the imminent shrinking of such funds for economic reasons, given the crisis that is sweeping across Germany. Falling birthrates, unemployment, the dissolution of rural cooperatives, and relocations are the most rapid form of assimilation, with a resulting decrease in the Sorbian community.

4. Every minority, but particularly a unique one like the Sorbs, which relies on the stability of daily life and sentimental loyalty more than on political struggle, can be found especially in its literature. The Sorbs—Germany's "Indians," as the writer Mato Kosyk described them—have a rich literature, resembling a landscape in which age-old memories are layered and fused in the earth, archaic legacies of migrations that came from all over, then vanished, remote lores and peoples erased by history's violence and glories in one long breath, slow and languid like the flow of great rivers in the plains, sung in their literature. Coming together in the small Sorbian crucible, which has tenaciously preserved its identity over the centuries and throughout oppression, is a fascinating mix of diverse elements from assorted peoples of that vast womb that blended Germanic and Slavic groups of all kinds. The ideal time of this literature is that which Bo-

browski — the German poet who was a model and teacher for contemporary Sorbian authors such as Kito Lorenc — called "Sarmatian," the time of myth, slower and more abiding than historical time.

It is a literature that portrays and judges history from below, from the perspective of the vanquished and of the land; the legendary Krabat, a kind of demonic magician redeemed by the help he gave his people and now depicted in a novel by Jurij Brězan, the most notable contemporary Sorbian narrator, is an emblematic figure of this lowly, vital world. A burden that certainly weighs heavily on Sorbian literature, though denounced by its best writers, is the umbilical link to a conservative tradition and a concern to serve the national cause; any constraint, even if morally noble, that sacrifices poetic creativity is a burden, and often makes it difficult, as Kafka wrote in a famous passage, for sparse populations, preoccupied with defending their identity, to produce great writers and great literature.[1] Still lacking is a modern drama production, the dialectic between inferiority complex and self-assertion continues to persist, folklore and traditionalism are often cumbersome; even the number of writers, high with respect to the small community from which they come, is dubious.

Now, however, things are changing, especially after what took place during the years of the GDR, which cultivated the Sorbs like a prize jewel and at the same time humbled them, primarily destroying their culture through unbridled industrialization, which demolished entire villages and thus the foundations of the Sorbian community. The land mined and ruined in the name of coal became, in the most exalted Sorbian literature, the true homeland, lost and found in the mind, liberated from any folkloric stereotyping and resurrected as a symbol of an "anti-world" in contrast to reality and of a less visceral, more universal identity.

Kito Lorenc, fond preserver of his people's literary tradition in the aforementioned anthology, which became a national vade mecum, is also an experimental author who scrapes the language clean of any sentimental pap and transforms it into a metaphor of historical and existential chaos: the Struga, his beloved river, is the mythical river of the oneness of life and at the same time a rivulet from a gutter carrying the dross and refuse of history. Jurij Brězan creates his Sorbian novel thanks to his awareness that as a writer he is not a bard but rather a "pariah" of a closed society; in a poem by Róza Domascyna the Sorb is a doleful, sarcastic "clown in Mitteleuropa's cage."

5. Literature produces contradictions; that's its task, which sometimes holds surprises. "We remain Sorbs!" proclaims a poem by Jakub Bart-Ćišinski, one of the classic authors, and you can find a great many citations like this.[2] At the Sorbian café in Bautzen, Kito Lorenc reminds me that his grandfather, Jakub Lorenc-Zaleski, he too a famous writer, urged people to be Sorbs and to put their efforts into serving the nation; it is from this direct, personal counsel that his commitment to his people and his poetry sprang. It is impressive to learn shortly afterward that he himself learned Sorbic as a boy, listening to the words and shouts of the peasants and laborers loading logs on carts along the banks of the Struga.

His Sorbian identity arose from within, from a remote calling suddenly recognized and embraced. Kito Lorenc is a poet in the two Sorbian languages, in addition to German, but his rootedness in his identity is virtually prelinguistic or extralinguistic, as if the Sorbian world were life antecedent to language. In the novel *The Shop* by Erwin Strittmatter, a German writer of the GDR, the protagonist's grandmother and great-aunt are also Sorbian and represent—like the Kashubian grandmother in Günter Grass's *Tin Drum*—the mythical, archaic forces of motherhood and vitality.

There are some Sorbs who declare themselves such without speaking their language, Lorenc tells me. He is a gentle man, whose gestures and eyes express an intense, reserved melancholy. He embodies Sorbian literature and identity; he is a voice that enables it to exist beyond the borders of Lusatia. But his children, he tells me, do not know Sorbic. He doesn't seem to regret it too much, although he admits to a tragic awareness of the possible end of the language in which he is a poet.

6. Like many national literatures, Sorbian letters as well owe much to Protestantism—despite the fact that Luther expressed himself in offensive terms toward the small populace; one of his early texts, which contains the Lutheran catechism, is the *Enchiridion Vandalicum*, in accordance with the tradition that links the Sorbs with the Vandals. Today things are very different. In evangelical villages Sorbian identity and especially its language are declining without much resistance, whereas in the Catholic villages—in which Sorbs sometimes make up 80 percent of the population—traditions, culture, language, and ethnic consciousness are tenaciously cultivated. As in other Slavic countries, the clergy are the aggressive guardians of national identity. It was Noack, a Catholic priest, who raised a strong protest against East Germany's plans which devastated the existence of the Sorbs through the development of the coal industry. It is in these villages that the Sorbian people live—somewhat mysterious and hidden, as though beyond the seven mountains of the fairy tale.[3] You can still see the ancient costumes, the big bonnets with the long ribbons, the full skirts, the chest bands heavy with coins. In cemeteries—such as the beautiful one in Ralbitz-Ralbicy—the crosses are in a row, white, all the same; none outshines the others, pompous tombs are not allowed, everyone reposes in the equality of death, a person who dies is not buried beside his family members, but with the last person who died before him.

At Easter, processions on horseback move from village to village, large banners in the wind; the riders wear black jackets and top hats, the horses' harnesses pass from one generation to the next. Another Easter tradition is the painted eggs with their various sophisticated techniques, requiring patience and consummate skill; fabulous colors, perfect, delicate decorative motifs, and meticulous geometries transform henhouse eggs into enchanting objects, poignant like any particularly fragile, fleeting beauty, such as snow sculptures, art that promptly calls to mind a humble attention to things, from which great art also springs, and the mortality of man and his works.

I am in Radibor-Radnor, another of these villages. It's cold, the sky is continually clearing, then clouding over; sudden snow flurries are sporadic ordeals. Here too the houses are mud-colored, that color that often makes Mitteleuropa so oppressive and melancholic, a landscape that wrings the heart. Everywhere, among the houses and in the fields, gilded crucifixes rise. The mass in Sorbian is over, people are coming out of the church, only a few older women are wearing the costume, you hear mostly German spoken. I turn to the sacristan, who dismisses me abruptly, with a peasant distrust of foreigners that perhaps echoes the still recent distrust of possible spies of the regime that fell with the Wall. In the welcoming inn Meja (May), the beautiful young woman, a blue-eyed blonde, who brings coffee to the table points out a photograph on the wall that shows her as a little girl in traditional costume. She is the innkeeper's daughter. Talkative and courteous, she tells us about her studies at the university of Dresden, about the town, about the harmonious coexistence that originates in the spirit of the people themselves, conscious of their dual identity. She speaks about the growing assimilation, accepted serenely, and about her mother tongue, which she thinks is destined to disappear. I ask if that fate saddens her. No, she says, because I won't see it. Perhaps that is the only prospect that remains before the inevitable end of all the things you love; the hope that you won't see it happen, that your end will come first.

April 3, 1994

THE ANONYMOUS VIENNESE

The photograph is not that good, which is not surprising given that I took it. The river is a branch of the Danube to Fischamend, in the vicinity of Vienna not far from the Slovak border, frozen during the period of that harsh winter. The three small figures seen from behind, to the left, are Alberto Cavallari, his son Andrea, and Marisa. As in a painting or a Chinese poem, the people are not presumptuously at the center but rather at the edge of the landscape, lateral presences in the greater scene who nevertheless give meaning to the horizon and without whom it would be difficult to love the woods, the sky high above, the boat imprisoned by the ice, the seasonal light. The death of a loved one carries away with it a piece or a color of the world; though the survivor tries to regain them to some extent, as in rehabilitation therapies following an injury, the absence remains.

Actually the photograph is merely a device leading to another photo, author unknown, which appears in this little story. It was March 1985, a very cold March with snow- and windstorms. I was spending a few weeks in Vienna, visiting the sites and shores of that stretch of the Danube as a guest of the Austrian Literature Society, which for many years—even in the darkest moments of the Cold War—has offered, under the intelligent, generous leadership of Wolfgang Kraus (at that time still its president), a possibility, at times the only one, to meet with writers and intellectuals of the East. The apartment provided for me in the Hotel Academia was comfortable, and I took the opportunity, keeping an old promise, to invite Cavallari and his family to visit for a few days.

He came with one of his sons, I was with Marisa. Various reasons, at the last moment, had detained other family members who were to have been part of the group; most likely some of those insignificant pretexts that seem so important with which the daily grind—a master at inventing traps and obstructions, passing them off as imperative necessities and duties—so often manages to prevent us from living, from drawing a breath, nipping in the bud any sincere attempt to live it up or spend a happy hour drifting.

It was several months since Alberto Cavallari had ceased being the editor-in-chief of the *Corriere*, which in the legendary three years of his leadership—a bleak time for the country, of infamous, gory mysteries—he had defended and protected from disgrace and failure, amid incredible difficulties and perils, and with intrepid, backbreaking effort, enabling it to maintain its place as the foremost Italian newspaper. A few months earlier, Cavallari had even lost the famous trial with the Italian Socialist Party (PSI), which had sued him for an article in which he wondered why the PSI was not fond of the *Corriere* for writing that it preferred carabinieri to thieves, and paid the one hundred million established by the judgment from his own pocket. The trial, obviously, had caused a stir.

Moreover—a fact that in itself has nothing to do with the matter and is only related to it through the little story of the second photograph—the scandal raised by the welcome that Austria had given Walter Reder was fairly recent. Italy had pardoned Reder, the criminal Nazi officer sentenced to life imprisonment for the monstrous massacre at Marzabotto, and he, having landed by plane in Graz, had shockingly been received with honor by the Austrian minister of defense, Frischenschlager, as if he were a glorious veteran instead of the man responsible for one of the most vile and heinous war crimes. On that occasion, however, the pardoned lifer behaved better than his unexpected admirers, since he did not encourage the celebration and said nothing.

God, says a character in Isaac Bashevis Singer, sets in motion grandiose, thorny events just to torment or test a poor devil; history too sometimes seems to bring down empires just because someone breaks a leg.[1] Even behind a silly, modest photo there can therefore be facts larger than it, such as a trial or a public welcome at an airport that caused an uproar in the court of public opinion and called into question the two countries' justice systems and political class. While destiny was preparing that camera shot, the four of us spent happy days doing nothing, days of laughter, of wandering, of conscientious visits to buildings, churches, cafés, and taverns, of amiable contretemps and misinterpretations, of time lapped up to the fullest with no nagging worries to escape or goals to achieve, time tossed away thoughtlessly like a coin in a beggar's cap, as if obligations did not exist, as if an unpredictable, pleasurable world were always within reach, and death, in the game of goose, had to take a big step back, until all but losing sight of us. Whatever came along was welcome, an occasion for laughter and abandon, as on school trips when the more your plans go amiss the more fun you have.

We were all, in our normal life, cursed by an obsession with work, but during those days we surrendered to the sovereignty of the gratuitous. Living that way is a gift that the gods rarely concede and that we must be worthy of, because an hour or a week of such abandon requires love and friendship, the instantaneous complicity that is the result of life, experiences, feelings, and values that are passionately shared. We must be able to travel together along the road to the final breakdown, doing as little bowing as possible to the Prince of this world — and Alberto was a master at this — or, if he insists, demonstrating your obeisance to him backward, ass first, so to speak, like Bertoldo.[2]

These magical moments of companionship carry within them the conscious sadness of brevity, of the separation that breaks up the group and puts an end to things — certainly not to what binds its members together, but to their chance to be together. It is not easy for me to talk about those days, because both Marisa and Alberto are gone, but having had that time together is no small thing, neither for the one who is gone nor for the remaining one, since it helps you to keep going, to hold your head up even with a broken heart. Without those excursions in the snow, without those encounters with the odd characters of a lesser-known Vienna—which our friend Hans Haider, a first-rate literary journalist for the *Presse* and a great *cotecio* player, led us to discover like an infallible bloodhound—without those grotesque, grandiose glimpses of a splendid, vagabond culture, I would not have been able to portray the Danube as a world both sensually robust and insubstantial as a soap bubble.

With a gaze that pierced things like a harpoon, as Bernardo Valli brilliantly wrote in *La Repubblica,* Alberto seized on detailed bits of reality in a flash, harpooned them like a fisherman, and put them before our eyes. He had his arrogant moments and his black rages, at times unduly peremptory, but he could be irresistible when it came to being hilarious and making those around him feel more positive and cheerful, as when he managed, with a fanciful quip, to turn our visit to the Cancer Institute in Milan, understandably fretful, into an occasion and cause for laughter. But we other three were certainly no slouches at the complex art of loafing about.

The days were frigid, forcing us to seek shelter more often than usual in brew pubs. Every now and then there were deadly gusts of wind, especially on the banks of the Danube, which we confronted head down. Alberto wore a kind of black wool hood on his head, rather undignified. One of my students, Patrizia Giampieri—a psychoanalysis major, now a professor at the University of Vienna—was lying in wait along with a few of her friends, and one day, without our knowledge, someone took a photo which appeared the following day in *Falter*, a Viennese politico-cultural magazine, often prone to satire. With the Hofburg as backdrop, in a blast of sleet and a setting resembling the Vienna of *The Third Man*, I am trying to assume an air of virile vigor, while Cavallari is bent over like a porter. Under a big headline, "On a Secret Mission?" the photo's caption read, "The noted German scholar and Austrian expert Professor Doktor Claudio Magris leaves the Hofburg, followed by his assistant Alberto Cavallari, until recently editor of the *Corriere della Sera*. According to rumors circulating in usually well-informed circles, the two are said to be in Vienna on a secret mission, to shed light on the intrigue behind the Reder affair. It would seem, according to the latest reports, that the much-discussed welcome Reder received in Graz was due to a misunderstanding that took place between Austria and Italy. That is, it would appear that based on agreements between the two countries, the individual who was expected to arrive in Graz was not Reder, but Craxi, which would explain the official welcome."

Various unverifiable conjectures have been circulating regarding the hand that wrote those unsigned lines, which appeared under the photograph in *Falter*, no. 5, March 7–20, 1985, as well as the hand that took the photograph. Someone sent the page from *Falter* to almost all the Italian newspapers, within the constitutional arch and not—as we once used to say—but the papers were all very meticulous and no one picked up the news of the secret mission.[3] In the end I sent a copy of it, with my card, to Bettino Craxi, then prime minister. I don't know whether he ever received it and if he appreciated the joke of the Anonymous Viennese.

August 23, 1998

SCHOENBERG'S TABLE

The image of goodness is often associated with an easy, personal relationship with things, with a respectful familiarity with objects, with a thoughtful, skillful ability to handle them capably, but also with care and regard. Kindness toward people, animals, plants extends, naturally, to things, to the glass in which a flower is placed; gentleness is also in the hands, in the way they reach out to others or take an ashtray from the table. Attention, it's been said, is a form of prayer, the recognition of objective reality, of an order, of boundaries; a way of looking above and beyond one's own self, of knowing that none of us is the tyrannical, capricious satrap of the world nor can we destroy it at will, as we do during those pathetic, impotent bursts of rage when, unable to destroy ourselves, others, or the universe, we smash the first object that comes within range. There is a vital goodness in the hands of those who consider others and don't just focus fruitlessly on their own longings; similar to children, whose imagination is stirred by a stone or an empty box of matches, and particularly similar to art, which does not exist without a sensual, curious, scrupulous passion for the physical, perceptible concreteness of details, for shapes, colors, and smells, for a smooth or bristly surface, for the epiphany that can come from the edge of the surf or from a mismatched button on a jacket.

All objects and substances can be cast in this light: rusty nails, skyscraper windows, or computer screens that come to life like Aladdin's lamp, but wood especially has a reverent association, perhaps because of the close affinity of the hand that holds and sculpts it, for the pleasure it gives to the touch, for its vibrant scent. It is not surprising that the carpenter is an ancient, mythical figure of protective paternal goodness, like Saint Joseph or *Pinocchio's* Geppetto.

The worktable of Arnold Schoenberg is crammed with objects, stacked up in profusion in the apparent disorder in which only the person who has put them there, scattering them about that way, can find anything, but which—for that same reason—represents real order for the man who lives and works there, arranging and organizing reality. On that table, piled up chaotically, are notebooks, pads of paper, inkwells, sheets of music covered with notes, pencils, penholders, and books, ingeniously constructed rollers for gluing stamps or sealing letters, a cardboard violin, complicated chessboards devised by him, unlike the usual ones, with bizarre chess pieces, examples and drawings of the celebrated playing cards he designed, squares of colored cardboard that he used to study the possible combinations of the twelve notes. On the floor are paper-folding sticks, saws, hammers, tools, and contrivances of various kinds. For the most part, those gadgets were fashioned by him, partly out of necessity, partly to save money, partly for satisfaction and pleasure. Schoenberg constructed his world like Robinson Crusoe: he cut, sawed, and pasted, he made baskets for wastepaper or cylinders to hold pens and pencils, he carefully wrapped pencil stubs in cardboard strips to make them last longer.

The table is not in Vienna but in Los Angeles, at the Arnold Schoenberg Institute of the University of Southern California—the most authentic Vienna, for that matter, perhaps survives in exile. The warm sea of things is found in the city where the musician had sought refuge to escape Nazism, not in the house where he lived—and where one of his sons, Ronald, now lives—but in the institute that collects the wealth of archival material made available in 1976 by three of his children: six thousand pages of musical, literary, and personal manuscripts, two thousand volumes often rich with handwritten notes in the margins, essays and articles, letters, photographs, journals, phonograph records and cassettes, paintings, testimonies of various kinds, from the furlough permits dating from the First World War to greeting cards, documents of all kinds, of great interest, catalogued and ordered clearly and precisely.

Schoenberg's table does not make you think of exile, of uprooting or distance, but of home, of the Lares, of a life deeply rooted in the family, in loved ones, in daily routine. That warm array of objects—which enable you to experience day-to-day life, makeshift and chaotic but indestructible in its passionate flowing—speaks of the sabbatical majesty of the idyllic Jewish family, which no pogrom and no extermination can destroy. It is the home of the Jew of the diaspora who has no homeland but has a homeland in his heart, which he always carries with him and which nothing can obliterate; the Jew inherent in tradition, in the Law, in the Book, who, according to the old story, when he is seen leaving and asked if he's going far, responds Talmudically with a question, asking in turn: "Far from where?" Because on one hand he is always and everywhere far away, yet on the other he is never far from his core values.

In that room of Schoenberg, maestro and creator of dissonance, we feel the mark of harmony, of a man who lived in harmony. It is the room of a fabulous father, grandfather, or uncle whom we perhaps knew in our childhood, a family member who might not have amounted to much and whom others regarded with suspicion, but who for us was the magician who made things come alive, transforming pieces of paper into mysterious creatures, building puppet theaters or crèches with shepherds and camels moving in the shadows.

In fact, Nuria Schoenberg-Nono, the daughter who for the most part looks after the museum and is working on a biography of the composer, tells me about cardboard traffic signals and other imaginative, elaborate toys that her father built for her and her brothers, or the special clothes hangers that he made for his wife Gertrude to hang her skirts on so that they wouldn't get wrinkled; in the essay written to accompany the publication of the delightful playing cards designed by Schoenberg, fifty-two cards for whist, Nuria recalls how as a child she loved to watch him prepare the models for his inventions, trimming and planing and gluing, and she loved to sniff the glue and the water-and-flour mixture that the creator of *Pierrot Lunaire* and *Moses und Aron* stirred in a pot.

Later, at supper at the Schoenberg home, the three siblings—Nuria, Ronald, and Lawrence—occasionally reminisce about games and birthdays, evenings with the family and funny stories around the table, admonitions to do well in school, jokes and laughter, with that fraternal complicity which is the best, spontaneous tribute to parents who were able to be such.

Looking at that table and listening to those stories, you think somewhat enviously that Schoenberg was able to master time, the time he spent on so very many seemingly trivial things instead of applying it, as often happens, to the feverish administration of his own talent, to conferences, to interviews, to self-promotion, to cultural concerns.

Schoenberg's greatness does not seem to weigh heavily on his children, as overused rhetoric would have it and as is often the case: it does not crush them but buoys them, and above all brings them joy; it does not cast a shadow over their faces but shines a fresh, sweet light, the bright, affectionate smile with which the daughter talks to me about her father. From their expressions, from their way of being, you get the feeling that Schoenberg, a great figure of the noblest, most exacting art, must have given these three children the love that teaches them freedom, that raises them to feel in harmony with the world—to the degree possible given life's tragedy and absurdity.

Schoenberg's music, with ruthless clarity, plumbed the depths of that tragedy and that absurdity of existence, of the dissonances of the heart, of history, and of destiny. Without the experience of scission and laceration, without venturing out like Moses in the desert, forsaking the consolations of reassuring images, there is no great art, nor is it even possible to express harmony and joy, which are authentic only after knowing and enduring tragedy and are otherwise bogus and false. The great artist knows, like Kafka, that his job is to take upon himself the negative and evil of his age.

But this descent into hell is not necessarily a fascination with evil and a rejection of humanity. Not far from the Schoenberg home and the towering waves of the Pacific that suddenly break, enormous, on the beach, was the home of Thomas Mann, he too an exile. The Schoenbergs sometimes went to visit the writer, but the children, though nearly grown, had to remain outside because in that house they weren't too fond of youngsters.

Schoenberg was greatly saddened when in *Doktor Faustus*, to represent the tragedy of contemporary art condemned to a perfection devoid of humanity and thereby aligned with Nazi barbarism, Mann identified this great though inhuman and demonic art in dodeca-phonic music. Of course Schoenberg knew very well that like any writer who invents a character, Mann had every right to endow his fictional protagonist, Adrian Leverkühn, with traits or features sug-gested by factual reality and actual individuals, without claiming to objectively portray them.

Doktor Faustus certainly does not presume to be a study of Schoenberg, but a novel. Nevertheless the greatness and fame of the novel may lead many to believe that Schoenberg's music is really the one that Mann ascribes to his infernal hero. As a Jew, deeply imbued with a sacred sense of humanity, Schoenberg could not help but be saddened at hearing that his music was in some way associated with the final, barbaric outcome of the decline of Germanic culture. "If Mann had asked me," he told his daughter, "I could have created a demonic, inhuman music for him, which he could have described in his book. I did not create it, because music like that did not interest me, my music is something else . . ."

Among many misjudgments, that one had particularly wounded him. But Schoenberg, the creator of a music radically new and so often misunderstood, rejected and denounced in various ways, had learned to tolerate even painful incomprehension with serenity. "He to whom the Lord God has given the mission of saying something unpopular," his deep, placid voice says in a Berlin speech of 1931 that I listen to at the museum, "has also received from him the ability to realize and accept that it is always others who are understood."

October 22, 1989

THE RABBI'S DANCE

A few years ago, during a literary conference which took place in Austria at the Jewish Museum in Eisenstadt, a rabbi who had come from Vienna who was attending our session at one point asked me with a faint note of caution: "You are not Jewish, am I right?" I hadn't quite finished answering him, telling him that I wasn't, when the rabbi hastened to explain, his hands outstretched in front of him, as if to dispel any possible misunderstanding: "It was just a question."

Like almost all Jewish stories, even this marginal anecdote is steeped in Talmudic humor, deriving its zest from what it alludes to and what it omits, from the millenary history of Jewish differentness that, unspoken, surrounds — with its grandeur and its misery, its comedy and its tragedy — that rejoinder and its art of paradox and of the abstract, the ability to overturn the problem by reassuring the person, the non-Jew, the other, and urging him not to worry. It is this imperturbable, ironic self-awareness that Judaism has used to counter persecutions, knowing that they arose from insecurity and fear, and that it was necessary to free the others, the persecutors, from that senseless fear of them, make them see that they had nothing to be afraid of.

The sabbatical majesty of the Jew, his indomitable invulnerability throughout history, have made him a mythical figure, regarded with nostalgic envy. Faced with Judaism, one has often felt the way Kafka — a Jew sadly persuaded to be not much of a one, to be uprooted from the religious, vital constancy of his culture — felt before the Eastern Jews of Yiddish theater who seemed to embody everything that Western consciousness was losing: a whole, intact sense of the cohesiveness of life, the affective, vital integrity of the individual, an epic and harmonious familiarity with all of existence.

Beneath the windows of intelligence of the West, which was more and more aware of its scission and internal laceration, the Jew, rich or poor, went around like the king of the *Schnorrer*, the undaunted, tenacious scrounging beggars: wandering and insistent, exposed to ridicule and aggression but ready to let it roll off his back unconcernedly, without a country but rooted in a Book and in a Law, ensconced in life like a king and capable of feeling at home anywhere, as if for him the whole world were a familiar neighborhood, the childhood street where his native dialect is spoken.

Judaism has been and is an example of extreme differentness, of an uncompromising otherness, that seems inaccessible and foreign in its rites, its customs, its language, but that mysteriously coincides with the universal human. For at least a hundred years, if we've wanted to regain a sense of perennial passion and feeling like that evoked by the Homeric shield of Achilles, we have had to open on many occasions the volumes of great Jewish literature, which recount fatherly love, the marital mystery, the anarchy of Eros, the Law and its infraction, the testimony and value of quotidian life, eating, working, making love, sleeping, praying. Jewish literature, stemming from a culture that often remains impenetrable to the laity, has expressed with incomparable intensity a process that does not only concern the Jews but involves all modern humanity: the breakup of cohesive values—which Judaism identifies with the religious cohesion of the Law—into the centrifugal multiplicity of contemporary existence, which Nietzsche called "an anarchy of atoms" and Robert Musil "a delirium of many."

Until some time ago, talking about Judaism in our world meant freely acknowledging this bond and this value, without a shadow of that anxious, hasty philo-Semitism that denotes a guilty conscience and discomfiture. Anti-Semitism, the horrific kind and the more superficial variety, seemed like a terrible disease against which Euro-

pean civilization had been inoculated forever. Now there is the disturbing sense that something is changing, albeit at a minimal level;
as if distrust of the Jew were surfacing again, the undeclared, abject
conviction that his differentness—his individual and cultural distinctiveness—makes him inexorably *other*, unreachable in his ambiguous
secret, and ultimately untrustworthy; as if it were doubtful whether,
in the diverse chorus of the human family, he could truly be the
bearer and representative of values that apply to all.

The attacks and spreading violence resoundingly echo an imperceptible change that has perhaps appeared in the tone of a voice
speaking about the Jews, a slight awkwardness that denies the voice
its freedom to agree or criticize: as if the Jew's otherness were once
again an issue, though merely murmured, or as if the question put to
me by the rabbi might imply a shadow of mutual discomfit.

The current controversy surrounding Israel's invasion of Lebanon
contributes to this fracture, but it is not the sole cause. Certain attitudes of the current Israeli government are offensive because of the
severity of the belligerent acts, which do not appear to be justified by
the political-military situation, but especially because of the arrogant
tone of certain voices, which do not indicate that they are taking measures deemed necessary, rightly or wrongly, though tragically painful,
but rather betray a sense of contemptuous superiority. It is a brutal
approach, bound to provoke irrational reactive moves, which must
be guarded against.

The controversy surrounding Israel and the campaign fostering
it might soon die down if a final tragedy is avoided in Beirut: not only
because the world has a short memory but because the Palestinians
who escaped Israel will go on being victims of the Arab states and the
tragic ballet that those countries choreograph around their fate, not
venturing to help them and continuing to incite them against Israel.
As a result the Palestinians are not allowed to settle in and blend into
a new country, putting behind them the wrongs and the trauma they
suffered at the loss of their land, as countless other refugees similarly

deprived of their homeland were able to do in many countries after the Second World War.

No Israeli government represents Judaism, and no criticism of Israel, just or unjust, applies to Judaism, nor can it be rejected only out of a concern to defend Judaism.

Jewish differentness, and its fate, is an exemplary universal parable of humanity. No one can render this differentness foreign or alien without causing us to lose a fundamental part of our culture. For that reason the tenuous but dangerous anti-Semitism that is spreading must be faced squarely, with no discomfit or concern for anyone, because the stakes are too high. Everything that feeds it must be discredited.

There is, for example, a complex with regard to Israel—one that is expressed both in criticism and in agreement, and that must be resolved by a rational, nonjudgmental finding regarding that state as any other—which was not summoned to build the kingdom of God, and has neither a duty to behave better nor the right to behave worse than any other nation. There is a false philo-Semitism in which some conveniently take refuge, seeking in a flaunted solidarity with the Jews, persecuted in the past and in distant countries, an excuse to ignore the victims of other persecutions, less remote in time and space, whose voice lacks the strength to rise up and shout.

The terrible Jewish primacy with regard to suffering endured and the dignity with which it was borne does not authorize us to award the Jews a monopoly on suffering and solidarity; they are the chosen people, a universal symbol of humanity, only if the tragedy of all individuals is read in their tragedy and if the solidarity that is owed to them does not stop at them but extends to the pain of everyone, including those who are unable to make their cries reach our ears. Otherwise philo-Semitism nurtures the delirious anti-Semitic hypothesis of Jewish conspiracy, as in the case of so-called revisionists who consider the death camps a Jewish fabrication.

In a world which on one hand splinters into the ravings of the many who do not understand one another and on the other flattens differences into an indistinctive leveling, the central issue is one of a differentness that in its particularity would embody the universal human rather than deny it. Judaism is one of the faces of this variegated universality. Two months ago in Mexico City, we were invited to a Jewish wedding. The groom was the nephew of a friend of ours, a rabbi's daughter and the youngest of ten children, younger than the nephew himself. After the ceremony, celebrated in the synagogue of a Syrian Jewish community, the reception was held at a huge hotel, beginning around ten o'clock at night and expected to go on until eight in the morning.

There were eight hundred guests, and they danced to the music of forty violins. Reigning over all was the great joy and vitality of familial pietas, the secret behind Jewish strength and tenderness. Our friend's brothers, sisters, sisters-in-law, and brothers-in-law were affectionate and happy; their faces wore an expression of contentment. Some of their marriages might have been arranged, but those men and women seemed cheerful and resolved: the sisters and sisters-in-law of our friend, a young woman, all seemed like girls, amiable, talkative, and joyful; some were grandmothers, one was about to become a great-grandmother, and in that invincible gaiety of the Jewish family I felt welcomed as though I were among classmates. I felt like one of them, as I had shortly before on the pew in the synagogue, among the groom's relatives.

At one point in the enormous hall, the waltzes and rock music flagged, and the hora, the Jewish round dance, began. The dancing became faster and faster, unrestrained, full of wild, joyous energy, of that Dionysian exuberance that Joseph Roth saw in Eastern Jews, yet always composed in a familial festivity. The rabbi who had performed the marriage, a smallish man, raised the massive groom to his shoulders, and zipped spryly through the dance moves without succumbing to that weight, demonstrating that the man of God is full of vitality and immune to the melancholy that Hasidic saints designated the blackest sin. At one point, the rabbi lifted the groom off his shoulders, then stood a liquor bottle on his head, upright, and continued dancing and leaping, not letting the bottle fall, challenging others to do the same — which many, not being men of God, tried impulsively but unsuccessfully amid the crashing of toppling bottles.

It was a celebration of the "eternally unharmed" Jew, as Roth calls him, indestructible and devoted to life, like his forefathers who sired children under the pharaoh's persecutions and in the Nazi concentration camps. We'd come from a trip to several Mexican villages inhabited by Indians; we still had before us the image of that depleted, oppressed people, rendered sterile, thwarted, and unable to have their cry reach the world. In those same days, only brief accounts in the local papers, and even briefer ones in the European dailies, reported on the massacres of entire Indian villages in Guatemala, the populations exterminated and tortured.

They too, like any oppressed people, could have used the strength displayed before me in that dance, that invulnerable resistance to any violence inflicted on a people, on its blood line and on its gods. The chosen ones, to whom a universal, not tribal, Law was given on Sinai, are such when their pain speaks for everyone. I, too, that evening, was one of them, but I knew that the most legitimate heir to that civilization was our friend, a young woman who at one time had left that world and had returned to it, rediscovering it in spontaneous affection rather than in a visceral bond: who loved her family of ten siblings and sixty grandchildren and great grandchildren, but who had also been able to transcend it. Dante knew that his love for Florence, which came from drinking the waters of the Arno, should lead him to feel that our homeland is the world, as the sea is to fish.[1]

August 18, 1982

MUSICAL AUTOMATONS IN ZAGREB

1. Count Ivan Gerersdorfer might be living in a tale of Hoffmann, like Councilor Krespel, who took violins apart hoping to discover the secret of music; instead he lives in a rundown, neglected
building in Zagreb, in the old, charming baroque city on the hill,
where he faces the straitened circumstances and sunset of his life with
unconcerned discretion and looks after his collection of automatic
musical instruments with meticulous love, the last private museum
in the Croatian capital.

The count is in his seventies, tall, thin, with a somewhat hollow
chest and slightly curved shoulders; strands of hair spill over sharp
cheeks, which frame a nobly hooked nose that suggests the indisputable authority of large noses; above it a pair of dark eyes, lit by a grim
fire, distant, indifferent. His jacket is threadbare, his thin, nervous fingers stained brown by nicotine. The building belonged to the Jelačić
family, that of the famous Croatian Ban who in 1848–1849 helped
put down the Hungarian revolution against the Habsburgs and under
whose statue, now removed, lovers would traditionally meet.

The count—says Ljiljana Avirović, the translator to whom
we owe precious versions of Italian literary works in Croatian and
equally precious versions of Yugoslav and Russian classics, among
them Mikhail Bulgakov and Boris Pasternak, in Italian—is also a de-
scendant of the family of the Ban, who for Zagreb is a symbol of
patriotism and for Budapest a symbol of foreign oppression. In that
building of bygone glory, once a theater of national history, there is
now dignified poverty: gloom, peeling walls, and the endeavor—no
less difficult than a pitched battle or the conquest of a city—of day-

by-day survival. The count gradually sold off most of the building, whose first floor now houses a nursery school, and retired to live in the few rooms given over to the museum, which we reach by way of a majestic staircase, decorated by teachers and children with carved jack-o'-lanterns and colorful drawings. Life is a strategy of retreat, as was well known by the wisdom of the Mitteleuropa of which Zagreb was and is a heart.

During the winter Count Gerersdorfer repairs, rearranges, cleans, and restores his automatic musical instruments, which are his passion and his reason for living, incontestable and self-justifiable as any love. His collection is a veritable museum, with its regular schedule of hours, although the host will open the door, if he deems it appropriate, even after closing time. Automatic organs, mechanical flutes, musical clocks, zithers; an orchestrion in the form of a Secession-style cabinet, which operates by weights and plays eighteen different compositions performed by piano, drum, and cymbal; a black, shiny, hand-cranked Herophon, the aluminum discs of an Ariston organette, a euphonion with its steel plectrum that reads the musical score on a rotating cylinder covered with sharp points, Biedermeier boxes that play pieces of classical chamber music, an owl-carillon, bellows that swell and shrink, filling the room with immortal melodies.

On the walls are damasks, here and there covered with cobwebs; a painting depicts a dead deer and a clock without hands, it too familiar from many stories and films, a blank eye of time. Rather than automatic musical instruments, the pieces are — or so it seems — more like musical automatons; the music seems to come from things, from the objects that in childhood we believed were living creatures, the stuffed bear who was no less real than the neighbor's cat, or the neighbor himself; the marionette of the paladin Orlando who really was Orlando.

Those cylinders, those perforated discs resemble punch cards, and in this baroque building you understand how foolish it is to see technology and computers as the death of poetry—here you sense that technology is wisdom of the hand, the magic of numbers, a familiarity with things and the hidden relationships among them, the ability to make them speak, play, and perform, to induce them to give us the gift of Mozart's music that now echoes in this old salon. By no means must automatons be the work of the devil; sometimes they were created by a saint, like Saint Albert the Great.[1]

In the count's museum there is also one of Edison's phonographs, the device that marked the end of the earlier instruments. But the phonograph or record or cassette—the count says proudly—can only play back music that has already been performed and recorded, whereas the automatons that he sets in motion actually play, each time anew, as when you grasp a bow and violin. It is clear that Count Gerersdorfer, though he maintains a respectful restraint, is none too fond of Edison. An aristocrat has the right to prefer the past. On the wall there is a portrait of someone who is the spitting image of him. One of us, thoughtlessly, asks if it is he. Indignant, he straightens up and waves a hand in haughty denial: "How can you think such a thing? I never would display my portrait in the room where I receive visitors . . ."

2. Built in 1876, the main cemetery in Mirogoj is truly "monumental" in the strongest sense of the term: the reassuring, maternal solemnity of domes that evoke the inviting protection of a womb, the sober decorum of its sepulchers and chapels, the solidity of its columns that counter death with a firm order, the tombs that encapsulate, through the many illustrious names, Croatian history and reaffirm an epic continuity against obliteration and oblivion, the sculptures and statues that impose form on formlessness and decomposition, the trees and earth. Here death appears still classical, a moment in the cycle of generations.

By contrast, the large crematorium, built in 1985, seems to belong to a world that does not yet exist, to an alien, foreign future like

the one envisioned by science fiction. The aseptic, geometric buildings allusively simulate a cemetery, just barely hinting at the traditional forms of steeple, organ, or bell, with a stylization that is immediately interrupted; the room in which the funeral ceremony takes
place—the urn mechanically swallowed up in a space below—is a
kind of chapel but it is not a chapel, neither religious nor secular. The
entire complex calls to mind an astronomical observatory, a model
prison, a space station—here it is harder to imagine that the urns
might inspire the soul to eminent things, death more on the order of
The Loved One than *War and Peace*.

The crematorium seems like the final destination of an unreal,
abstract life such as the one many prophets of the future predict for
us, a life in which palpable things, colors, scents, actions no longer
exist, but only their simulation, a TV feature about the sea instead
of waves and salt water in your mouth, vacation photos without the
vacation, sexology in place of sex. It may be that this crematorium,
whose dynamism asserts itself imposingly, is a brilliant anticipation
of the future. I don't know if the future will look like that, and it
seems to me that at the moment rather than guess how it will look,
we must ask ourselves if we will have a future and at any rate try to
have one. Perhaps this crematorium, which is so little reminiscent
of a cemetery, whether people are buried or cremated, is fitting for
the grotesque, absurd unthinkability of death, which it tries to eliminate with maximum efficiency. Nevertheless, I can understand why
a friend, close beside us, murmurs that she would not want to end up
here, not even when dead.

3. Being presented at the headquarters of the Croatian Writers
Association is the translation of Marisa Madieri's *Verde acqua*, dedicated, in part, to the exodus of a great many Italians from Istria,
Fiume, and Dalmatia at the end of the Second World War. The subject, which might well be controversial, is treated with great civility
and great openness, with frank discussion of reciprocal wrongs and

common tragedies. In Croatian culture—a rich, deep culture, European in scope—there is an interesting rediscovery of the Italian component, the Veneto, in Adriatic culture, perhaps to counter the intense nationalism which is also present in Croatia, in effect a desire to find common roots in a supranational dialogue. Novels are being published that, for example, focus on the Italians' exodus from Istria—like that of Milan Rakovac, who relies on a linguistic pastiche of Venetian elements already seen in his title—or on the Italo-Slavic encounter, like that of Nedjeljko Fabrio set in the composite world of Fiume/Rijeka.

Among those in the room is a charming elderly gentleman, rather short and stocky, with a modest, gentle air. Those kindly, serene eyes have looked the Leviathan in the face, unperturbed. He is Karlo Stajner. Of Austrian origin, a militant since his youth in the Yugoslav Communist Party, Stajner was arrested in the Soviet Union by the Stalinist police in 1936 and disappeared into a gulag. Rehabilitated and released by Khrushchev in 1956, he wrote a book, *Seven Thousand Days in Siberia*, which is a great, epic testimony of that inferno, from the nightmare of universal betrayal to the prisons of the NKVD, the secret police, from interrogations to torture to the frigid cold of the Siberian Lager. Back home, Stajner would not publish the book without the consent of the Yugoslav Communist Party; he had survived, he said, to tell about Stalinist horror, but he did not want to bring harm to communism, in which he believed.

Watching this man you understand that faith can truly move mountains; surviving in Siberia was no less difficult than moving a mountain. The horrific experience, testified to without reserve, did not warp his soul, did not—as Danilo Kiš, the Serbian writer, wrote—leave scars in his heart. With him is his wife, Sonia, a gentle, shy Russian lady. She waited twenty years for him, when everything led her to believe that he would never return, when it was so awful to be the supportive wife of a man accused of treason. I study this petite bashful woman and I realize that heroes may indeed exist.

The twenty years Karlo and Sonia endured are a great epic poem. Meanwhile, the evening is at an end, and the association president, after thanking everyone, offers a public salute to Stajner. Everyone applauds. Karlo, who feels insignificant, thinks that they are still applauding the author and he too claps his hands. His sufferings have not robbed him of the pleasure of participating in the joy and celebration of others.

December 2, 1987

ISTRIAN SPRING

In Pula, two hundred yards from the Roman Arena, Guido Miglia shows me his aunt Catineta's house, where at Easter he would go to eat *pinza*, the delicate panettone, golden-yellow like a sunflower; now in that house, which has become a mosque, the muezzin proclaims that Allah is the one true God and Muhammad is His prophet. The ancient elements of a city, like the Roman arches and Venetian palazzi in Pula, are like the features of a face, whereas fresh, recent traits, like the mosque, seem like rouge or hair dye, which give the impression they can be removed without altering the face.

Just a short walk is all it takes in Pula to move in and out of different eras and cultures. In the Habsburg era, palazzo Stabal, behind the Arsenal, housed the Austrian Naval Engineers and Admiral Horthy, the maritime strategist of a continental empire that loved the torpid plains more than oceanic distances, and the future fascistoid governor of Hungary.

Situated on the Corso, at 30 via Sergi, now Prvomajska, was the workshop of Colarich, the dreadful serial killer of long ago, daringly captured after an elusive period on the run. Sentenced to life imprisonment, Colarich had been pardoned after many years, and made a living as a glassmaker in that workshop. When parents sent their children to buy or have something repaired, the kids stopped to exchange a few words with the old craftsman, who spoke good-naturedly, blithely unconcerned, as if those distant crimes no longer had anything to do with him and had become blurred and lost in the darkness of the years, like times spent running in the park as a child.

In 1904–1905, James Joyce, as an English teacher, lived on the third floor of 3 via Giulia, now Matko; the nameplate on his door, beside a wall with peeling plaster, now bears the name of a Mr. Modrosan Rude. On the first floor was the editorial office of the *Arena di Pola*, the newspaper that Miglia as a young man edited in the terrible days preceding the great mass exodus in the winter of 1946–1947: thirty thousand Pulians out of a total city population of thirty-five thousand. Lack of interest and ignorance persist in Italy with regard to the exodus of Italians from Istria, Fiume, and Dalmatia—approximately three hundred thousand people between 1944 and 1954, at different times and in various ways, sometimes more dramatic, sometimes less so, but always extremely sad given the anguish of leaving, the poverty, the future uncertainty, the wretched conditions for years in refugee camps.

The errors and faults of Fascist Italy as well as anti-Slav prejudices preceding fascism were paid for firsthand by those people who lost everything and found themselves in the eye of the storm when the Slavs, oppressed by fascism, took their revenge. As inevitably happens, a trampled nation that rises again gives free rein in turn to an aggressive nationalism, indulging in indiscriminate violence and trampling the rights of others. Italians for centuries have made up at least 50 percent of the total population of Istria, situated along the coast in cities that were cultural jewels of Venetian art, from Capodistria to Pula; the rural interior was Slavic, largely Croatian, and to a lesser degree Slovenian, with a mixed intermediate band between the two zones.

Italy, "so distracted," as the poet Giacomo Noventa wrote, paid no attention to that historical tragedy, ignoring and dismissing it, unlike Yugoslavia, which played the game with greater awareness and commitment.[1] The best progeny of these lands are those who have been able to overcome nationalism, developing, despite painful uprooting, a common feeling of belonging to a composite borderline world, seeing in the other—in the Slavic and in the Italian, respectively—a complementary and fundamental element of their own identity.

The epic of Fulvio Tomizza or Marisa Madieri's *Verde acqua* are examples, though not the only ones, of this sentiment, which represents the only salvation for border lands, in Istria as in Trieste and elsewhere.

That is yesterday's story, little known in spite of excellent volumes, from the great, fundamental work by Diego De Castro to the one put out by the Institute for the History of the Liberation Movement, to those of Miglia himself and many others, up to the recent *Trieste* by Corrado Belci; at age twenty, Belci had become editor of the *Arena di Pola* on February 10, 1947, the day of the signing of the peace treaty which assigned Istria to Yugoslavia—it was for that reason that a great, loyal anti-Fascist like Leo Valiani voted against the treaty in Parliament, having experienced Mussolini's prisons and the armed struggle and having always defended the Slavs.

Today history is turning the page, particularly with the upheavals in Eastern Europe, which are bringing about the fall of the Iron Curtain behind which Istria found itself after 1945. Throughout this period censuses have seen the community of Italians who had remained in Yugoslavia dwindling; today they officially number fifteen thousand, although there are many more Italian speakers, at least fifty thousand, and enrollments in Italian schools are rising, though mostly comprised of Croats.

Apart from the offspring of increasingly frequent intermarriages, for years many Italians were hesitant to proclaim themselves such, partly because they feared that as Italians they would be equated with Fascists, doubly ridiculous for those who had chosen to remain in Yugoslavia. Moreover, the Italian minority is not concentrated in a compact area but spread out in small, patchy groups, making it more difficult for them to preserve their identity, although it is evidenced by literary output, cultural initiatives, newspapers such as *La voce del popolo* and *Panorama*, and magazines, among them in particular *La Battana* in Fiume.

Starting in 1987 a true political "Istrian Spring" began, coming together in Group '88, formed by seasoned intellectuals led by the young, charismatic Franco Juri. Aided by developments of Slovenian and Croatian glasnost and concerned about the decline of the Italian minority, Group '88 vigorously addressed the taboo of past history and the oppression of previous years. Far from any irredentism, Group '88 demands not only the most effective protection of the minority, with measures necessary for its survival, but also an active role in the overall Yugoslavian context, beyond falling back exclusively on themselves.

The Group's activities resulted in a series of initiatives, meetings, debates, and position papers. At the moment there are two conflicting trends in the Italian minority. One, traditionally represented by the Union of Italians of Istria and Fiume, looks toward a more intense cultural relationship with Italy; it is a position shared by Antonio Borme, former member of the Federal Parliament and former president of the Union itself, ousted in 1974.

The other trend, expressed mainly by Group '88 and part of the Eastern European process that is insistently causing communism to crumble, has a transnational vision, advocating Istrian identity, that is, a close unity among the three ethnic groups that have lived together for centuries in Istria—Italians, Croats, and Slovenes—and that are now reduced, all together, to about 40 percent of Istria's total population, while 60 percent is made up of those who arrived after 1947, Slavs from the South, nomads or Muslims like those who look to Mecca near the Roman Arena.

There is much ferment: an interethnic Istrian assembly appears at the Slovenian elections to demand, within the "diversity" proclaimed by Slovenia, Istrian distinctiveness; such formations exist in many areas, such as "Club Istria," the Italian community of Pirano which poses as a minority party, a proposed tributary of a Constituent of the Italians of Yugoslavia and specifically the assemblies of Group '88, like the recent one in Gallesano. An interethnic consciousness is being formed that often encourages people to call themselves Istrian rather than Italian or Croatian, in a medley that is also reflected in the Riviere Hotel's menu, which promises *njoki sa sguazetom* and in which the objective is not hybridization, but the solid preservation of one's specific national features.

The autochthonous Istrian identity has none of the local government chauvinisms that throughout Europe have given rise to rancorous alliances of parochialism, more regressive than the great nationalisms. The 60 percent came afterward, certainly, filling roles and deserted cities, but the children and grandchildren of the newcomers must also feel at home in the places where they were born, in the streets or on the enchanting beaches where they played as youngsters.

As in other European countries, Istria's future now also includes, legitimately, the mosque installed in Aunt Catineta's house, even though it will be a difficult future, because every uprooting entails harsh clashes, and the current Muslim expansion in particular often has an encompassing intolerance that triggers defense mechanisms.

Even from Yugoslavs, especially in Croatia, you hear today that the Italian exodus was a loss for everyone, including Yugoslavia itself. One way or another Italy must materially help the Italian minority in Istria that has been so long neglected, apart from the meritorious local efforts of the University of Trieste and other similar institutions. The year 1989 shuffles the deck and liberates the truth, even in Istria. Perhaps Ligio Zanini's *Martin Muma* will soon be released, after being banned for years; the novel recounts the history of the camps on Goli Otok, the island to which orthodox Communists were deported, those who, like Zanini in 1948, refused to follow Tito in his great split from Stalin. Zanini believed in a strictly observed communism; I don't know what he believes in today, in freedom certainly— as well as in the freedom of his intense verse, a poetry in the Venetian dialect of Rovigno, in which, having retreated to be a fisherman, he speaks with the sea and with the seagulls. This poetry too is a sign of a centuries-old Venetian culture. "If the tendency of the World decides to expunge the Istro-Venetian presence from the Adriatic," Biagio Marin once told me, "I will bow my head and say '*fiat voluntas tua*,' but then, on my account, I'll add 'f . . . you,'" and here he came out with a fine, classic expletive that not even our bold secular times and anti-clerical battles allow to be printed in the *Corriere della Sera*.

February 20, 1990

CICI AND CIRIBIRI

1. "Cicio no xe per barca," an old Triestine saying goes, the Cici are not made for seafaring. Evidently the shepherds and charcoal burners who came from Romania centuries earlier and settled in the Istrian interior must not have been at home on the sea, if for the Venetian coastal populations and those in Istria's cities they've remained a prototype of the wariness inland people have for the disquieting depths, in a proverb that still today in Trieste indicates by definition an individual's ineptitude in any field, one for which he is not cut out. On the other hand, the Cici (or Cicci) in their valleys and mountainous highlands have tenaciously preserved their language, Istro-Romanian, and their identity, which can be quickly transcended and lost on the unfaithful, magnanimous sea.

The Cici are in all likelihood the smallest minority in Europe, if you can even consider them a minority; in the past century they numbered a few thousand, and in 1991, the year of the most recent census, 810 people declared themselves Istro-Romanian and 22 Morlachian. There may be more if you count those who have emigrated, as claimed by the representatives of the Andrei Glavina Association that recently formed in Trieste to save this small ethnic group from oblivion; there may also be fewer, because many of them, especially the young people, consider themselves Croatian or Italian as well, and their feelings toward their culture resemble the affectionate pietas felt for old family traditions rather than a sense of national belonging. Life is tenacious and in Briani (in Croatian, Brdo), a small village near the town of Labin where at one time, people in a nearby village tell me proudly, as many as forty confirmations were performed each year, now only two or three people still speak Istro-Romanian. "Dance, oh legs of mine, for tomorrow will be too late," says a *bugarenje*—an ancient form of epic poem sung by one or more voices—that until a few years ago was sung in Seiane (Žejane in Croatian, Jejani in Istro-Romanian), one of the two towns in which the Cici persevere and survive.

2. The Cici are a small tile in the composite Istrian mosaic, primarily Italian and Slavic but with a wealth of other minor components, which the Fascist regime, the regime of Tito, and today Franjo Tudjman's sought and seek to "purify" ethnically. The Cici were originally Wallachian, Vlach, refugees, who reached Istria mainly in the fifteenth century (although sporadic earlier appearances are recorded), fleeing before the Ottoman advance and welcomed by the Republic of Venice and by the Habsburgs as a means to repopulate areas devastated by invasions and plagues. The term *vlahi* was generally used to indicate populations of Latin origin in the Balkan peninsula, in turn divided into various subgroups, including for example the Morlachians; Romanians mixed with the Slavic majority were also found among the Uskoks, ferocious pirates of the Dalmatian coast who made things very difficult for Venice, for the Ottomans, and for the House of Austria, though it incited them against La Serenissima.

The more diffident Cici shepherds settled in the region north and west of Mount Maggiore, in a few isolated cases going as far as the environs of Trieste—as testified by Irenaeus of the Cross, an eighteenth-century historian and Barefoot Carmelite. Istro-Romanian, tenaciously preserved over the centuries, is one of the Romanian language's four groups, along with Aromanian of Macedonia, Megleno-Romanian of Thessaloníki, and Daco-Romanian of Romania itself. Ciceria (or Cicciaria) is divided into two enclaves: Žejane (with nearby Mune) and, on the other side of Mount Maggiore, several villages—chief among them Valdarsa (Susnjevica in

Croatian, Susnjevita in Istro-Romanian) and Villanova d'Arsa (Nova Vas, Noselo) — where the Cici have assumed the name of Ciribiri.

Ancient chronicles record the Cici as tall and strong, astute, rowdy, hardworking, faithful when they gave their word, oblivious to hardship and death, scruffy, used to making deals by counting on their fingers, and inclined to *straderie*, robberies on country roads, which led Marshal August de Marmont, governor of the Illyrian provinces during the brief Napoleonic period, to issue strict edicts and enforce repression. The traditional occupations of the Cici included trading in vinegar — which they went as far as Vienna to sell, authorized by a permit from Maria Teresa — salt transport, smuggling, when their territory found itself on the border between Austria and La Serenissima, and in particular the sale of "sweet coal,"[1] which they would bring to Trieste on donkeys, as Tatiana Silla records, shouting "Carbuna, carbuna!," Coal, coal!, through the streets.

For centuries lacking any cultural institutions, schools, official recognition, and written literature, easily prone to assimilate with the much more numerous Croatians or Italians, the Cici endured owing to their language, a subject of interest among the great linguists from Cattaneo to Ascoli to Bartoli to eminent Romanian scholars. Emil Petru Ratiu, president of the Glavina Association, recalls that in the nineteenth century the Triestine historian Pietro Kandler appeared at the erudite Society of Minerva wearing the traditional Cician costume to draw attention to their neglected culture; in 1887, the Cici addressed an appeal to the Italians of Istria, like them subjects of the Habsburg Empire, to ask for solidarity. An Istro-Romanian school existed only between 1921 and 1925 in Valdarsa thanks to the efforts of its teacher Andrei Glavina — author of the first book written in Istro-Romanian, a calendar-almanac — and was closed when he died, because there were no other teachers.

In the history of the Cici, at least the recent one, everything happens among a few people who know one another personally and see each other regularly at the tables of a tavern or at a shop; it is a history whose processes are visible to the naked eye and in which the family epic has not yet become sociology. The reclamation of Lake Arsa by the Italian state in 1932 improved living conditions and attracted other people, transforming Valdarsa's ethnic features; after World War II many Cici emigrated to America, where today Istro-Romanian is still the mother tongue of their descendants. In the thirties, Ervino Curtis recalls, two young boys were sent to Romania, a Cicio from Seiane and a Ciribiro from Valdarsa, to soak up the mother culture and bring it back to their small towns. I don't know the fate of those two boys, which recalls the sad lot of the two young Tahitians, Aotourou and Omai, brought to Paris and London at the time of Captain Cook's voyages. Today there is a return to an awareness of Istro-Romanian identity, thanks to the above-mentioned association, to the *Sabor* (assembly) formed in Valdarsa and to other initiatives. Naturally trilingual, the Cici and the Ciribiri, observes Fulvio Di Gregorio, the association's founder, emerge as a symbolic focus of the Istrian crucible, irreducible to a sole nationality.

3. I am in Seiane. In 1904, one of my learned fellow citizens, Prof. Dr. Ugo G. Vram, traveled through these towns on behalf of the Adriatic Society of Natural Sciences, charged with measuring the cephalometric and facial index of the Cici; he concluded that they belonged to the category of brachycephalic-mesoprop, established the minimum frontal diameter of adults, and compiled tables of "ellipsoid, sfenoid, spheroid, ovoid" heads, of "square, pentagonal, or triangular" faces, and of concave and convex noses. In the photographs that accompany his research, the faces so measured smile back, shy and gentle.

I would hope that the people of Seiane would not be so patient with me if I had craniometric intentions toward them. In the autumn fog the town seems semi-deserted, a dog and a few sheep roam through the streets, the smell of manure is in the air. The horizon is a barren, gilded panorama, splashed with the black of fir trees and blood-red splotches of sumac. At the only tavern, the Bife Tina, a few customers are talking in a mixture of Istro-Romanian and Croatian. They tell me, in Italian, about the *zvončari*, players who stroll around at Carnival time with paper flowers on their heads, wearing colorful striped garments and bells tied around the waist, which tinkle owing to the rhythmic movements of the body shaking them.[2] Lacking words and literature (fairy tales, lullabies, calendars), the Cici had dances of remote pagan origin as well as musical instruments: Franco Juri Sanković recalls the *cindra* with two strings, the *mih* or *meh*, Istrian bagpipes, and the *dvojnice* or *vidalice*, double flutes.

Carnival begins on January 6 and lasts for weeks; an intense love of festivity, all the more poignant the less there is to celebrate. The houses and streets suggest loneliness, a life that has gone elsewhere, a culture that perhaps lives on mainly through overseas emigration, through someone in New York who with an American accent speaks the language of a land never seen, or in the verses of Ezio Bortul—perhaps the only Istro-Romanian poet—which celebrate the far-flung, wandering vlahi. But the beautiful young hostess at the Bife Tina, a Croatian who married into an Istro-Romanian family, says she is content to live in Seiane; in her words, the village becomes a place of life, not one of decline, which happens when a person who is footloose and fancy-free is satisfied with her surroundings, because she gives meaning to things, thereby transforming even the smallest setting into a world stage.

4. I am in Susnjevica, Valdarsa, among the Ciribiri. On any trip the first-person pronoun is uncertain, reduced to being practically a grammatical convention. Who is it that is traveling? The "I" of the traveler is little more than a gaze, a hollow shell in which the shape of reality is molded, a container that is filled by things, giving them at best—with his idiosyncrasies, his longings, his anxieties—a form, just as a container shapes the water that fills it. If literature, as has long been said, must reject the stereotypical puppet of a coherent,

unified "I," in vain reinstated by commercial, albeit quality, fiction, the travel essay is the epic form best suited to a civilization in which the "I" — of the character and of the author — is a fleeting, oscillating juncture of events and sensations, the sediment left by a volatized tradition and history.

Valdarsa is close to the Arsa's dam and coal mines. Many houses are dilapidated and closed up: of the four hundred inhabitants of one time only about seventy remain; an elderly man encountered along the street recalls, though not sadly, that there were once four pubs, two smithies, a nursery school, a shoemaker's shop, a bakery, and a police station, while today a squat, reddish building houses the town hall, a grocery store, and the post office. The telephone arrived five years ago, electricity in 1967, and indoor running water in 1984. A few miles away, visible to the naked eye among the hills that begin to slope down toward the sea, is the controversial coal-fired power plant of Fianona. At one time men went to work in the mines of Arsa every day; they dug for coal or smuggled tobacco over the mountain. The women were nannies for the well-to-do Germans who vacationed at the shore in nearby Abbazia; other families in the nineteenth century earned money raising the children that one Romanian scholar, Ioan Maiorescu, called "the fruit of the sins of Trieste's plutocrats."

Here is the school of Glavina, the teacher, with its deserted classrooms; set among chestnuts, pines, cypresses, and a few palm trees are houses abandoned by those who realized that working the land cost more than they earned by selling the harvest; in one family only three people remain, while forty-three are in America. A pair of trousers hung out to dry is a sign of life; on the wall of a tottering house a climbing red rose dissimulates its caducity, as the baroque essayist Torquato Accetto wrote, almost as though the beauty of its color could make us forget that it and all the things around it are mortal.[3] Some retell timeworn stories about the Germans who burned the rectory and town hall with all the documents, or about two rich, greedy old sisters who lived in a house with a thatched roof, now collapsed, kept piles of money under the mattress, did not feed their workers, and ended up in the poorhouse, their money left to rot away or, according to anticlerical gossip, pocketed by the parish.

Not far away is the cemetery, with its Church of the Spirito Santo, frescoed by a painter named Biagio of Ragusa, its tombstones and a view from a hill densely covered with junipers, behind which stood Lake Arsa. The dry bed left by draining the lake is said to be a place where witches gather; a woman who collected nettles and slept on the church steps saw them often. In accordance with established custom families took turns digging graves in the cemetery. But neither death nor despondency prevails in Valdarsa or in nearby Villanova. There are bright, well-kept houses inhabited by open, friendly people, young, smiling faces, children playing, a refined, cordial hospitality offered to the traveler. At the table, deliciously laden, Italian, Istro-Romanian, and Croatian are spoken. For this free, relaxed people, the Istro-Romanian identity is not a visceral obsession, a purity to be protected from any contamination, but an added richness, which coexists peacefully with ties to Italy and being part of Croatia. That is how a border identity should be, an enrichment of the individual, whereas instead the border often exacerbates barriers, divisions, hatred.

Before leaving, we pay a visit to Barba Frane, the blacksmith, who is said to possess the only book in this community, a primer. His father and grandfather had once worked in the same smithy, full of tools scattered among corncobs to be roasted; people not only lived in that house, with its wooden floor and thick walls, they were also born there, like his grandmother, and died there, like his father. Outside the door, rabbits, cats, and chickens live together peacefully.

Embedded in the stones of his house are marine fossils. Istro-Romanian words are fossils as well, clearly distinguishable in the diverse mosaic that encompasses them. "The dying and death of things goes hand in hand with forgetting the name that designates them" wrote Gian Luigi Beccaria in *I nomi del mondo* (Names of the

World), a delightful labyrinth of lost words and the stories buried in them and exhumed. Frane, who is lame like the blacksmiths of mythology, from Hephaestus to Volund, sees us off with a smile: "In the world, nothing ever stands still." It's hard to tell if he says it regretfully or with relief.

November 7, 1995

IN BISIACARIA

1. The name—*Bisiaco,* in dialect *Bisiàc*—means a fugitive, an exile, although its etymology, a science moreover that is often tested by adulteration, has been distorted.

In the Fascist era, concerned with negating the presence and traces of other peoples and nationalities, especially Slavs, in the lands on the eastern border of Italy, the official etymology, still today borne out by public opinion, held that the name derives from the Latin *bis aquae,* that is, from the area near Monfalcone between the Timavo and the lower Isonzo. Like the course taken by rivers—the Isonzo, over the centuries, has modified its path as well—every identity is ephemeral, the advancing or retreating edge of a beach, a scar on a face. Not even "bislacco," which would be an honorable and enviable etymon, can hold up against the glottologists' chisel. As Silvio Domini and Aldo Miniussi write, the origin of the word dates back to an old Nordic verb, *baegia,* through the Slovene *bezati,* meaning to flee; progressing along the border between the seventh and eighth centuries, the Slovenians called the Italic peoples who withdrew *Beziaki,* so that *bezjak* came to mean exile as well.

Bisiaco—which the Slavs in the Middle Ages called *Vlahicum,* neo-Latin—is primarily a language; the dialect that arose, according to Giuseppe Francescato, when Aquileian Latin dissolved, diversifying into Friulian in the Lombardy area and into Venetian (of which Bisiaco is a variant) along the Adriatic coastline. Today about sixty thousand people speak it. A few years ago, a never-approved bill, which provided for the teaching of Friulian in schools in Bisiacaria as well, sparked protests from the Bisiachi, fearful of seeing their

centuries-old individuality absorbed and obliterated by Friulian culture, much more widespread and robust. An ethnic group that asserts
itself often does so at the expense of another, weaker group, thus vio-
lating the principle in whose name it protests against the stronger
state or nation by which it in turn feels oppressed; history is one big
frothy fermentation in which bubbles eager to emerge continuously
destroy one another, bursting one by one.

As a synonym for fugitive and refugee, *bisiaco* indicated in past
centuries a person who speaks the language poorly and therefore
struggles to understand, a dimwit; anyone who doesn't speak our
language is always, for each of us, a barbarian, as such people were
for the Greeks. Always something of a nomad, a traveler can easily
be spotted as a foreigner who doesn't understand the language well,
much less the gestures, feelings, or gods of the inhabitants, just as he
is unable to distinguish the variety of bird songs—on the island of
Cona, at the mouth of the Isonzo, a hundred different species can
be seen in a single day—or the sounds of the wind and the weather
changes they herald.

2. The distances between stops along the way, from one town in
Bisiacaria to another, are quite short, one time eight miles, another
two and a half. But space too, like time, contracts and expands according to what fills it; it shrivels up or swells like a balloon, magnifying distances and things, altering their proportions. A curious, attentive idler
who wanders about in a confined space is like a photographer blowing
up images, causing ever new details to emerge from an indistinct blur,
revealing universes cubbyholed one inside the other. A swamp on the
island of Cona is an undifferentiated expanse, but gradually the eye
distinguishes and brings into focus countless worlds, the motionless
head of a frog just above the surface of the water, the squiggles of a
snake that glides along the muddy film, hard to tell whether swimming or slithering. Distances open up between objects, and a reed
bed stared at for a long time with eyes dazzled by the intense summer

sun undergoes a process similar to words which, when repeated over and over again, end up losing their significance and become other words, echoes of other meanings.

A journey without an itinerary and without obligatory destinations—because after all, in Bisiacaria there is almost nothing to see—is a school of perception, Paolo Bozzi, a master of the science that teaches not how the world is made but how our senses grasp it, patiently explains. Perceiving requires time, leisure, the idle freedom that allows you to linger over an effect of light refraction or a showy oleander flower; it requires that you not be harried or feel you have to achieve a result, but that you be able to squander time, letting it flow by or heedlessly tossing it away like a slice of watermelon you've barely tasted, unconcerned since there is still a lot of the big beautiful red melon, enough to stain your shirt with the juice that squirts out as you take a bite.

Bisiacaria is one of those parallel spaces, contiguous to our day-to-day reality, which we skirt very often but almost never enter, like certain streets in our own city or certain towns along the highway. I had circled, crossed, and bypassed these low-lying lands of rivers and sea many times, without ever really seeing them, touching them; Turriaco, San Pier d'Isonzo, Staranzano were mere names. The act of wandering among these fields and villages is a search not for memories, nostalgia for the past, fond, precarious relics of the "I," but for the world beyond the hedge. It is not, in the end, a search for anything: it is letting oneself drift, like a piece of wood in an irrigation channel.

3. The first stop is Pieris. In the Church of Sant'Andrea is a primitive, plain-spoken Via Crucis, whose overly large heads and toes have the graceless, absolute vividness of flesh. In the sultry heat, we enter a courtyard where a few people are playing cards beneath dense horse chestnuts. It is the headquarters of ARCI, the Communist recreational association, which hospitably also offers refreshments to non-member foreigners. As we enter, Margherita Bozzi hears someone at

a table mutter, "These people are not our comrades." For a moment we get the wrong impression, the feeling of undeserved discrimination, but then it's nice to hear that word again and especially to see that there is still a healthy working-class instinct, capable of distinguishing who is really a comrade. Under the horse chestnuts, the *sessantottini* activists of 1968 and extra-parliamentarians with radical sympathies would have little luck; they would be unmasked even before their preordained conversion to the right.

In Bisiacaria you see solid Case del Popolo, streets named after Antonio Gramsci and Tina Modotti, posters announcing partisan rallies. The farmers and workers of Ronchi, in particular those of the shipyards of Monfalcone, suffered harsh Fascist repression and opposed it with dogged resistance, which—thanks primarily to the Communist organization—was never entirely crushed, like an army that even in a losing battle does not crumble. For the most part, the two thousand Communist militants—survivors of the partisan struggle (some from the Spanish Civil War), Fascist prisons, and German concentration camps—who in 1947 voluntarily went to Yugoslavia to aid in the construction of socialism were also Monfalcone workers; in 1948, when Tito broke with Stalin, they were deported and subjected to atrocious abuses in two Titoist gulags on two Adriatic islands, where they resisted heroically in the name of Stalin, who for them symbolized the revolutionary ideal and who, if he had won, would have turned the whole world into a gulag, in which free, ardent men like them would have been the first victims. Those who years later returned to Italy were pursued as Communists by the Italian police and boycotted by the Communist Party, for which they were inconvenient witnesses of the Party's Stalinist policy, which everyone wanted to forget.

4. Although Monfalcone, with its history and industries, is the most important center, the capital of Bisiacaria is perhaps Ronchi. It was in one of its old inns that Guglielmo Oberdan was arrested in

September 1882 as he was preparing an assassination attempt against Franz Joseph, counting on dying rather than killing for Trieste's Italian identity; he has remained a symbol not only of patriotism but also of an exceedingly sublime morality of those inclined to sacrifice themselves and others. Ernestina Pellegrini has spoken of an "Oberdan complex" on the part of Triestine writers, present—to her fond regret—even in those she loves the most, who are also able to surrender happily to the waters of the Danube and the sea, to the flow of life.

At 59/61 via D'Annunzio, a plaque recalls that in that house, on the night of September 12, 1919, the Vate, "ardent with fever and heroic will," had awaited "the radiant dawn" of his legionaries' march on Fiume.[1] Other figures are perhaps more willingly recalled in Ronchi, from Franz Joseph, who in 1912 elevated the countryside to a village, signing the imperial certificate in Italian, to the teacher Rodolfo Kubik, half-Czech and half-Bisiach, who in 1926 refused to have the town band he directed play "Giovinezza" and who, as an anti-Fascist exile in Argentina, celebrated General San Martin, the *Libertador*, with a cantata. Ronchi did not erect a monument to Gabriele D'Annunzio, but one was put up instead, perhaps out of spite, by the Monfalconesi a few yards from the castle marking the border between Ronchi and Monfalcone.

"Quis contra nos" is inscribed on the monument. A few years afterward, some of the former legionaries of Fiume had to face each other, weapons in hand, from opposite barricades, in the clash between Fascists and anti-Fascists; twenty years later they would become heroes of the Resistance, such as Ercole Miani, whom the Nazis tortured without being able to get a word out of him, and Gabriele Foschiatti, who died in a concentration camp. In Fiume, D'Annunzio caused the Lloyd restaurant belonging to Marisa's family to go bankrupt when the legionaries—as she recounted in *Verde acqua*—were invited to eat there gratis. A photo shows the Poet, smiling and unavoidably charming, surrounded by all those enthusiastic relatives of ours.

5. In Ronchi I meet Silvio Domini. A history and linguistics scholar, author of numerous publications of various kinds—among them, a formidable *Vocabolario fraseologico del dialetto "bisiàc,"* a phraseological lexicon of the "Bisiach" dialect—Domini knows everything there is to know about Bisiacaria; he is much more than an intellectual, however, since his writings, celebrating his land but devoid of any particularistic, rigid exclusivity, are marked by a broad view of things that combines a love for one's birthplace with the feeling of belonging to a vaster national community and a fraternal dialogue with other cultures that are part of a border world, such as that of Slovenia. He is above all a sincere, vigorous Bisiach poet; his verses, free of any local color, speak of passion and melancholy, of slipping into the shadows, of the blaze of sumac on the Karst, of disturbances of the heart that soon become insignificant as sawdust, of death, which, under the white wing of birds flying high above, seems lighter to the worn-out, splintered vessel that awaits it. It is hardly a misfortune to be a poet in Bisiach, which has six distinct terms to indicate the different love warbles of the finch and in which the word *sleep* is feminine, as befits its maternal regenerating harmony. A poem by Domini expresses one of the most intense (even irrational, devastating) passions of life and the most neglected in literature, the love for one's children—the fear, as he writes, of not being able to show them the way to go confidently into the tumultuous waters that lie ahead of them.

6. Villages close together, but each one distinctive, virtually unique on the plain. In Turriaco a barista, whom Alberto Cavallari asks about a gifted, deceased lute maker, a Signor Clemente, reproaches me for not having been critical enough in my article in the *Corriere* of some swimmers who were unmoved by a corpse lying next to them on a Trieste beach.

In this small town in 1945, during the terrible time of defeat and violence against Italians by Yugoslavian occupiers, Silvio Benco wrote a sorrowful essay, *Contemplazione del disordine* (Contemplation of Disorder), in which the entire century and its ethos seem to result in decadence and chaos. That noble, misguided work is the grief of a man who sees his world destroyed and mistakes it for the decline of the entire world; one should always be able to say, as Evelyne Pieiller did, "It is not the end of the world, it is only the end of our world." But grief is a poor teacher, it clouds the gaze, and it is easy and unfair to criticize its bias: to do it justice, one must be able to empathize with it, to lose, along with the person grieving, the global vision of the situation, which puts the pain into perspective but also enables it to be forgotten, to fully experience that extreme moment of life when only grief exists.

In San Canzian d'Isonzo a passerby vigorously discourages us from visiting the Church of San Proto, which contains a sarcophagus of San Grisogono, a martyr to whom tradition attributes several graves, including one at sea, and my presumed ancestor, on my maternal side, whose epic portrait Giorgio Pressburger traced through the history of its palazzo in Spalato.

In San Pier d'Isonzo, after complying with an elderly lady who stops us on the street to have her photograph taken with us, we go in search of Giuseppe Ermacora, who writes poetry under the name of Pino Scarel. We have to ring the bell a long time before he opens the door, after having put on a shirt and woolen knee pads, because he's hard of hearing. He's old and has worked all his life in construction sites and as a bricklayer; he's published some slim little volumes, other poems of his are posted on the church door and on the wall of a club. He is pleased to see us, but the interest of foreigners doesn't overawe him or make him swell with pride; he shows us his poems with absolute naturalness, the way he shows us the rosemary in front of the house or the way a carpenter displays the piece of furniture that he has just made. The images in his verses are strong and muted, materializing like objects fashioned by capable hands. "Fogo al veciun," reads one of his poems; the withered grass that is burned is also old age. But he tells us about his grandmother, more than ninety years old, who though she complained about her aches and pains added that it is better to stay down here, "because there is always something to see"; she took life, rightly, as a film. Death, writes Paola Cosolo Marangon in her intense *Storia di Rosa* (Story of Rosa), set in the Lower Isontine, exists only for those who believe in it.

"Tempo de soto" they said at one time when the scents of the sea and of summer, the season of Eros, wafted through these fields. Benito Nonino has never forgotten how as a child he heard people talk about a Bisiach woman who was a "lover," without saying whose lover — it's quite a thing to be able to say of someone that she is simply a lover, that that's her primary label. The sea is nearby; it mixes with the fresh water of the river and marshes. Staranzano beach is strewn with dried mud, the water is very low, big fish swim between your legs, a crab that's picked up brandishes its claws, placed back on the bottom it burrows into the sand. Many large houses, built as at one time and quite beautiful, are unauthorized and the subject of a bitter dispute between those who defend the traditional landscape and those who defend the law. In ancient times the Amber Road passed through here. The mud cracks underfoot, seaweed and empty shells rot in the sun, it's late in the afternoon. "Eusebius grows old with dignity," says a Latin inscription found not far away in the urn of a noble Roman family.

7. The linguistic boundaries are imperceptible, requiring a special ear. Carlo Luigi Bozzi, for example, distinguished the slow enunciation of the inhabitants of Sagrado from the harsh, fast diction of Fogliano, his adjoining hometown. A historian, educator, and poet, he endures here in two streets, a school, and a memorial stone bearing his name, in numerous scholarly volumes, and in his poetry, indissolubly bonded to a Bisiach dialect free of any folkloristic vernacular, transformed into universal expression. In his verses we find Fogliano, with its churches, the mountain and the "compagnoni be-

verendi," drinking companions, whose obscure existences are lived out between church and tavern. Fogliano, the commune of Fogliano Redipuglia, is also home to the great sacrarium to the fallen; what is sacred is the feeling that everyone is equal in the face of death, each of us—even those who have a name—is an unknown soldier.

A little farther on is Sagrado, whose inclusion in Bisiacaria is debated. Small but with a city feel, respectable old buildings and ornamentation, colorful bright flowers; a place of battles, of river transit. Crossing the bridge over the Isonzo, in early June 1882, was the hearse of Angelo Musmezzi, the prosperous "pirate" who had adventurously plied the seas at the time of the Greco-Turkish wars, accompanied not by ecclesiastical chants but by the tune—the chronicles say "bawdy song"—of the bocce players. Paolo Bozzi recalls that in the piazza, at the time he was a boy, there was a waterwheel fountain, and the kids were unanimous in interpreting its murmur: the creak the wheel made as it climbed up said "my love" and the piston pump, plunging into the water, added, "it's you." "My love—it's you; my love—it's you."

We go down to the Isonzo's pebbly riverbed. Uprooted, rotted trunks lie among the rocks, the water glistens, the sky's gold, the color of time, slowly turns brown, like an immense autumn leaf. Meandering here and there, splashing about in the water, lying on the stones, imagining, as in childhood fantasies, being swept away by an engulfing flash flood. The vast riverbed is almost empty, but in that emptiness you notice reflections, echoes, sounds, leaves dropping, water flowing, the chirping of birds. Now it is a little more difficult for me to perceive and distinguish all this, to recognize nuances, variations, changing colors, accustomed as I was to seeing the world not only with my own eyes but also and especially with those of Marisa, so much more observant and perceptive, more lovingly able to capture things. A marriage, a shared existence can in large part be this as well, traveling through the world together to view everything or nothing there is to see. The sun, scarlet and huge, almost touches the plain.

The human eye sees it as all the more gigantic when it is on the horizon than when it is at its zenith or at any rate high above. It seems that for lemurs, according to experiments performed by the great Viennese psychologist Johannes von Allesch, a friend of Robert Musil, the opposite is true. In any case, right now it is really big, fiery. "Al'ros / de na zornada finida," says a verse of Domini, the red of a finished day.

September 21, 1997

A FATEFUL HYPHEN

Bratislava. Czechoslovakian or Czech-Slovakian? In *The Man Without Qualities*, Robert Musil recalls how, in the now defunct Habsburg Empire, a complex, initiatory science was required to distinguish the institutions and authorities that were to be defined as Imperial-Royal from those that were to be called Imperial and Royal. To make an error was dangerous, fraught with consequences that could be dire, almost like the imprudent presence or absence of an "i" in *omousia* or *omoiusia* at the time of the theological disputes between those who advocated the same exact substance and essence between the Father and the Son in the Trinity, and those who argued instead that there was merely a resemblance between them.

Vowels, conjunctions, and hyphens that are omitted or added incorrectly can lead to squabbling and sometimes even to slaughtering; for that matter killing and dying over a question of race or over a monopoly of bananas is neither nobler nor more rational. Even the disagreement over the plural of the imperial royal monarchy(ies) helped lead to Sarajevo. Now a similar antithesis is likely to ignite passions in Slovakia—fortunately on a lesser scale and to a more moderate measure, at least so far. Emerging in the controversy over the spelling between those who want and those who do not want the hyphen in the name of the republic headed by Václav Havel is the centuries-old problem of relations between Czechs and Slovaks, of their solidarity and rivalries, of their fate in some ways shared and in many other ways distinct, of the mutual distrust of arrogance on the part of some and resentment on the part of others.

Days ago in Bratislava, in front of the Hrad—the castle where a summit promoted by Havel took place between the heads of state and government officials of Czechoslovakia, Poland, and Hungary with the participation of Italian, Austrian, and Yugoslavian foreign ministers—alongside the honor guard were girls wearing national costumes, waving flowers, and singing celebratory songs, but also groups displaying, albeit in a polite, civil manner, signs demanding the self-determination of the Slovakian people and protests against the treatment suffered by the Slovakian minority in Hungary, protests which the Magyars replicate with similar accusations about the condition of their minority in Slovakia.

We shouldn't be too amused by those spelling altercations, since contained in them is the memory of centuries, of passions, sorrows, and hopes which history has engraved on men's feelings and entwined with the fate of generations. But a tree, to grow well, must also be pruned; being free also means putting past sorrows and spites behind you, forgetting the abuses endured at the hands of a malicious superior or a petty colleague, the harassment of neighbors who muddy the stairs and keep the radio turned up at full volume; it means no longer keeping meticulous track of when you were right and when you were wrong.

The charm and curse of Mitteleuropa consists instead in the poignant, bitter inability to forget, in a punctilious memory that records everything and that each day rereads the transcript of the centuries, eager to avenge the defeats suffered in the Thirty Years' War with the same passionate intensity shown toward events of World War II.

This dogged loyalty is touching, full of pietas for everything that dies, a quixotic challenge to time and oblivion. But at times this central Europe transfixed by hyphens ends up becoming obsessive and unbearable, a cell in an asylum, a café in which the smoke and reek of epochs fester; perhaps this is why it is a truthful, which is to say distasteful, mirror of the world. Sometimes you just can't wait to get away, to go to a relaxing, uncrowded beach, to put out to sea.

In recent times, strong winds have shaken that café, throwing wide its doors and windows and opening up new horizons, new possibilities, and hopes for a new history. The summit in Bratislava, lavish and almost chaotic in the anti-protocol spontaneity officially proclaimed by Havel, was a tangible, physical experience of this changing central Europe, of the role it may play tomorrow on a global level, as well as the role that Italy might have within it; Italy is proving to be its most receptive interlocutor in the West and could play an increasingly active role in promoting an integration process that will no longer see an oppressed and forgotten "other Europe."

Of course, the claims of the past are tenacious and obstructed the meeting in Bratislava as well, with various reservations and mutual distrust up until the end. Freed from totalitarianism, which had frozen national tensions, central Europe risks falling prey to devastating ethnic divisions, to long-standing, still smarting turbulences that we illuded ourselves were buried forever.

No ghosts of yesteryear hovered in Bratislava; instead there was the exhilarating feeling of being in a cauldron of the future, chaotic and even contradictory, but creative, cosmopolitan. Havel, in his inaugural speech, also stressed the fundamental importance of the tragic, unsolved problems of the Third World in order to prevent the interest accorded to the new emerging Europe from degenerating into an insular, egocentric Europeanism; everyone spoke in terms of real supranational openness, looking beyond the vast yet still too parochial confines of Mitteleuropa. Wojciech Jaruzelski, whom I actually saw smile and even laugh, sat cordially beside the other members of the Polish delegation, some of whom—among them friends who are close to me—had been jailed after his coup d'état of December 13, 1981.

Looking at the general, stiff and erect, and recalling many dramatic days in Poland that I had seen with my own eyes, I thought that he deserved respect and even gratitude for the sacrifice he made, at least for a time, of himself and of his figure, assuming an odious role to avoid the worst, exercising it in the least odious way possible and slowly anticipating—thanks mainly to the opposition, of course, with which he ended up practically collaborating—the transformations that later on took place in other countries with such intensity. In his speech, speaking of Lithuania and how the phasing of its independence must be subject to the continuation of the trials under way throughout the East, he mentioned in passing, with impassive unconcern, that it was from Lithuania that the Soviets at the time had sent him to Siberia.

It is not only the babel of national struggles that threatens this new Europe. The president of Czechoslovakia (Czech-Slovakia? or . . .) is a writer, until recently persecuted and imprisoned. In his courageous works written as a dissident, Havel defends life against ideology; he strenuously distinguishes truth from appearance, accusing totalitarianism of obliterating the first with the second; the struggle for authenticity versus lies, for values versus the reduction of all of existence to the mere gratification of needs, for the significance of life and for art that expresses it. In one of his striking passages he recounts how one evening, watching a television anchorwoman give the weather forecast, he saw a sudden bewilderment cross her face as the result of an unforeseen transmission problem; Havel speaks about that look, about the difference between the stereotypical, programmed expression and the abrupt change when confronted with the unexpected, about the difference between being and acting, between life and performance.

In the West an opposite culture often prevails, exalting the end of values and the triumph of an automated social mechanism in which there is no difference between life and its representation, between being and appearing, person and role, significance and success. As the journalist Gianni Riotta reports, American political propaganda consultants want to teach the Hungarians not how to produce advertising and propaganda commercials, which is legitimate and useful, but how all politics and all life can be reduced to a commercial and to the lucrative imbecility of a "Say *cheese*" smile.

In the darkest years of the Brezhnev dictatorship, Havel, fighting it, wondered whether that tyranny weren't also "a caricature of modern life in general" and whether the Czechoslovakian situation at the time were not "really a kind of warning for the West, revealing its latent destiny." One can only hope that the East's legacy is not lost, that the West may teach democracy and economic efficiency but also learn or relearn a sense of values.

I don't envy Havel, the poet-president, forced to reconcile those two antithetical roles. Devotion, duty inspire them both, the writer and the politician, even in the same battle. But a politician, even the most unconventional, must represent, mediate, mitigate; at times keep silent when he would like to shout out, or at least use a more diplomatic tone than the one the poet would. A writer cannot be reduced to a representative role. Georges Bernanos, in his harrowing novel *Mouchette*, is more Christian than many popes are in their sermons, but a pope cannot afford to write the story of Mouchette, with its grim, naked violence.

The politician has many responsibilities, which he cannot shrug off — even in an age that is fortunately less formal, which abolished the double-breasted suit and loosened neckties for authority figures as well — because he can't say the hell with the consequences. The writer has a right and a duty to tell his truth, regardless of the consequences. If Shakespeare — Havel himself wrote — had worried about not maligning nurses, often so laudable, and parents who arrange their children's marriages, he would not have written *Romeo and Juliet*.

Though the political-literary symbiosis in the Slavic world is a more deeply rooted tradition than in ours, I think the presidency truly weighs on Havel, despite the understandable joy it may have given him at the beginning. As I listened to the speeches, I could see the river from the castle of Bratislava and I thought about the day a

few years earlier when—just over there, watching the water flow by
and the curious inscription on a sign—the idea of writing *Danube*
had occurred to me, there on the border where "the other Europe"
still began at the time.

Meanwhile, it seems the dispute over the hyphen will be resolved
with a third option, the words "Czech and Slovak Republic."

April 14, 1990

ON THE CHARLES BRIDGE

1. *Prague.* On the Charles Bridge, in front of the statue of Saint John of Nepomuk—thrown in the Moldau by King Wenceslas IV because his tongue, which for this reason has been preserved miraculously fresh and red for centuries, refused to tell him the sins murmured by the queen in the confessional—two wooden carts pulled by sturdy horses proceed forward, leaving extensive traces of their passage. The cart drivers are dressed in somewhat unusual garb, and it's been a while since those country wagons have been seen around, but on this bridge those shabby jackets and funny hats don't seem strange, as they would elsewhere, and were it not for the gestures of someone who, a little farther on—looking a bit ridiculous, like anyone insisting on organizing things—orders them to stop, start over, and do it again, directing someone else to move a few feet forward or backward, you wouldn't realize that they are shooting a scene for a film, Steven Soderbergh's *Kafka*. The scene, moreover, is marginal, it doesn't involve the leading actors or the central moments of the story.

As usual the scene is repeated several times, except the horse does not consent to bestow more manure; above the Moldau that courses along slowly, the camera, which will narrate a story that gives the illusion of the flow of life, unbroken like the course of a river, isolates the fragments and details of actual life, plundering them from reality to recompose them later, as in a Meccano. The art of the cinema, which disassembles and reconstructs the pieces of reality, is particularly suited to Prague, which Angelo Maria Ripellino compared to a lunatic shop in which time, the great junk dealer, has amassed the shattered remains and relics of history in a disarray that has the lucidity of a fairy tale. In Prague, despite the overall enchanting landscape that surrounds you on all sides, the eye is captured continuously, with commanding seduction, by the details, especially the roofs and dormers, the pantiles transformed into fanciful ornaments; a person could wander through the city for hours just looking up, even while captivated by so many other unforgettable sights.

Strolling through the streets and squares, gazing near and far, is reminiscent of the character by the German-Prague writer Gustav Meyrink, the author of *The Golem*, who aims a telescope on the city and isolates individual images of it, faces in the crowd or friezes over a door, the wing of a statue, a spire, a pillar of the bridge sinking into the water. Czech literature as well is often characterized by the incursion and rebellion of individual things, of objects that break free of any totality and any comprehensive order and appear in the foreground in their separate, secret lives. From Jan Neruda's nineteenth-century *Mala Strana Stories* to *Tales from Two Pockets* by Karel Capek to the many short stories and novels of Bohumil Hrabal, Czech fiction is often an epic of little things or seemingly minimal events, tavern chatter, and country walks where there are flashes of a more authentic sense of life, experiences threatened by the violence of history and by the abstraction of social mechanisms.

Especially, though not only, during the Stalinist and Brezhnevian regimes, Czech literature was an ironic, grotesque, acrobatic resistance against the alienation that renders things unreal; Václav Havel too, in his essays written as a victim of persecution, defended the tangible, concrete authenticity of existence against the generic counterfeit of all-encompassing ideology. Jaroslav Hašek's soldier Švejk also defends life from the perspective of the little man; he defends his simple, guileless physicality from abstraction. In the most intense of his novels, *Life Is Elsewhere*, Milan Kundera sides with warm, familiar everyday existence against ideological totalitarianism disguised as sacred and against inspired poetic furor, which would subject the humble multiplicity of things to its narcissistic ravings: even those who preach "all power to the imagination" are often tyrants.[1]

At this time of euphoria and sadness, euphoria over their regained freedom and sadness for the bitter future that looms ahead, the Czechs can mainly or almost exclusively put their trust in that tenacious, anarchic fantasy. The shots filmed in old-fashioned costumes on the Charles Bridge attract little attention primarily for another reason. It is unlikely that something would appear anachronistic in this Prague setting made up entirely of multiple, stratified eras, superimposed and entangled with one another. A journey in Czechoslovakia, as in other central European countries, is also a journey through time, which now and then makes the heart skip a beat. It is not just the vivid, urgent presence of centuries-old memories, typical of Mitteleuropa. It is like suddenly being back in the fifties, in their fervid, impoverished atmosphere, plagued by everyday scarcities.

It is primarily the smells, a great informer of reality, that abruptly take us back to those years: the smells of doorways and buildings, of stairways and corridors, an indefinable smell that is reminiscent of oldness, of poverty, of washing soda and coal; a smell that belongs to our past, to a period we left behind, to a kind of adolescence of our present society, poignant and bitter like every adolescence. The actual chimney sweep I see go by, covered with soot, on his way to work, with his brushes and curved rods strung over his shoulder, is an image almost as far back in time as the actors on those wagons. Forty years of communism return a country—at least those countries that were already in an evolved social phase at the time, not the backward ones that communism nonetheless modernized—to the desolation and hope of the immediate postwar period.

Even the trepidation, fervor, and anticipation that are felt in the air recall those years when our life was miserable and difficult. In Czechoslovakia last year there was a radical, magnificent renewal, but other changes lie in wait that could be more prosaic and negative. The catastrophic legacy of communism is as yet held in check by precarious economic and social safeguards, which have so far postponed the shock of radical global change; next year, when a free economy is launched, there could be tragedies in store for individuals and sectors that will see the liquidation of the purchasing power of the money which today enables them to live, and the destabilization of the foundations of their existence. A great momentum can be seen in the country, initiatives full of hopes for the future, together with the impending presence of a kind of expropriation, which could damage its identity.

On the Charles Bridge, the strolling puppet theaters, musicians, and painters are still those of magical Prague, but the faces of the sharks you see around—former Party officials who became rich illegitimately thanks to the nomenklatura, who are about to become the new capitalists, and profiteering foreigners, especially Germans and Italians—are the faces of characters out of Dickens or George Grosz, ready to exploit those puppet theaters or get their hands on them. Three of my compatriots, at the table next to mine, are making shady arrangements with the maître d' to get a lead on some building to snatch up at a bargain price, bypassing the legal obstacles. One of the three—short, with a prominent belly and a fat, sweaty neck—is whining that the night before he'd wanted to bang the girl who was with him, but he'd had too much to drink and he couldn't get it up. The girl can thank one of the saints whose statues adorn the bridge— I'm not sure whether the matter falls within the province of Saint Ludmila or Saint Luitgarda—since being spared such an experience, even just one time, is no small favor.

Thanks to their culture and imagination, the Czechoslovakians, who must start over again virtually from scratch, have the intelligence of a centuries-old civilization accustomed to having to struggle to survive. But in the face of hurdles and powerful neighbors, they do not have, on an economic level, huge battalions, for which, fortunately, there is no need in military terms. Many soldier Švejks, it has been said, do not make an army, despite their inordinate virtuosity. I believe, however, that, in spite of the certainly harsh difficulties of the near future, Czechoslovakia will manage to retain its identity, essential to European civilization. Mitteleuropa is essentially the result of the encounter between German civilization, which afforded a certain fundamental unity to its heterogeneous mosaic, and Slavic culture, which enriched that of the Germans with the mythical, fairy-tale gentility that Prague displays in its towers and bridges. What happens in Prague concerns the entire world.

2. Apropos of pentagonals. It is called Prague, but that is a reductionist concentration of which others, Moravians and especially Slovaks, rightly complain. In Bratislava and in Brno, apart from the small and at times emphasized diversities, there is an extraordinary vitality of cultural interests, an intense intellectual fervor, and in particular a strong interest in Italy and the Italian language. The pentagonal partnership, proposed by our Foreign Ministry, is favorably received in part because a protective solidarity toward neighboring titans, such as Germany, is deeply felt. The initiatives under way are numerous and energetic, but Italy could do more—as the Germans, Austrians, and French are doing—in the small arena of daily necessities that is the true playing field of culture: not conferences, exhibitions, and other impressive demonstrations, which are ineffectual like all impressive things, but simpler forms of aid, such as sending books, many books, for which there is so great a need and which would cost us relatively little, paltry sums compared to those spent on sensational endeavors. Making the classics of yesterday and today accessible, or art history texts with quality reproductions, is worth more than organizing exhibitions, no matter how splendid. It would be easy, at a time when these countries are looking to us with great attention, to give them some real, small but important support.

3. In an interview with Giovanni Firmian in the *Europeo*, Prince Karl Schwarzenberg called himself Citizen Karel Schwarzenberg. The prince, belonging to one of the greatest families of the Habsburg nobility, left Vienna and returned to his native Prague, which he had abandoned when he was ten, where he became chancellor, that is, Havel's chief adviser. In this act a great many things are at play: a touching loyalty, the assumption of responsibility in an as yet uncertain country, not as easy and comfortable as Vienna, the feeling of belonging to a nation combined with that of belonging to a supranational central European culture. At a time when national dissensions are becoming a threat everywhere, even in Czechoslovakia, this attitude is particularly valuable. Moreover, when Hitler invaded Czechoslovakia, many of the great families of the Habsburg aristocracy who resided in Prague, and who had always considered themselves in some way supranational though mainly of German culture, declared that at that moment they identified with the Czech people.

In the aforementioned interview Schwarzenberg rejects any Habsburgian nostalgia, even indirect, which is often kitschy sentimentality. However the catastrophe of communism, which has tragic aspects as well, is not only a victory of Liberal Democracy, but is likely to involve, beyond the fall of communism itself, democratic and liberal thought as well, and cause a reemergence, in very different countries, of dormant forces and traditional forms of social aggregation; a return, in technically updated ways, to some ancien régime. In Italy, the criticism, often unrefined, of the Risorgimento is one of the many indicators of this process, which has many regressive aspects and which is aimed at art and literature as well, as if after two centuries the modern poetry of absence and schism, which found its truth in painful renunciation of any peaceful harmony, should give way to a literature newly and blissfully unaware of laceration and exile; as if slick novels with handsome covers were getting back at Musil or Beckett. One must be aware of these reverting tendencies, especially if one rightly wants to fight them. We are faithful to truth and happiness if we know, like Kafka, that we do not possess them, that we have been banished from the Terrestrial Paradise; if we respond, like the character in Borges when asked if he is from Prague, "I *was* from Prague."[2]

October 30, 1990

THE COUNTRY WITHOUT A NAME

1. It is curious to find oneself in a country so rich in history and centuries-old culture that, for a few weeks now, hasn't had a definite name. Following the split from Slovakia, Prague became the capital of a country, the Czech Republic, which is searching for a designation, a term to be written on maps and used in everyday speech. The country can no longer be called Czechoslovakia, of course, or Bohemia either, because it includes Moravia and Silesia as well; perhaps the most likely name in Czech, "Cesko," may be acceptable, whereas the Italian translation suggested by someone, "Cechia," sounds imaginary, like the made-up countries in operettas; a corresponding version in German, "Tschechei," seems even more dubious, evoking infamous Nazi nomenclature.

This reticence and indefinability are appropriate for Mitteleuropa, whose labyrinthine, tangled history is unlikely to permit the establishment of precise identities and the drawing of distinct borders; even the Habsburg Empire struggled to adopt an unambiguous name, racking its brain over designations in which a conjunction and a hyphen more or less could be disastrous. According to Robert Musil, that very inexpressibility may perhaps have been the cause of the empire's downfall. The lack is particularly fitting to Prague, the magnificent Slavic-German-Jewish city irreducible to any unequivocal definition, whose literature, full of enchantment and specters, has mainly evoked the voids and shadows of life, the longing for everything that is wanting. Now in many parts of Europe, and especially in central Europe, names are changed and expunged, borders are moved and signs modified, in a relocation of history that adds to apprehension over the precariousness of life, as though that were necessary. In Prague and in the country of which it is the capital this undoing, which elsewhere triggers bloody atrocities, occurs with distinguished civility, not only peacefully but with ironic, resigned melancholy, a great lesson for anyone who is exhilarated by separations and divorces.

A name is needed, of course; neither an individual nor a state can afford the luxury of being Nobody, like Ulysses, or of having only initials, like Kafka's characters. The task of finding the right name would be up to the poets, and perhaps someone might have the ambition of becoming the Baptist and father of the country. But it is unlikely that Czech writers, with their glorious anarchical, picaresque tradition of taverns and cafés, will give in to the temptation of becoming a vates. In the particularistic delirium that is infecting Europe with a fever to proclaim roots, ethnic purity, and coherent identities, it might not be a bad thing if this beautiful country were to remain nameless; it would be—as with Kafka's anonymous creations or the absurdity prized by Czech literature—a lesson in human truth and irony, in tolerance and humanity.

2. Prague is being transformed, invaded by McDonald's and spaghetti eateries, at a pace deplored by Prague citizens certainly not nostalgic for the old regime. The city is teeming with currency exchanges in particular, which are met at literally every step; rather than admiring towers, statues, and pinnacles, the eye focuses on obsessive signs, vertical and horizontal, of every size and color, reading "change money," "exchange," "convert." There is no point in pouring out anti-consumeristic rhetoric, easy for Westerners who have not suffered poverty and restrictions; the fact that there are currency exchanges close at hand attests to the presence of foreigners important for the Czech economy and consequently for people's actual lives, for their needs and their desires.

But like every excess, that exorbitant forest of "exchange" is caricaturist and seems to symbolize a mania for change that is accelerated, as in the slapstick comedies of silent film, a convertibility that extends to all of life. It is understandable that many Praguers are concerned about the adulteration of their city. "We want to be Europeans, not Americans" can be heard, alluding to the lifestyle. But in Prague the diffusion of the American way of life is paradoxically left mainly to the German economy, that is, to Germany, though it is the economic rival of the United States. Present-day Germany is, for better or worse, the opposite of the old Holy Roman Empire Germany, which had founded its first university in Prague and was a fulcrum of Mitteleuropa. Today there is an efficient, economically aggressive and culturally lackluster Germany—aseptic, like certain perfect, beautiful, and undesirable women—which on one hand competes with the United States, while on the other is the clone of a certain American way of life whose model it helps promote. On the banks of the Moldau one can understand the desire, in all likelihood unsuccessful, to resist German-Americanization; indeed in an essay written when he was persecuted by the Communist regime, Václav Havel wondered whether the alienation caused by that tyranny wasn't also a caricature of contemporary life in general and of the West's veiled destiny.

3. The current uncertainty over the name of the country, or rather the division of Czechoslovakia, is certainly a defeat for Havel, which does not detract from his rare lesson in integrity. Elected president, Havel has maintained the genuine simplicity of a poet who loves rambling walks more than honor guard parades, cafés and brew pubs more than chancelleries and castles—the qualities thanks to which he at one time faced totalitarian oppression without buckling, with the quiet courage of one who believes in the eternal and in a glass of wine enjoyed with a friend rather than in the world's ostentatious displays.

But Havel was also able to accept the prosaic and not very agreeable weight of the presidential office, the sacrifice that it imposes on his gypsy-like freedom. He has proved to be capable of a virtue that poets rarely possess, and on which nearly everything that can be achieved for the good of others depends: a sense of responsibility. Which also means accepting the price that must be paid to achieve your ideals, being aware of the compromises that doing so sometimes entails, and being able to assess, from time to time, whether they are acceptable or not. Havel is immune to the narcissism and facile confrontational rhetoric that are often found in literary figures, quick to point to abstract, impossible social goals in order to justify the right to take no notice of any small, tangible progress, to love the act of protest more than the cause for which they are protesting, to get more fired up—even in political debates—about their effect on matters pertaining to literary factions than over the fate of the people around them, to proclaim "all power to the imagination" while unable to actually imagine the labyrinths of power and its unpredictable developments. It is easier to believe you are changing the world by reciting libertarian verses to Odéon, as in 1968, than by dealing with government paperwork. Havel retained his rebellious spirit because he was able to assume the distasteful, gray duties of the world's prose, abandoning his beloved taverns and wine cellars for a while and settling into the boring castle.

4. In Stredokluky, a suburb of Prague, we find the studio of Aleš Veselý, a prominent Czech sculptor. The studio looks like a farm, open as it is to the surrounding countryside, and has a workshop, crammed not only with sculptures in iron, wood, and various other materials but also primarily with objects and tools of all kinds, which Veselý uses in his work. His atelier sometimes looks like one of those shops described with such love in Angelo Maria Ripellino's *Magic Prague*, jam-packed with things, balls of yarn, spools, handlebars, harps, looms, mannequins, and all sorts of odds and ends. Amid the

proliferation Veselý moves about, shy and gentle; his open, melancholy smile suggests mildness, which is perhaps also a characteristic of his people.

Sometimes the visitor cannot immediately distinguish between the sculptures and the materials or even the tools prepared to make them, between the poetry of the completed work and the poetic spirit present in things before the artist's intervention. Things—as well as gestures, faces, landscapes—certainly possess poetic qualities, and a piece of reality set in an empty frame is a painting. Perhaps, in that case, one should not insist on affixing a signature, the personal name of an artist, just as a viewer who points out the breaking of the waves does not claim to be mentioned in the encyclopedias, even if such a person rightly feels that he or she is no less a poet than one who has the honor of an entry in those volumes. Nevertheless in Veselý's workshop and yard, many beautiful works, unique and compelling, emerge from the fascinating accumulation of poetic possibilities inherent in things, works which in the boldness of daring forms bear a classic stamp, like the monumental, tragic Kaddish, the Jewish prayer of mourning, which towers over the items around it. Sculptures like that cannot be mistaken for the prolixity of reality.

5. According to a surreal postcard given to me by Václav Jamek, one of the most interesting contemporary Czech writers, the Danube flows to Prague. It does not strike me as strange, at least on an evening when my *Danube* is being discussed. I see Eduard Goldstücker again, who gives me his memoirs, *Prozesse* (Trials). In a few months he will turn eighty, eighty magnanimous years of a difficult, but fervent, intrepid life. A great Kafka scholar and a leading figure in the Prague Spring of 1968, Goldstücker, a militant Communist since his youth, experienced Fascist and Stalinist persecution, several years of prison following an unfounded conviction at the time of Stalin of life imprisonment, and exile following the Soviet repression of 1968. The hardships and abuse he endured did not bow his courage,

his faith in humanity, his will to live and to laugh, the goodness of a heart so capable of affection and friendship, his humor, and his taste for life's pleasures.

For me he is a fraternal and paternal friend, whose presence provides a sense of security. Goldstücker has known honors and darkness; there is a tragic historical irony in the fact that a great interpreter of Kafka's *Trial* such as he was arrested one morning many years ago, like Josef K., for a crime unknown even to his Stalinist accusers. In exile after 1968, Goldstücker had not hoped to see Prague again, but the irony of history, this time benevolent, brought him back home.

In the last lines of his memoirs, he says that he had dreamed of leading an individual life and that instead his was one of many typical Mitteleuropean destinies; perhaps human greatness consists of this acceptance of a common fate, of the ability to be Everyman.

February 13, 1993

THE TRAGEDY AND THE NIGHTMARE

Life, it has often been said, imitates literature. In the novel *Minor Apocalypse* by Tadeusz Konwicki, one of the most significant contemporary Polish writers, the protagonist is asked by two friends who serve in an unspecified opposition force to douse himself with gasoline and set himself on fire, as an act of protest, outside Party headquarters in Warsaw. Two weeks ago a man actually did set himself on fire in Poland, but—at least according to the official version—it would seem he did so to express his agitation over the country's strikes and rebellion; Polish television, taking pains to confirm this interpretation (in all probability true, but in any case agreeable to the government), aired his image and his injuries, fortunately not fatal, with a taste for the sensational not unlike the pursuit and consumption of exciting visuals that generally characterize the West's social style.

But life moves on and changes more quickly than literature; after less than two years, Konwicki's novel seems virtually surpassed by events, by a reality that has become different, by life that has been newly invented, with a bolder imagination than that required to revitalize poetic language or formulate a narrative.

The Warsaw that is displayed to visitors during these weeks is not the spectral city that evaporates into thin air evoked by Konwicki in his novel, it is not the unreal or surreal setting of a minor, insidious end of the world. Poland today reveals a completely different face and seems to embody—perhaps because it is on the brink of a serenely faced, potential disaster—a closely woven, solid world, full of contradictions, but free of ambiguities, abounding in feelings and values, a world which we, the heirs of ambivalence and uncertainty, are no longer used to. If we feel foreign or alien, it is not because we feel as if we are venturing into a nebulous country, but because we feel that we ourselves are nebulous creatures or the effect of shadows walking among living people, somewhat more threatened by death than we are, but alive. In Poland you sense the tragedy, not the nightmare; and the tragedy entails a human dimension of greatness and strength, a full, integral sense of life that is attacked or destroyed, the intuition of a destiny and a significance. The tragic fall does not diminish the individual; it hurls him off the wagon like a Homeric warrior struck in battle, it does not break him and does not dissolve him into nothing as occurs to those who are sucked into the unreal labyrinths of a nightmare.

The tragedy is there, but you don't see it, and that is what is most striking. Except for the long but very orderly lines in front of grocery stores, you don't notice any ferment or unrest in the streets, you don't sense the tense atmosphere that forms in our cities, like a high-voltage electric current, as soon as some incident disturbs the everyday routine. Though national flags displayed on buildings indicate, with intentionally nonprovocative, conventional language, support of Solidarność and readiness to strike, an unsuspecting viewer might think they are simply waving, festive and patriotic, with no particular purpose.

Monday, March 30, when for a few hours many prepared for the worst as the possibility of a clash, which would probably have been bloody, intensified, a tourist who did not know Polish and had no occasion to talk with a friend would not have been aware of anything. The looming tragedy did not disturb the normal day-to-day existence. I was a guest at the University of Warsaw and Kraków for a conference on Austrian literature, and I had set out with an obvious feeling of embarrassment, because it seemed painfully comical to hold forth on Robert Musil in front of people who had to stand up to hunger and the possibility of tanks in real terms. But instead the conference was culturally passionate and warmly welcoming; the students asked questions about Arthur Schnitzler's narrative technique and colleagues discussed the interpretation of Hugo von Hofmannsthal's *Rosenkavalier* or expressionist opera. The attendees, coming like me from Italy or mostly from Austria or Yugoslavia, could easily forget that between sessions of the conference their hosts went off to their combat committees to plan for provisions and medical assistance should a decision be made to occupy the university, that they took part in union meetings and were essentially preparing for the possibility of a tragic confrontation.

The ominous shadow did not cloud the pleasant warmth of the encounter. The Kraków cafés were welcoming in their amiable Habsburgian tranquillity; the conversations, which of course centered on the tension of the moment and the continual wait for news that could be decisive, soon strayed onto the historical and artistic curiosities of both cities, indulging in banter and good-natured pleasantries, the great art of laughter.

The lack of drama with which our friends were ready to stake their entire existence, hoping not to have to do so, was striking. A young journalist from the daily *Życie Warszawy* said that the previous day the thought of fleeing on the first plane had crossed her mind for a second, but then, after describing an interview with Lech Walesa done a few hours earlier, she went on to cheerfully recount a reporting assignment in Japan. I thought that in their place I would have been frozen with fear or gripped by obsessive exhilaration. The lesson passed on by such courage was not drawn only from a willingness to risk danger, but primarily from a love for everyday harmony and routine that transpired in those men and women, able but certainly not eager to face the chaos, the exceptional event.

We often forget this love of ordinary familiarity, the ability to feel satisfied and content by ever new repetition, by that which makes the passage of time delightful: watching, walking, constructing, reading, sitting at the table among cherished faces, talking, getting together, loving, being friends. Individuals who have all this are privileged and should know it, should be aware that their happiness is the flowing of each day's hours, normal and customary but always new. Those who have a greater capacity to love are able to give up this privilege in order to fight so that others, who are deprived of it due to natural or social adversities, may also have it; the revolutionary's actions, like those of the Christian, are the generosity of one who reluctantly sacrifices the joyous harmony of individual existence and faces disruption for the sake of those who are denied that harmony.

Such love, capable of renouncing the pleasures of living—certainly not with an ascetic's sense of fulfilment, but rather regretful for it—has nothing to do with the frenzied ineptitude for joy and everyday gratification that drives so many poor unhappy souls to seek disruption out of a love of disruption, to find comfort in the exceptional and dramatic, to get worked up over every tense situation and every disaster, large or small, that gives them the illusion of playing an exhilarating role.

Life in the West is often drugged by such impotent childishness, which produces public and private failures. Countering the pervasive insubstantiality, the dramas and ferments taking place in Communist countries hold up a great lesson in reality and truth, in humility; a colleague in Warsaw told me that following a strike at the university, the students who had participated in it had immediately asked her to resume their usual literature seminar.

On Monday, March 30, I, like everyone else, wished for a peaceful outcome of the conflict, but I was aware that my wish was driven primarily by my petty personal interest, by the desire that everything might remain essentially as it was, that the equilibrium from which I too derive a modest gain—relationships and exchanges with colleagues, conferences and trips—might not be altered by a violent shake-up.

My instinctive reactions expressed, like everyone else's, the West, which rejoices at any difficulties of the Communist regimes provided that they remain contained, so as not to change anything. I sat beside my friends, but in a few days I would be leaving; I did not share their fate as far as the essential aspects of living and surviving were concerned. The irony of history weaves such affinities together and widens separations; the tragic history of Poland is scored by such irony.

There is also perhaps a Polish face, a facial expression lined, as if by wrinkles, by the vicissitudes of that fate. It is the face of certain old people, for example that of an impassive, mocking old man playing a complicated drum at the Kraków Cloth Hall: a face made up of respectful melancholy and indifferent derision, like the mask of the great comic actors. Familiarity with catastrophes produced that face. It is also the face of Poldy Beck, who in his *Book of Whistles*, a kind of parodistic treatise in verse on the art of whistling, summarized his endless flight from one disaster to another, from the collapse of the Habsburg Empire to Nazism to Stalinism.[1] Serious and imperturbable, Poldy Beck—an Austrian Jew living in Łodz, at the café when not at home—is a professional joke teller who drops pieces of history like ash from his cigar. "Just imagine," he told me, "a young critic spoke of political commitment in connection with the *Book of Whistles*; the only politics that interests me is that of the ostrich."

April 13, 1981

POLAND TURNS THE PAGE

Warsaw. On a street corner in the Old Town, a blind man plays the accordion and sings; in front of him is a saucer for coins and a cardboard box with a slot, for bills. It is Sunday, and passersby do not prove indifferent to those songs that welcome them with the carefree call of fleeting, passing life as they leave the church, where they've listened to promises of eternity. The Old Town is familiar and unreal: completely destroyed during the Second World War, like all of Warsaw, it has been reconstructed with meticulous fidelity; it is a perfect imitation, a copy of the neighborhoods and buildings where Polish history unfolded, a fake. In this re-created antiquity there is also something spectral; one wonders what would happen if everywhere, throughout the world, people were to continually reconstruct, with impeccable restorations, what time, inclement weather, attrition, and wars destroy. Airplanes would land in Roman *castra*, near the temples of Mercury, stockbrokers on Wall Street would create and destroy empires not among skyscrapers but among Dutch cottages or brand-new Indian wigwams. We would all do what the nomads of the desert do, put the same tent back up again after the wind has torn it down.

But this artificial antiquity is real, and becomes ever more so; in these houses people live, events take place whose history is no less grand and tumultuous than that of the past that they evoke. The buildings are a stage set for the present, and little by little they too will grow old and deteriorate; there will come a time when they must be rebuilt, as though one were restoring a copy of the *Mona Lisa* painted a few years earlier. The Old Town is the heart of Warsaw, it embodies the historical memory, a fidelity to the past, to tradition, to itself that has been Poland's strength of resistance against everything that has, many times over the centuries, threatened to destroy and obliterate it, to dissolve its identity.

Totalitarianisms obliterate memory, and even the rapid transformation of dynamic, opulent societies, which offers individuals many opportunities for freedom and spiritual growth, tends to uproot and eradicate recollection, to store history away in the attic or in a museum. The reconstruction of the Old Town also has the distinction of fidelity, a bold, intrepid contempt for change without which, most likely, certain of the acts of courage and defiance that abound in Polish history would be less comprehensible.

The blind man with the accordion performed one of those acts as well. He was still a boy, fourteen years old, a friend tells me, when he took part in the epic Warsaw Uprising against the Nazis in 1944. Seeing a bomb that was about to explode near a powder magazine, he threw himself on it, and it blew up in his face, thereby saving the storehouse and above all preventing the catastrophe that a conflagration would have caused. His face, in fact, is disfigured by scars, grooved with troughs and irregularities that denote rough territory.

Looking at that face, one thinks uncomfortably that our culture, pleased with itself at that, often proves to have lost a sense of courage and mocks what makes those acts possible and therefore insurrection as well. Bertolt Brecht rightly described a time in need of heroes as sad, but he knew that at sad times — such as that of Nazi rule and many other dominations and threats, political and individual — there is indeed a need for heroes. Not for monumental and rhetorical heroes, certainly, inflamed with bellicose ardor and proud to act brave and endanger their own lives and those of others; the bodybuilder's display of muscle and boldness, dear to regimes that love to show people marching, is a parody of courage and provokes tragicomic disasters. But there is a courage which is essential to life: the courage of one who detests marching in rows and would rather take a walk or go to the tavern but knows that in order to defend his right and that of others to take a walk or go to the tavern, it might sadly be necessary to sell his cloak and buy himself a sword and, though scared stiff, with legs shaking like jelly, stand up to the Leviathan that is spreading tyranny, cruelty, and death.

That boy too, whose wide-open eyes cannot see me now, would rather have played cops and robbers and let his schoolmates prompt him during class quizzes. But there are times, in which clearly no one hopes to find himself, when only someone who is willing to lose his life can save it. I lean toward that face so far removed from the smiling "Say *cheese*" faces or the intellectual–self-important ones that we are used to, and—without taking credit, because I don't know what to do with the zlotys that were given to me, which I can neither convert nor bring to Italy—I slip a considerable sum into the box. After a few steps, wanting to call from a pay phone, I realize that I don't have a 20-zloty coin; I go back and, mumbling a few words, embarrassed, ask him for one and take it from the saucer. A passerby looks at me, puzzled at seeing me ask the blind man for charity.

The roundtable between government and opposition is of course the focus of general interest. Without wishing to diminish its importance, certainly it is not a point of arrival but undoubtedly a significant step. There is the physical sensation of a dismantling of the Communist regime in the countries of the East, the attempt to transform Eastern Europe into a Finland. Apart from the countries still held in a vise and excluded from this process—Czechoslovakia, Romania—tomorrow it may perhaps be said that as craftsmen of the process governments were as praiseworthy as the opposition forces, the latter being necessary—to some degree to please the old dialectic—to initially allow governments to embark on that road, to give them the impetus or two that they then exploit, regulate, and contain, at times when a pause is called for so as to be able to move forward again.

The high hopes that are opening up in the East are threatened both by fear of a regression to authoritarianism and the danger of destabilization that would throw the geopolitical continent into chaos. In some countries, which may be moving toward a parliamentary, multiparty democracy, there is already a centrifugal swarm of movements and groups that might soon risk precipitating a democracy, newly formed, into an ungovernability that as the Weimar example teaches, facilitates in turn a reemergence and triumph of tyranny. I do not envy the leaders of the Socialist countries who find themselves having to steer this course in the midst of so many Scyllas and Charybdises. What is certain is that, unlike at one time when it seemed that anything that happened in the "other" Europe did not concern us, nowadays we sense that this bout is also ours, that our destiny, that of Europe *tout court*, is also at stake here.

In that church, a friend tells me, you occasionally see an old priest who heard the confession of Rudolf Höss, the commander of Auschwitz, before his execution. I am amazed that Höss confessed; a few weeks earlier he had written his autobiographical volume about Auschwitz, an appalling, arresting book in which the horror is depicted with imperturbable objectivity, with no repentance and no holding back, with no attempt to mitigate or conceal anything, with no commentary and no judgment, as if nature, indifferent and impassive, were describing that inferno, a nature which does not hide or justify anything and regrets nothing. The confession lasted thirteen hours, spaced out over three sessions. I can't understand why it took so long. One of us, if he or she hasn't confessed for many years, would require many hours to list the countless small, petty, assorted sins with which we debase ourselves each day. But half a minute would have been enough for Höss, just time to say, "I murdered millions of people."

Breslau-Wrocław. Chaotic, disfiguring reconstruction, which in the fifties defaced the historic urban landscape here as everywhere, did not obliterate the old German stamp from this Polish city with two names, the center of a mixed, composite area like Silesia, with a past that is not only Polish but also Austrian and Prussian. The Aula Leopoldina, the university's great hall, in which even today the academic year is launched, has the baroque majesty of knowledge conceived as the mirror of order and of the world's splendor; beneath its ceiling fresco that opens out toward infinity, with the illusionistic effects dear to painting of that era, saints, angels, scholars, and kings guard the universality of the empire and of science.

Angelus Silesius, the great German mystic poet of the seventeenth century, is buried in the church of Saint Matthias; Joseph von Eichendorff, the Romantic lyric poet who penned the Lieder set to music by Schubert and Schumann, was married in another church; a short distance away, Andreas Gryphius, the gloomy tragedian, sang the vanity and transience of the world; all of Silesia is a vast terrain of German as well as Polish literature.

The market square, with its Gothic town hall, is found throughout central Europe, from the Baltic to Transylvania: the familiar mark of a culture that has bestowed a certain unity on a multifaceted mosaic of peoples and civilizations, as the Roman aqueducts did at one time. After the war, the multinational past—now attested to, for example, by a German writer such as Horst Bienek, who lives in Munich— had been erased from Polish consciousness. Now it is beginning to be talked about as the German traditions of Gdansk and Silesia are recalled. There is movement in this sense as well, in the resurgence of minorities and of the national complexity of those countries; recently, in a literary café in Wrocław, an anthology of Polish poets from Lwów (Lemberg, L'viv), now in Soviet territory, was presented.

Until a short time ago, such a thing would have been unthinkable. The upheaval that is taking place in the East is also restoring the historical memory, giving new voice to peoples and minorities, to centuries-old traditions that had been buried. Even this great, liberating reawakening can have its dangers, the risk of degenerating into resentful nationalisms that repeat the fatal acrimonies of the past.

The German squares that extend throughout Europe like milestones along a road recall the need for cultural unity, respectful of all diversities though not fragmented into a babel of particularisms. The unity of central Europe under German hegemony and under Soviet rule failed; the new Europe that we hope will arise from the current turmoil must, in its variety, be a culture that is in some way united, not a seething archipelago of nations and ethnic groups obsessed with their own singularities.

A great Polish poet, Czesław Miłosz, recalled as a painful loss the time when, due to political tension, families had had to choose between their Polish and Lithuanian origins, amputating a part of themselves. Yet the same Miłosz writes about one of his relatives who had taught him to defend his threatened identity, certainly, but had warned him not to let himself be wholly absorbed by such defense, to remember that beyond his individual identity was a higher one. Not surprisingly, the title of the book that contains this passage translates roughly into "my Europe."[1]

April 9, 1989

ON RASKOLNIKOV'S LANDING

The nameplate on the door, though anticipated, gives you an undeniable thrill; we aren't used to thinking of the name Dostoyevsky as that of a tenant. Yet Dostoyevsky not only lived in this apartment on the first floor of 11 Kaznacejskaja Street in Leningrad, writing *Crime and Punishment* in these rooms, but was the bard of these landings, of these attic cubbyholes and poorly lit stairs, of the squalid housing in which Raskolnikov indulges his delirium of rising above good and evil.

With an intellect in which Christian charity was intertwined with the murkier experience of modern nihilism, Dostoyevsky showed how tragic and at the same time gauchely trite is transgressive seduction, which urges us to violate moral law in the name of the unfathomable, turbid flow of life; his heroes, like Raskolnikov and like each of us, excel at suffering and ultimately at the arrogance that leads them to be blinded by the claptrap of evil, taking literally the first books that come to hand, devoured hastily and not well digested. Perhaps only Dante is as successful at making his characters express their drama from within, without overpowering them with his own decalogue of the values he firmly believed in. Dostoyevsky does not superimpose the gospel on his abject figures, on the voice of their tormented depravity; on the contrary, it is the gospel that enjoins him to listen, without censure, to the most dissonant expressions of the human heart. In the modern *Commedia* that is Dostoyevsky's narrative, Dante's circles have been transformed into the dark corridors and stairs of the metropolis's working-class neighborhoods, the most authentic setting of our poetry, our theater of the world.

A visit to this house forms part of the most predictable tourist agenda for any trip to Leningrad, but that does not diminish the fascination and surprise at crossing its threshold. A cane stands beside the entrance along with an umbrella and a hat; a little farther on, in the children's room, we find a rocking horse with a bristly mane, a doll, a blue inkpot, and the notebook in which his wife kept the household accounts, the debits and credits. In these rooms is the mystery of a life that was lived, and not just because the one who lived it was called Dostoyevsky; condensed around the objects is the existence that they marked, the time that slipped through them on its way to nothingness, the day-to-day rhythm, pleasure, and disappointment, the incredulous astonishment with which one reaches the end of a day and of life. The coffee cups are brown, there is a supply of very strong tea on the table, the desk is covered with a green cloth, an icon discreetly watches over the domestic order and over a feverish imagination, some Laferme cigarettes seem only temporarily spared from the consumption that, more than a century ago, transformed their pack mates into smoke and ash.

In these rooms in which *Crime and Punishment* was written, one does not imagine the ritual of a great writer, but rather the act of a man who, having returned home, puts his umbrella back in its place. How unreal, by comparison, the house-museum of Maxim Gorky looks, visited a few days ago in Moscow, at 6/12 Kacalova Street, a mansion built in the early years of the century for the millionaire Rjabusinskij.

In that house, where Gorky lived from 1931 until his death in 1936, there is almost nothing but literature, the table around which meetings of the Writers Association, chaired by him, were held; even his books on the shelves seem like the volumes of a library for public display, rather than those a man picks up at a given moment, out of interest or by chance. Photographs show Gorky, with his slanting eyes and sweeping paternal mustache, among delegations of authors or schoolgirls come to visit the Great Writer.

That beautiful Liberty-style house suggests a literary institution, which is not well suited to life; it's not surprising that before Gorky lived there it was the seat of the State Publishing House. There is the table with his pens and pencils, but these indicators of the venture of writing are overshadowed by signs of the administration of writing and of work that has been written; the photographs capture exemplary moments, the young people have come not for pleasure, but to admire the famous author, who here appears distant from the truth he reveals, from the vagrants and slums of his stories. As in all ritual occasions of the republic of letters, the writer here does something else, he plays another role—which, depending on the situation, may be meritorious, blameworthy, or inane, but has nothing to do with writing, just as a sexology conference is quite another thing from love and sex.

The fault is not Gorky's, who—as Vittorio Strada writes—deservedly occupies in literary history "a significant secondary place, different from that of the grand vizier of realism" assigned to him in Soviet tradition; neither is it the fault of socialist realism, which Gorky represented in those years. A writer, as such, simply cannot represent anything, not even less dangerous institutions than Stalinist realism. Perhaps Goethe was the last poet who was able to reconcile poetry with a representative role—though he too not without paying a heavy price. The very idea of Baudelaire as an official exponent of anything, if only of transgression or of *fleurs du mal*, is ridiculous, irreconcilable with his greatness. Maybe that's why the great writers of the twentieth century were authors such as Italo Svevo or Franz Kafka, whom a benevolent fate spared the possibility and therefore the risk of becoming official figures of literary society.

The writer cannot embody anything, not even a trend or a poetic world, both of which are authentic only if he expresses them as he experiences them, without worrying about what will happen to them, what effect they will have in the real world. Once he touches them up and worries about them, out of a spirit of lofty moral duty, his poetic venture is over and his administration of it begins, which must take into account many things and consequences extraneous to it. In *Buddenbrooks*, Thomas Mann told a great story about Lübeck and the decline of bourgeois society; when the success of his masterpiece transformed him into a representative of that world, he had to become its conscientious guardian and pedagogue; his beautiful, polished Ciceronian essays on Lübeck and Hanseatic culture are excellent lectures, but quite another thing from the poetry of *Buddenbrooks*, because weighing on them is the sacrifice of a man who is determined to provide for his family—and depending on one's personal commitment, the family may be called revolution, progress, order, liberty, or the struggle against repression.

The conflict can be dramatic, because the writer has all the duties of any man, which he cannot sacrifice to art; he is responsible to his family, the nation, liberty, justice, other people. He may also be asked to give up art for something higher: Aeschylus wanted his epitaph to recall his military service at the Battle of Marathon, not his poetic work. Yet he did not claim to fight for his country as an exceptional case, as a tragedian; he knew that he could and should do so only as a simple citizen, like everyone else.

When circumstances summon you to unavoidable responsibilities, you may or must put down the pen, but without fooling yourself that the preceding performance of the pen attributes special authority to the exercise of that moral duty. The fact that Gorky received schoolchildren is not disconcerting—on the contrary, it's nice that he stole hours away from his literary work to devote time to them—what's disturbing is the fact that those meetings with students, which should have been something artless, simple, and natural, become, in those photographs, something contrived though frequent, something edifying. Sometimes the writer must have the humility to use even the pen in the service of a cause, knowing, however, that at that moment he is not being a writer. Thomas Mann's speeches against Nazi Germany may, on a certain level, count for more than his novels, but they are something different, they are expressed in a language that has nothing to do with the spirit of the narrative.

Today the writer is in no danger of representing the ideology or the poetics of a regime, as Gorky did, but rather, which is just as bad, risks becoming the full-time spokesman for a literary establishment that tautologically reproduces itself, a participant at a permanent roundtable on society and life, an expert on Reality. Rhetoric, namely the organization and systematizing of knowledge, requires such useful functions, but poetry—to use Carlo Michelstaedter's terms—has to do with persuasion, or rather with the endeavor, successful or failed, to possess one's own life and face it without diplomatic concerns. Biagio Marin relates that once, in Grado, when he told a little girl that he was a poet, she had replied derisively that "poets are dead." Perhaps she was right because as long as he's alive, the poet, like it or not, is on the professional register of reality, which necessitates circumspection, duty, restraint, compromise, human regard, palliation, and nuance. Only when he is struck off that register does his poetry shine free, disinterested, regally indifferent to all the rest.

May 18, 1988

THE BIRCH WHISTLE

Jyväskylä. The town, an industrial center and university site, is located in the heart of the Finnish lakes, silent waters, forests of conifers, and birches bright as summer nights, a poignant enchantment that is as vigorous as the good, fresh scent of wood. Here Eastern Europe, which is under discussion, is not Danubian but Russo-Baltic-Scandinavian; Finland, which fifty years ago was able to maintain its freedom, fighting with epic courage, is destined to play a prominent role in the new political pole that is forming in the Baltic, with its mixture of cultures and its reemergence on the international scene.

The recurring theme is the extension of European unity to this Northeast, with the sole opposition of a Marxist deputy or former deputy who dreams of a self-sufficient, national-Communist Finland. But what is noticeable above all, disturbingly so, are the first cracks appearing in the Soviet state. A Belarusian, Jakub Lopatko, denounces the Russianization of his homeland and Ukrainian Oles Zavgorodni chimes in, planting the blue-and-yellow flag of Ukraine on the podium and recalling its past glories. Galina Starovoitova, Russian, a member of the Soviet Parliament, and a specialist on minorities, attacks the CPSU and the shortcomings of perestroika and declares that in light of the new situation, the Helsinki Accords should be revisited and many European borders reexamined.

The Baltics, the most directly involved in these prospects, are a lively presence, full of fervor and humor. When I ask if, beyond the current anti-Soviet solidarity, there are latent tensions among them, they tell me that in 1929 or 1930 some Latvian students entered Estonia, climbed Suur-Munamäki — at 1,040 feet the highest moun-

tain of the Baltic, 13 feet higher than the highest Latvian summit—
and shoveled away those 13 feet to steal the record from the Estoni-
ans; the latter, however, reestablished it immediately, piling the 13
feet of dirt back on top and even adding a tower. "But the Latvians
are better than us," laughs Estonian Gennadi Muravin, "everything
of theirs is better, even their neighbors are better than ours . . ."

These peoples have suffered many tragedies, translated also into
individual griefs: Pirkko Peltonen recalled in an article that Marju
Lauristin, leader of Estonia's movement for independence, is the
daughter of the secretary of the Estonian Communist Party who in
1940 asked for his country to be annexed to the Soviet Union. As I
talk with a young Latvian writer, I see that among the designs on her
shawl are some swastikas; though she explains to me that they are
certainly not Nazi emblems but rather the old ornamental motifs of
her people, I still find it a bit strange for her to go around with those
hooked crosses and would rather she'd chosen other ancient Indo-
European symbols.

Anxiety is also stirring in this Baltic wind of freedom. The dissolution of the Soviet Union seems to be a foregone conclusion, but this
perspective, I believe, may well lead to dire consequences. Hearing
talk about borders that should be revisited and therefore contested,
about national sentiments that are rightfully being revived but that
can easily become charged with antipathies, the specter reemerges
of possible future national wars, which we thought were over and impossible ever again, but which perhaps were prevented only by the
threat of world conflagration. Galina Starovoitova says that peoples
are eternal; however, they only last a little longer than individuals
and it is right to love them, but not idolize them. The ungrateful
indifference to Mikhail Gorbachev—to his attempt to manage the
transformation of the Soviet Union in an orderly, gradual manner,
in the world's interest as well—doesn't seem just to me either; like
almost everyone who performs a good, courageous action, he risks
being punished for it.

Proletarian internationalism has been perverted into an instrument of domination, but it had created a supranational consciousness for which there is extreme need, if we do not want the liberation of 1989 to also entail regression. In this sense the ideal legacy of socialism should not be lost, and every effort is required to make European unity as solid as possible, against all centrifugal tendencies — maybe, I tell the Ukrainian delegate, by having everyone go back to speaking Latin like Ivan Mazepa, the hetman of seventeenth-century Ukraine who spoke Latin with Charles XII of Sweden.

As I say these things, I encounter the disapproval of an old Finnish farmer, a diehard Communist isolationist who heatedly supports theories that are unpopular with all of those present; perhaps he remembers difficult times for Finnish Communists, the oppressive camps in which so many of them ended up after the civil war of 1918. But I must not have been totally antipathetic to him; at the end of the discussion, he goes out, cuts a branch from a birch tree, and with his knife begins carving and whittling, until he hands me a beautiful, elaborately fashioned whistle that emits shrill shrieking sounds. I put it in my pocket with gratitude; life will certainly present me with an opportunity to use it.

July 1, 1990

A HIPPOPOTAMUS IN LUND

In a fine book released last year, *On How to Recognize the Saints*—identification based on Stefano Jacomuzzi's narrative with drawings by Gigi Cappa Bava—a childhood episode of Saint Aloysius Gonzaga is recounted. A relative, seeing the boy playing, asked him what he would do if he knew that he would die in a few minutes; the child calmly replied, "I would go on playing." If this anecdote is true, Aloysius deserves a halo, much more than for the other penitent acts that are attributed to him by an often tiresomely prim oleography, unsuited to the greatness of true saints who are not sanctimonious doubters but adventurous navigators in the inexplicable sea of existence.

In that apologue there are a great many things. On the one hand there is the stupid, cautionary gravity of the adult, who needs to feel important through lofty thoughts because he is not capable of living, simply living: he must have goals and commitments that distract him from his impotence, he can't just take a walk but must always be going someplace, he spurns the futile present hour and plans for the future. When the adult sees someone who, like the child, lives and plays unmindful of concerns and objectives, he cannot tolerate such freedom beside him, since it humiliates him in his pompous wretchedness; consequently he resorts to a higher repressive authority, to death, which has the solemnity of all authority—every rite, even the most innocent, like the start of an academic year or the opening of an exhibition, is in some way a funeral; whoever cuts the tape or opens the meeting is always a bit like one who soberly throws a handful of dirt.

That relative of Aloysius wants the child to think not about play-

ing but about death or, rather, the future, because death is the culmi-
nation of every future. Perhaps, in his parochial devotion, he thinks
he can call him back to the thought of faith. But the boy continues to
play because he is suffused with grace, with the gospel that urges us
to leave suffering behind each day without adding that of tomorrow
to it, to not destroy life by worrying about holding on to it. The act of
playing—I don't know why, but I picture the child simply running
back and forth—is enough in itself, it doesn't need anything else,
neither prayers nor report cards nor final motions. It resembles joy,
without the foolish arrogance that every alleged happiness often has.

It is difficult to approximate childhood, the child running up
and down in a race that comprises the world and the things that are
his playmates. It is easy to talk about playthings from a sociological or
pedagogical viewpoint, study them as products of an imposed culture
and appreciate or deplore their educational effects; it is inevitable to
long for them with sentimental nostalgia when they remind us of our
childhood, a season which we identify with the poetry of life, though
it was merely the time when we discovered the poetry of life, in ways
and in forms neither better nor worse than those of other generations.

The toy becomes mysterious, unlikely to be accessible in its
essential quality, as an object in which the absolute present of the
child playing with it is condensed, the self-sufficiency of an article
suddenly imbued with meaning. There are not many children—
credible children, not the intolerable, false kind—among the great
characters of world literature and not many toys either. A few great
writers, from Hoffmann to Baudelaire, have captured the enigmatic
or sinister aspect of toys, the disturbing alienation that sometimes appears on the face of a stuffed monkey abandoned on the ground or
in a parrot's expression.

Hoffmann's tales masterfully depict the ambiguity of toys, which
transforms their familiar gentleness into a menace, as if dolls, toy soldiers, rocking horses, and teddy bears were also or primarily a nocturnal army awaiting the moment to rise up hostilely, meanwhile rag-

ing scarily in the dreams and nightmares of the children who until recently played affectionately with them. The treacherous caginess or perfidy, which some writers reveal a glimpse of in lead cowboys or cloth clowns, symbolizes the dark disquiet of childhood, its ambivalences, its traumas and separations, the pain and cruelty that mark a youngster's growth with deep scars. A stuffed dog with its strabismic glass eyes may be the first epiphany of the indifference of things, of the solitude and melancholy of life.

This aspect of a toy is the easiest to represent: painting perverse dolls does not require too much imagination. It is much more difficult to capture the secret of familiarity without distorting it into mawkish pap. In museums and exhibitions toys are generally educational; the displays cannot evoke the non-time of play, but detail the history of how and when games were organized, suggested, or imposed; they arrange them in categories—airplanes and teddy bears, erector sets and robots—but don't let us see the unique individuality that a toy assumes in a person's life. The inevitable mistake of almost all museums and exhibitions is that of the professor who always wants to teach and explain things rather than simply showing, the way poetry does; perhaps the best museum might be a storehouse that makes no claims other than offering anyone the chance to go and see whatever he or she likes at the moment, without having to submit to didactic routes and acrobatic productions.

In the cultural history museum in Lund, in an inconspicuous room—which on a hasty visit one is likely to overlook, attracted by a more ambitious display of ceramics—is an unassuming, enchanting world of toys, simply gathered together, as if only to make a little order (though not too much) once the children have gone to bed. There are very few explanations, no commentary; there is no catalogue. The toys span about one hundred years of childhood, roughly from the second half of the 1800s to the 1950s.

There is a cozy intimacy in the little room that houses the delights and sorrows of childhood. An intimacy that is encountered throughout this old Swedish town, with its tranquil streets, its low houses whose uncurtained windows reveal sedate domestic interiors, the Romanesque cathedral, a sturdy fortress of the faith, and the centuries-old university, rich in freshly preserved tradition. In Sweden one enjoys the refined, festive intellectual curiosity of people interested in others, in what comes from across the border, completely free of the frenzied insecurity that assails so many peoples and cultures, especially in Mitteleuropa, obsessed with themselves and their own identity, who require continuous expressions of esteem and regard. One of the greatest injustices of life is the one sadly recognized in the gospel: "Whoever has will be given more; whoever does not have, even what they have will be taken from them." Those who are well off—individuals or a people—who are free from need, from oppression, and are not a minority, are often also generous and sympathetic, while those who are starving and humiliated are sometimes distasteful in their insistent, resentful craving for self-assertion.

The stuffed hippopotamus in the Lund museum is like the donkey that Prince Myskin, Dostoyevsky's idiot, sees grazing in a Swiss meadow and can no longer forget. As big as an actual bulldog, the hippo is all battered and ripped, the glass eyes are missing from its face, but the signs of the worn-out fabric in their place are a more genuine pair of eyes: they seem like the myopic, good-natured gaze of a person who doesn't rely on things too much, like an affable old man who persists in not putting on his glasses and squints his eyes instead. The hippopotamus is stumpy and awkward, with crooked legs and a large behind, and looks like a creature who goes around wobbling uncertainly, hoping only to be left in peace; he's a poor soul whose back bears all the blows inflicted by life and history, which he counters with quiet dignity, evidenced by his patches.

Beside him a rocking sheep is losing a bit of its still thick reddish fur, dolls are settled comfortably in tidy, warm houses with sloping roofs, a miniature train is stopped next to a chair, soldiers on foot and on horseback mark out the tumultuous geometry of a battle and suggest the pathos of closing ranks against the chaos, building blocks on a shelf compose changeable figures, occasionally distorted by a block face turned the wrong way, bizarre and innocent chimeras. The toys are old, they show the perishability of things and existence, the desolation of so many childhood days, but also a tenacious resistance to consumption. The hippopotamus stands up to the severe storms of time no less courageously than the red and blue hussars; life tears you to pieces but a good pair of pants, after all, can be mended many times.

I would like to hear the hippo's story, to know what he saw, in what rooms he was tossed about and cuddled, what happened to the child who played with him. That gruff face reproaches us for the fact that we always stop playing too soon. Even with completely different toys, of course, for example, the electronic devices that are certainly no less seductive for the imagination than the old wooden blocks. Outside that room, adult life rarely gives in to the seriousness and passion of play, muffling them with the inconsequentiality of obligation. Playing in itself would actually be simple; anything can become a toy: an empty match box, a button. A pediatrician friend of mine told me about a child seriously ill with leukemia who, after the I.V. drip, took the pole used for the infusion, and started running through the wards, hoisting it straight ahead; at that moment he was happily in a bumper car in an amusement park. There's no need to read the lives of the saints to see how one should live.

December 9, 1990

THE WOODLAND CEMETERY

The North is essentially its light and in particular that of late afternoon, when the day passes into an evening announced for some time but never seeming to come, indefinitely postponed by a tenacious luminosity. A clear light, which makes the air transparent and cloaks things in the glow of a poignant distance, in a longing for everything that is wanting. Under tropical or equatorial skies, where darkness falls suddenly and goes abruptly from a dazzling, unbearable sun to night, a European notices the lack of lingering twilight with a feeling of estrangement. In the pages of so much great Scandinavian literature, the light becomes the aura of true life and of its absence—promises and disappointments, happiness and sadness, the sense of life that shines beyond the immediate reality, as it shines beyond the snow-covered mountains for Ibsen's character Borkman, the poet who, studying the discontents of civilization in depth, said that claiming to live, to really live, is megalomaniacal.

Among the trees of Stockholm's Woodland Cemetery it is still light, despite the hour, and the white trunks of the birches break up the dark green of the firs and foliage the way foam crests on a dark sea. The usual cemeteries are forests of stone that crowd and smother the vegetation, increasingly sparse between one tombstone and another, reduced to an occasional boxwood hedge or some meager rows of cypresses, sometimes to simply a few flowers in a vase. They are cities, marble necropolises and metropolises, majestic triumphs of death and its order. The cemetery in Stockholm—constructed or rather designed by two great architects, Erik Gunnar Asplund and Sigurd Lewerentz, in a lengthy project of planning and realization that started in 1915 and lasted half a century—is instead a forest that surrounds, invades, and covers the stone, and in which the irregularity of life seems to triumph.

Many graves are sprinkled randomly and asymmetrically among the trees, and in the twilight they seem like crouching animals concealed in the grass; no imposing slabs of rock but small scattered memorial stones, a discreet understory of names and dates, which poke out from the ground like roots. Some graves are more prominent than others, but none is really pretentious; the pomposity of many family chapels with dome and columns, which often make our cemeteries garish, is impossible and unimaginable in this setting, where it would be as grotesque as an evening gown worn to go tramping through the woods, watching for animals and following their tracks, picking mushrooms, smelling the scent of resin and damp earth.

Here death suggests equality, fraternity; the naturalness of a familiar, spontaneous act like breathing, sleeping, walking, which knows no distinctions and hierarchies and ignores ceremonial pomp. Some chapels, like that of the Resurrection, conspicuously draw attention to themselves and play a central role in the topography and memorial services, but others sprout unexpectedly at a bend in a path, the simple huts of woodsmen rather than churches, shelters in which to take cover from the rain rather than places for worship or funeral rites—even though a tree, beneath which you sit to catch your breath, can perhaps be a good spot to pray, more so than other places officially designated for devotion.

Our cemeteries of stone are a space-time continuum dedicated to death, which is dutifully thought of during a brief, penitent visit and forgotten as soon as we leave. Here the visit is not a funeral ritual, but rather a stroll through the forest perceiving its breath; one is attentive to the trees, the ineffable tenderness of the slender birches, the red of the leaves, the branches that the clear, crisp light outlines against the sky, the footsteps of some animal, the call of a bird. The deceased scattered around are no longer anonymous or unreal, or any more disquieting or sublimated than the crowds we move among every day on the streets. There would be nothing profane about it if one of them were to come and play or make love among these meadows. The thought of death comes and goes, benevolent and indifferent; a memorial stone calls it up and a stand of fir trees on a hill, like a regiment of knights with spears ready to rush into battle, sweeps it away. Some graves have only a cross or not even that, just a piece of wood stuck in the ground; the flowers are a small, fresh bunch laid on the ground or on the grass. Margit, who rests at the edge of a lane under tall black firs, has only a first name, no surname, as does Vilhelm, a few steps away from her.

The intent of the cemetery's architects was to divert the attention of the living from the sorrow of death, to create a sensual intimacy with nature, with the forest that speaks to the senses through its scents, its colors, the rough touch of bark, the bitter taste of berries chewed and spit out. The forest is a fitting setting for a person who does not feel alone with his anguish, but feels part of the world around him and of generations, of the history of the species and the even vaster history of which even the species is but a brief moment.

But grave and forest, stones and trunks are and say the same thing, the triumph of time, destroyer of Margit. Christianity — virtually absent from this cemetery — made classical objectivity and serenity impossible, perhaps forever: the placid acceptance of the fact that the individual is predestined to be nothing and therefore is nothing; this forest is full of enchantment and poetry, but it is nothing more than the Button-Molder's foundry spoken of in Ibsen's *Peer Gynt*, in which every used button — every individual — is ground up, melted, destroyed forever and reused, at least in part, for the manufacture of other buttons.

In the eyes of those who die, Christianity dictates reading a deep-seated, terrified, or astonished absurdity asking to be redeemed. In an extraordinary Jewish parable, recounted by Enzo Bianchi in his unforgettable *Vivere la morte* (Living Death), when Aaron's final moment comes, God says to Moses, "You tell him, because I don't have the heart to." Faced with God's sorrow over a man's death, there is no forest that can hold up. After the Judeo-Christian revolution of all human sentiments, not even a skeptic like Eugenio Montale, hardened against all absolutes and faiths, can be content to walk quietly among the dead as among the flowers; when he loses a loved one he looks for an opening on the horizon, an impossible way through; he wants to devise a whistle, a signal "for the afterlife," even though he doubts any afterlife.[1]

In an apocryphal Apocalypse, Eve, dying, asks to be reunited with Adam—who had preceded her and with whom she had lived, transgressed, and atoned, enjoyed and lost the Terrestrial Paradise—and the ground in which she asks to be received is like a huge body, cherished flesh. Even the forest, after all, is a triumph of death, though so much more generous—and more ambiguous—than stone mausoleums. Of course it's easy to say that life is tougher than death—there are shoots, buds, flowers. For that matter, life is also tougher than wisdom and intelligence. Asplund and Lewerentz, the architects of the Woodland Cemetery and the setting that should teach us to overcome all dismay and individual misery before the great law of the Whole, ended up arguing pathetically in a squalid battle that sidelined Lewerentz, the more gifted of the two. Everyday pettiness is more universal—and tougher—than death and life.

October 26, 1998

THE FJORD

The most remote arm of the fjord begins in Midtfjord; the cruise boat which left from Bergen, continuing its journey to Flåm, comes alongside a ferryboat in the middle of the sea, and two or three passengers, to whom the previous route's solitude actually seemed too crowded with things, transfer over and look for a place on deck that is sheltered from the wind. The fjord, on the way to Gudvangen, narrows, the ferryboat passes between gray and greenish rocks, through a barren landscape that on shore becomes a fleeting forest, dense and somber. The world has two colors, green and blue — dark green along the banks, tender as a newborn leaf where the water ripples or murky as a rotten trunk where the current stagnates; blue deep as night, and pale blue that seems more like light than color. In the clear, fresh air, rinsed by the previous day's rains, there is still summer, that glitter that makes it resemble life's brevity, the pleasure of squinting your eyes when looking at the sun.

Colors are an alphabet of the world; it's not just the sea, meadow, or fire that have colors, but feelings, words, situations, even ideas have them. Filippo Burzio, the fervent Piedmontese writer, speaking of the wars of the Risorgimento, wrote that *Quarantotto*, Forty-eight, was blue and *Cinquantanove*, Fifty-nine, red;[1] Paolo Bozzi, in his *Fisica ingenua* (Naive Physics), a crystalline narrative disguised as a scientific treatise, focuses on the colors that words, the strangest as well as abstract ones, assume in the mind.

The fjord has the tints of distance, a precise receding distance. The gaze thinks there are few things to take in, rocks, a rather limited variety of plants, some seagulls, occasionally a solitary house on shore. In reality there are countless things, they escape the eye that wants to seize them like a predatory animal but sees them slip away, too numerous and too diverse to be captured: the nuanced color of the water, gradations and transitions of gray, green, blue, ivory, lead, silver whose impossible catalogue would be a multifaceted songbook; the streaks of bright, dazzling light that every so often slice through the water like sabers, the golden brown of a reverberation that sinks in a small vortex, the dark gorge through which the ferryboat moves that gradually grows lighter like smoke vanishing into the sky. The clarity and transparency of the air that make things stand out yet defy the ability to see, to be aware of the world's inexhaustible surface.

This intensity of perception is especially possible in scenes that appear empty or nearly so: the sea, where there seems to be nothing, or at most a disappearing sail or hull, deserts, barren steppes with only the monotonous swaying of grass. In actuality those places are infinitely diverse, like the changing colors of evening, and the most patient observation never ceases to probe their variety and significance. But to grasp the shifting shades of grass, waves, or clouds requires that preliminary impression of emptiness, of nothing.

In lush places, teeming with life, is the danger of not seeing, as when you can't hear anything in very noisy surroundings; the superabundance of things to perceive hinders the perception of them. In this northern light, a leaf illuminated by the sun appears unrepeatable, momentary but essential; a branch that snaps streaks the air. Perhaps reality, to reveal the inimitable significance of all life, needs to be pruned, trimmed down.

Little by little as we advance, the rock walls loom higher and grow more constricted; the surroundings at certain bends are bleak, but where the passage is wider the sea shimmers with light. Strindberg said, contentiously, that in Ibsen's drama one is always aware of the narrowness of the fjord and a wintry harshness. Like many great writers who in their personal journey feel a need to factiously attack other great writers, Strindberg was wrong. The narrow Norwegian fjord did not constrict Ibsen's great art; it gave it—to extend the metaphor employed by Strindberg—the sharp essentiality that is one of its greatest gifts.

Between the mid-nineteenth century and the beginning of the twentieth, Norway, a peripheral European province that still lacked an independent national identity, produced an extraordinary, world-renowned literature that examined in depth the darkest twists and fundamental contradictions of modernity, in part still unresolved. Ibsen is the greatest voice, though certainly not an isolated one, of this literature—that of Jonas Lie, Alexander Kielland, Knut Hamsun, and others—that reveals the world by watching it from the edges of the fjord. Ibsen observes the impossibility of living an authentic life and the delusion of any claim or hope to live one; few have grasped civilization's disquiet, with no qualms and no illusions, as he has. Ibsen exposes the inadequacy with troubled melancholy but denounces it with stark objectivity, devoid of wistful abandon. The constraint of the fjord, for which he is reproved, teaches him to drain life of every superfluity, to trim away every ounce of sentimental fat, of rhetoric, however noble; under the stiff frock coat he liked to wear, his arid extremism can sometimes even appear cold, almost a puritanical frigidity, or erotic self-repression. But that was his coherence, which pruned redundancy even from the heart, so as to represent life's isolation with the imperturbable sobriety that alone can underscore the tragedy. No nostalgia, no elegy, but rather sharp, austere rigor, a karstic harshness that exposes only barren rocks and through the barrenness of the rock lets you feel, all the more intensely, the lack of any maternal, aquatic tenderness in life.

The rigor of the fjord, essential to all true art, ensures an unspoken purity of sentiment; for Thomas Mann the ideal homeland of sentiment was Nordic, a retreating interiority sensitive to the call of distances, able to center on the minimal and the near at hand, in the intimacy of a remote house in a desolate landscape.

Empty spaces often become, in Norwegian literature, landscapes of the soul, its silences and resonances. Not only in classic Norwegian literature but in more recent works as well. Contained and concealed in those silences and in those denials is a fierce, intense passion, which assumes the appearance of an ineptitude for living.

The Birds by Tarjei Vesaas is an example; written in Nynorsk, the old peasant folk language (as opposed, especially in the past, to that of the more illustrious literary tradition, closer to Danish), Vesaas's novel is the story of a mentally disabled, simple-minded man. Undertaking a theme already addressed in so many masterpieces, the writer tells the tender, bitter story of a mind unequal to the struggle of living but open, almost to the point of confusion, to the silent flow of things, which courses through him like a faint rustle, like the flutter of birds' wings in the evening, fading into the distance. This too is a story left unspoken, a solitude that ends, without complaint and without sentimentality, in the waters of a lake. The waters barely moved by the wind which are enough to swallow Mattis, the good-natured, limited man, resemble those of the fjord: they shimmer, they ripple and close; the wake behind the boat disappears and there is nothing left to say.

September 29, 1991

PARISH OF THE NORTH

Nesset, on the west coast of Norway, is situated at the intersection of Andfjorden and Eresfjorden fjords, which form practically a right angle. Where the two arms come together the water gets slightly choppy, a brown line slices through it like the blade of a sword, dividing pale green from a gray blue that blends with the color of distance; beyond the black forests and other fjords the mountains are spotted with snow. Bjørnstierne Bjørnson — Ibsen's poet friend, so bound to the Norwegian landscape that he became its passionate, more or less official bard, author of the national anthem of the new independent Norway — celebrated the unlimited dimensions of Nordic nature, nights and days as long as seasons, a sun that in the evening appears enlarged behind the veil of fog that rises from the sea, large flocks of birds and schools of fish, the violence of waves against the cliffs.

From the immense landscape, in his view, fantasies and legends equally grandiose were born. But the silent distances that were so dear to him evoke an absorbed restraint rather than titanic pathos, a subdued enchantment as fleeting as a brief summer; the horizon of water, forests, and solitudes is a pensive, gentle infinity.

The parish of Pastor Peder Bjørnson, the writer's father, was in Nesset; his family had moved there in 1837, when the future Nobel laureate was five years old. Compared to the harsh desolation of Kvikne, the mountain village where he'd been born, Nesset and nearby Molde, the district capital, had seemed like serene, idyllic places to the boy, graced by a breezy freedom and openness to the world, characteristic of cities on the sea. There is the tall ash tree in front of the new parish house, planted by Elise, the writer's mother, the childhood tree where Bjørnson and his five siblings played. There are many wild roses; there is also the grave of Blakken, the horse that had transported the tree trunks required to build the new rectory, which Pastor Peder decided on because the one he had found, some centuries old, was falling apart. The gravestone recalls that Blakken had been attacked by a bear once, in the woods, but he had fought back and ended up killing his aggressor.

The poet never forgot that horse; the grave in the bosom of the parish complex is also a challenge, a question which the great religions are embarrassed to answer, an inquiry into the life and suffering of animals and their significance in the history of salvation. Saint Francis preached to birds and Saint James of Compostela spoke to salmon, but it is not enough. No Glorious Mystery recalls the ox and the ass in the stable in Bethlehem.

In the big wood-paneled room where the community of the faithful gathered, a grim portrait of Pastor Peder Bjørnson in clerical garb with a wide white collar evokes centuries of austere devotion, generations of pastors—about thirty of them—with their psalms and sermons and belief in an inscrutable God. Bjørnson is also one of those "pastor's sons" to whom the literature and culture of Germanic countries owe some of the proudest poetic passages and some of the most extreme spiritual experiences. It was in the setting of the Lutheran parish that personalities like Gotthold Lessing and Friedrich Nietzsche—to cite only two major examples among many—absorbed an absolute need for moral rigor and truth, in whose name they subjected the doctrines, dogmas, and overall structure of Christianity and its churches to ruthless analysis, only to reject them on the basis of rebellion and censure learned from Christianity itself.

Bjørnson too, the son of Nesset's pastor, learned to rebel against the Lutheran Church from the air he breathed in his father's parish, to reject what he viewed as a rigid, fossilized orthodoxy, although his rebellion, unlike those of other great authors to whom he cannot be likened, sometimes falls into rhetorical excess, in a facile, progressive, and radical-leaning optimism, ill-equipped to comprehend the fractures of modernity, religion, and rebellion against it.

Compared to his friend and compatriot Ibsen, one of the giants of modern literature, Bjørnson often seems like an eloquent lecturer. But even in a vehement, bitter conflict, he is able to listen to more profound anxieties: in the novel *In God's Way* the fervent depiction of the heroine, Ragni, and her courageous rebellion against social conformity in favor of the heart gives way to a painful intuition of the coldness that threatens lives and feelings, namely, contradictions that no emancipatory enthusiasm can resolve.

The polemic against Christianity and its churches is much more complex than it might seem to facile anticlerical thinking. Christianity is opposed in the name of a morality that is seen as more authentic — especially in comparison to a national church such as the Lutheran Church, which bears the weight of a double institutional function — but this morality, by the very fact of being more rigorous, weakens the individual all the more, stifling his vitality on behalf of duty and truth, as it proceeds with exacerbating the consumption of life by the conscience that Ibsen — with quite a different poetic power — attributes to religion in *Rosmersholm*.

Christianity — which is also criticized in the interest of life, which it would repress — reveals instead a primal force, capable of confronting face to face the heinous demonicity of life and death, of the ephemeral and the eternal that annihilates it. It is this force that secular morality has lost, because the latter eliminates the abyss and tragedy of living, which do not follow any commandments or moral prohibitions. In the drama *Beyond Our Powers* (or rather in the first part, the only one poetically valid), Bjørnson expressed the humanistic horror, found in every moral vision, of everything that transcends human measure, including that of good and evil. But since life itself, with its disasters, tragedies, and injustices, crushes human measure and smashes the tablets of its law, the strong man, able to withstand the destructive violence of living specifically because he is intent on the transcendent, is Pastor Adolf Sang, to whom Bjørnson is ideologically averse.

Christianity therefore appears to be not a pious unction but a devastating familiarity with that which is beyond our powers and which lies not in a seraphic sky but in the daily tangle that every individual is called upon to experience despite being unequal to it, just as each of us must die even if we cannot face up to the incommensurability of death. As Aldo Magris—an author with whom I share a surname, though we are not related—wrote in his wonderful book *L'idea di destino nel pensiero antico* (The Idea of Destiny in Ancient Thought), every moral vision of life is appalled when confronted with that which transcends and thereby disrupts and shatters the human attempt to impose order, justice, and rationality on the abnormity of events. Bjørnson's exhortation not to go beyond our powers is very human, and would, if we could follow it, bring us joy or at least serenity, but it is unrealizable because a good part of our being, loving, and dying is beyond our powers. The moralist can only teach us to value as much as possible the little, precious little bit that is in our hands.

Life in the parish community was an integrated, cohesive whole. In the big room people prayed, met together, studied; within these wooden walls Bjørnson had learned and then taught other children to read and write. Bibles, kitchen utensils, arithmetic manuals, tubs, and casks are shared for daily use. The court convenes here as well, and the last death sentence carried out in the district of Molde was issued here. A young, wealthy farmer had seduced one of his peasant workers and wanted to marry her, given that she was expecting a child, but her mother was fiercely opposed to the marriage, and in the end he lost his head and killed the girl. He was sentenced to decapitation, and the whole town, children included, Bjørnson among them, had to witness the execution, performed with an ax. It was only fifty-nine years later that the writer was able to put the horror of that experience on paper. In another wooden house, among the kilns and shed for the harvest, there is a counter with a drain where the animals were slaughtered.

Prolific and uneven, Bjørnson wrote too much; he contributed to the creation of "Norwegiomania," the stereotype of the Nordic idyll with its blonde young women, silent waters, and solitary forests, but he also created—for example, with the novel *Synnøve Solbakken*, inspired by these places—an enchanting landscape of the soul, animated by distant echoes and resonances. Democratic and generous, he fought for oppressed minorities, such as the Slovaks; it was his misfortune or crime to become an official poet, representative of values and a nation, taking on a role that our age does not forgive a poet, because no one can represent Humanity without distorting it into a decorative monument. "False as an after-dinner speaker," Strindberg aggressively described him.

The remote places among the fjords belong to the geography of universal literature; a building in Molde is linked to Ibsen's *Rosmersholm*, another location to *The Lady from the Sea*. On an island across the way is a museum that preserves the old boats of Nordland celebrated by Jonas Lie, boats whose shape, suitable for breaking through the surging waves, seemed to him to have been forged by the protracted, anonymous toil of generations, by experience of routes and currents, winds and coasts built into the contour of a bow or the proportions of a keel.

One of the greatest contemporary European literatures was born in provincial Norway, Europe's periphery, a literature that has thoroughly understood how each one of us, in the historic season that he is called upon to live, finds himself at the periphery of life. Ibsen— but also Lie or Alexander Kielland, whose novels about a bourgeois family inspired *Buddenbrooks*, and not long afterward Knut Hamsun, or other Scandinavians such as Jens Peter Jacobsen or Strindberg— laid bare contradictions that are still at the heart of our civilization's crises, of the nihilism that surrounds us.

Claiming to live, wrote Ibsen, is megalomaniacal; this laconic landscape instills a yearning for true life and invites us to retain a touch of megalomania, like the melancholy, intractable drifters who, in many pages of Norwegian literature, persist in seeking it.

July 31, 1995

WATER AND DESERT

1. "American tourists are welcome in Iran," a senior official of the Interior Ministry in Tehran declares at the beginning of the summer, "and they may feel secure, much safer from Al Qaeda attacks than in the United States." The few Westerners, valued for their dollars, are welcomed warmly and viewed with benevolent curiosity by people, and it is hard to imagine a September 11 or a March 11 in Isfahan or Shiraz; in the streets, at the bazaar, or in the garden of a museum it is not uncommon for women wearing the chador (or in any case fully covered as prescribed by strict Islamism) to stop and chat, and politely pose questions to the foreigner—naturally without giving him her hand, which is forbidden under any circumstances between people of different sexes. The war in Iraq does not seem to have aroused anti-Western violence, unlike in other Muslim countries; the protest against the British Embassy—the only street demonstration during the weeks of our stay—stems from a more ancient grievance.

Many indeed are rejoicing over the war in Iraq and they have many reasons to: the satisfaction of seeing a country and a regime thrashed that, goaded and assisted by the United States, had bombed them for eight years with missiles reaching as far as Tehran; the gratification of seeing the West embroiled in a bloody quagmire that risks weakening its world leadership role; the hope that the ill-advised mess may result in a Shiite Iraqi government, a possibility envisioned by Colin Powell in a statement prominently reported in the newspapers; the conviction that the unexpected (and grossly underestimated) difficulties encountered by invading Iraq will keep the United States from attacking Iran.

There is, however, an obvious and huge difference, even in this regard, between representatives of the regime (as well as the population, not very enthusiastic about the regime but even less so about being bombed by liberators) and the cultured upper middle class, opposed to the ayatollahs though prevented from expressing themselves. An intellectual who lives and has lived for long periods in Europe tells me that he had hoped at the time that Saddam Hussein would achieve victory over Iran and that he approves the support the United States then gave the Iraqi tyrant against fundamentalist Islamic Iran.

2. "Clash of civilizations," "war of cultures," slogans that are heard more and more often at the beginning of the third millennium, just as they resounded a century or so ago during Europe's great irrationalist crisis, with legions of prophets proclaiming the decline of the West, preaching war between the races, announcing the birth of the new man, a transformed, pure Adam risen from regenerative bloodbaths. Millenarian, apocalyptic pathos becomes heady with sweeping, empty formulas ("the end of history") and distorts the course of events into cheap melodrama, dominated by a dark, exhilarating fatality, which engulfs men in scintillating, spectacular, doomsday-like sequences.

First among the many things that Western culture has to impart is the sober, lucid criticism of any bombast and any arcane sentimentalism; what is needed to understand the overwhelming transformations of reality, which take place before our eyes at a bewildering speed, is solid, distinct analysis, not flamboyant, vacuous synthesis. Conflict characterizes the existence of human communities—at various levels, barbaric or civilized—and can be a source of progress if it is channeled within the rules of humanity. If war, as Clausewitz said, is the continuation of political conflict by other means, civilization and democracy consist in developing mechanisms that prevent moving on to violent means, just as they prevent individual conflicts from being solved by physical force. The current anarchic-ultraliberal fundamentalism—which today pollutes Western society with its factious irrationality and vilifies liberal thought, mistaking it for chaotic license and an untamed jungle world—foments violence because it undermines the rules by which civilization holds it at bay.

It is not "civilizations" that clash; conflicts and wars arise from tensions and transformations that fail to act within the structure ordained by a nation or a complex of nations conjointly associated in a balanced system. The First and Second World Wars were not a twilight-of-the-gods clash of Germanic, Latin, and Slavic civilizations, but an outcome: the horrific bloody purging of upheavals that rocked a centuries-old European order. Civilizations have a physiognomy of their own, but they do not have a fixed, immutable identity that wholly coincides with a country. Democracy is infinitely superior to a murderous dictatorship, but that is not to say that Denmark, which has not known the abomination of the latter, is superior to Germany, where it was practiced to a heinous extent. It is futile to wonder whether Islam is a superior or inferior civilization, adding and subtracting the Alhambra, the Shari'ah, Avicenna, and infibulation. What counts, each time, when faced with a concrete question, is to know where civilization stands and where the affront that is inflicted on it lies. Today undoubtedly Islamic fundamentalism, whatever the reasons that facilitated its rise, entails serious and sometimes extreme attacks on the individual's basic rights, which should arouse more protests from Western libertarian movements; there have not been many demonstrations against the stoning of adulterers or the decapitation of homosexuals that have occurred in Muslim countries.

3. At the University of Tehran, Roberto Toscano—the Italian ambassador to Iran, who in that difficult context performs a particularly enlightened role, combining a great solicitude toward that country with a steadfast defense of our values—holds a conference on human rights and ways to respect and ensure them internationally. Though

there is general agreement among the audience, one intellectual insists on equating religion and law; religious commandments and precepts, in his view, should not only inspire a vision of life which will then, independently, also generate a judicial system, but should themselves be the laws of the country, directly; in that way, not going to mass on Sunday would become, for a Catholic, a crime to be prosecuted.

There is an indisputable, insurmountable borderline, which cannot be negotiated but must be affirmed and defended, namely the distinction between the ethical-religious sphere and the judicial. This distinction is a universal value and is one of the cornerstones of Western civilization. The gospel's sublime Sermon on the Mount is greater than any legal code, but it is not suited to be a code of law. Civilizations, however, are not static, but dynamic and contradictory; the West has also known, though to a limited extent, hierocratic forms of government: for example, the church-states at certain periods, or theocratic rule, such as, for a brief time, the Calvinist republic of Geneva. That is not to say that the countries in which the Calvinist religion prevails are totalitarian today; indeed, they are among the most democratic, and Calvinism is at the origin of many modern liberties. Islam, at the time of Arab dominion in Spain, was more tolerant and liberal than Christianity. At times the face of a civilization changes deceptively, in the collective imagination of others as well. Only a few years ago, when the Serbs were foolishly and falsely demonized or when the Soviet Union unwisely invaded Afghanistan, Muslims—in Western media—were viewed as good and decent, valiant champions of liberty; today they are villainized as a whole in ways that seem drawn from the worst Serbian nationalism. Civilizations and their images evolve and change over time, splitting into diverse and sometimes conflicting elements. They cannot be photographed—Roberto Toscano wrote—and captured in a still image, as if they were motionless, but must be video filmed, caught in the movement that transforms them.

4. For centuries, Iran has been a country with a flair for gardens, waters, and mirrors, celebrated in a poetry and mysticism that are intrinsic to the loftiest universal literature; "paradise," in Persian, means garden. In the Bagh-e Fin, near Kashan, the city-oasis dear to Shah Abbas the Great, the waters course gently through smooth-flowing canals and the world seems cool and peaceful; no one can capture water's mysterious grace like peoples familiar with desert and drought, its crystalline transparency, its fluidity and mutability even as it remains itself, its force that becomes channel, irrigation, geometrical yet unfathomable order. In great Persian poetry and its brilliant adaptation–re-creation which is Goethe's *West-East Divan*, water, assuming a mobile yet perennial form in the play of fountains, becomes the face of life and its flow, of the continuity and unpredictability of Eros, of the enigmatic association of nature and civilization, primal disorder and the ordered fabric of existence.

Traveling through Iran — its cities, its barren mountains, its arid plains, the unexpected, tender oases of greenery, flowers, and pools of water — is a continuous abrupt transition from a sensation of strangeness, rejecting many intolerable aspects of Islamic fundamentalism, and a feeling of familiarity, almost like commonly belonging to an enduring, far-reaching civilization. From the ruins of Persepolis to the vestiges of the Sassanids, from the Abbasid dynasties to the Timurids, there is a great sense of empire, of a country that is a crucible of races, cultures, and religions, traces of roads that cut through deserts and mountains connecting peoples, laws, and aqueducts, the proud battle against Time and the glory of ruins crumbled by time and reduced to desert dust. Undoubtedly, Marathon and Salamis, which saved Greece, are still today our victories, but at the same time we are also heirs of the Persian empires which brought East and West together, the ancient Mesopotamian civilization and Judaism; of the Iran which opposed the central-Asian region of Turan just as Greece had opposed Achaemenid Persia.

Whereas Qom, the holy city teeming with priests, gives the impression of an East that is exotic and, for us, alien, and Tehran is a huge metropolis that proliferates in disjointed suburbs, vital and precarious, other cities, despite the regime's tribal repression, present a sense of *civitas:* enchanting Isfahan—with the incredible beauty of its blue mosques, its squares, its bridges over the river, where families gather in the evening in joyful tranquillity—or Shiraz, the city of roses and poets.

Persian poetry bears the stamp of classicism; its *ruba'i* (the quatrain in which Omar Khayyam, in love with life and convinced of its nothingness, wrote his celebrated *Rubaiyat*) is a universal poetic form like the hexameter or the hendecasyllable. Remembered during these weeks is Firdusi (in Farsi, Ferdósí), the poet who more than a thousand years ago wrote Persia's epic poem, *The Book of Kings;* to commemorate his anniversary, a 24 × 9–foot carpet, on which four people worked continuously for three years, was placed on his grave, which is located in Tús, in eastern Iran. Like life itself, the epic is a carpet, a weaving and unraveling of destinies like threads of different colors, events, figures, and characters woven together and undone by time, by chance, by God, by inexorable necessities or fortuitous coincidences, experienced, enjoyed, and suffered with the same passion. *The Book of Kings* is not an exotic, remote text but a great poem of war, adventure, love, faith, disillusionment, and destiny that is as much a part of our world and of our imagination as the *Song of Roland* or the *Nibelungs.* I was fortunate enough to read and love it as a young man in Italo Pizzi's nineteenth-century translation, one of many examples of illustrious Italian philology and its universal receptiveness.

Among the stories that are interwoven in the poem is an archetypal tale that appears in many literatures, even remote ones: the tragic confrontation on the battlefield between father and son, with the father killing the son, thus destroying himself and his survival. Rustem, the Iranian Achilles, is forced to kill Sohràb, the son unbeknown to him who fights under other flags.

The Book of Kings blends Islam with the pre-Islamic heritage of Persian tradition; the verses of its preface invoking Allah are one of the grandest expressions of Muslim monotheism. Authentic spirituality—when not distorted into a caricature of itself that negates it, as occurs with fundamentalisms—is always universal and does not pertain only to those who explicitly profess it as believers and practitioners. In Shiraz, in the marvelous mausoleum of Shah-e-Cheragh, the dazzling crystals reflected by countless mirrors and colors that become light, as in Dante's paradise, transform the world into a mirror of something else. Here the chador no longer seems cloyishly picturesque, like a Venetian gondola in a glass dome, or like a grotesque imposition, but like a ritual garment suitable to that place of devotion, which we choose to ask to visit, and thus respect its rules. The atmosphere is intense, the praying has an almost physical density. A suspicious glance toward the foreign infidels quickly returns to absorbed concentration. Leaving the sanctuary, whose rooms for men and women are strictly separated, and meeting up again in the courtyard, J. and I discover that each of us instinctively recited a Hail Mary before the tomb, the prayer that is perhaps the most conciliatory toward different faiths—or even no faiths—and makes fewer claims of superiority over other faiths; in any case, the most acceptable Catholic prayer for a Muslim.

5. Mohmmad Khatami, president of the republic, begins his "Letter for Tomorrow"—published prominently, amid heated discussions, in Iranian newspapers, in Farsi and in English—with the image of the desert, which is aridity, death, menace, but also challenge, patience, journey, a search for the water of life.[1] Water for Khatami becomes a symbol of hope for a renewal—in his view essential, indeed "irreversible"—in the life of the country. He is fighting against fundamentalist obscurantism for a separation of religion and politics, so that national independence, gained by opposing colonial exploita-

tion and domination by other powers, will no longer mean repression but rather stand for democracy and civil rights.

These secular—which is not to say irreligious—values are the great distinction of the West, which has often renounced them, however, in its politics of power and exploitation, resorting to acts of violence in countries it wanted to exploit to repress modernizing, liberal forces in particular, which, inspired by the Western model, wanted to make their country a free, independent, and democratic state that would then no longer let itself be enslaved by other powers. If today in Iran a tyrannical Islamic revolution is raging, rejecting Western progress and liberalism, it is largely due to the Western governments which fifty years ago saw the overthrow of Mohammad Mossadegh's government in a coup, along with his attempt to make Iran a democratic, secular country, master of its destiny and resources.

According to Khatami, the Islamic Revolution, having accomplished its purpose of liberating the country, must transform into an open, advanced, normal state, in which—he says, quoting Brecht—there is no longer the unhappy need for heroes.[2] In reality, his letter stands in bitter conflict within the regime, with an outcome difficult to predict. Ali Khamenei, the supreme ayatollah whose power is much greater than Khatami's, is set on harshly intolerant positions, and he is followed by the intransigent clerical wing. It appears that the regime is sending intentionally contradictory signals. It sentences anti-fundamentalist intellectual Hashem Aghajari to death, but the Supreme Court annuls the trial; squads of guardians of the revolution and of sexual morality are no longer seen in action, but flagellation for even moderate erotic displays, although practiced to a lesser extent or hardly ever, is still legally in force and can always be applied, perhaps to someone whose ideas make him unpopular with the regime, which takes advantage of his attentions to the opposite sex to get its revenge. One is not allowed to even shake hands with women when greeting them, yet they hold eminent social roles, they constitute—

according to *Le Monde*—60 percent of university students, and they widely use contraceptives. Those more favorable to reforms are not the young women, who were born and grew up in a world where the earlier Khomeini regime was already established, who therefore did not experience it as a shock but as a given reality. It is their mothers, one of them tells me, who feel that having to wear the chador, for example, or in any case a headscarf, is an outrage, because when they were young they experienced Western modernization, albeit based on repression and even torture of political opponents, as practiced in the regime of the last shah, so quick to flee when his throne was tottering, his chest covered with medals not earned on the battlefield.

Farideh Lashai, a painter and writer of great talent, was at one time held in the prisons of the shah's infamous secret police and wrote of the experience in a book that aroused the perplexity of her fellow supporters and victims of political persecution for the anti-rhetorical sobriety with which she describes her own searing suffering and that of an entire generation. To speak with restraint and objectivity of cruelties endured is the best sign of inner liberation, both premise and consequence of civil liberty. Iran will be a free country when it is no longer necessary—and therefore will no longer be possible—to write books like the very interesting *Reading Lolita in Tehran* by Azar Nafisi, a dissident now emigrated to the United States. That is, when reading Nabokov's masterpiece will be a natural act, neither transgressive nor undertaken with transgressive vanity, because the end of the foolish, despotic ban on a book like *Lolita* (and others) will make it clear that its value lies not in its theme, neither more nor less provocative than others, but in the poetry with which it is narrated, and that pedophilia in itself is certainly no more interesting than the premarital virginity of Renzo and Lucia in *The Betrothed*. At the bookshop of the Hotel Abbasi, in Isfahan, you can also buy the *Decameron*, Kipling, and Brecht, but only in English.

Moralistically repressive societies are also responsible for the

vices that they engender, and on the whole, seeing perversion everywhere, for an upsurge in the idiotic fascination with perversion or
what is presumed such. To the pure all things are pure, the gospel says.
Though Nietzsche adds, "To the swine all things become swinish!"[3]

6. Though early on the Khomeini regime was more explicitly violent and repressive, it now seems to prefer a tacit intimidation. You
can do what you want, they say, but they can do whatever they want
with you. It is surprising to hear even people with a clear-cut role,
such as documented tour guides, openly criticize the government,
affirm that at most 10 percent of the population supports it, and state
that a double moral standard applies, which no one speaks about but
of which everyone is aware. At times the criticism might even seem
to be deliberate, made at the suggestion of the authorities to give foreigners the impression of a more open country. Prostitution does not
officially exist, but fixed-time marriage, only between Muslims, does
officially exist: a man and a woman celebrate a marriage in front of a
mullah, specifying the duration of its validity, in theory even a week
or a night, after which anything is permitted. There is a saying: chador
and nothing underneath.

7. Poets like Sa'di and Hafez repose near the water in Shiraz;
their verses — especially those of Hafez, the Persian lyricist par excellence — change color and flow, unique and infinitely variable, like the
murmur of the waters and of life itself. Revered religiously as well,
Hafez extols God, the eternity of His breath and the dissolution of
every life, at every moment, in that breath — it too perhaps a puff that
vanishes — but he also celebrates wine, roses, nightingales, the intoxi-
cation of an inexhaustible, passionate, undemanding Eros. To love
a fleeting rose is to love the rose that blooms forever, for eternity, in
the mind of God, as the verse of a great seventeenth-century mystic
and Catholic priest, Angelus Silesius, proclaims, a verse which could

be by Hafez or another mystic poet of a different time and place. Mysticism is in fact the abolition of time, the equation of life and death, of the individual "I" and the All in which it is absorbed, dissolving into the shadow of a God so indefinable as to resemble nothing. God is a great Nothing, many German Catholic mystics repeat in the late Middle Ages. The boundaries are blurred between faith in a transcendent God and that in a pantheism in which neither God nor man exists; for Rumi, another great Persian poet, reaching God is the shadow annihilated into light, the breaking of a wave in the sea. Happiness and despair, joyous abandon to love, which envelops and dissolves everything, or sorrow at its waning are almost the same thing; they depend not on a religious or philosophical concept but on a state of mind, maybe on how endorphins react to the same stimulus, to the rose that reminds you of an identical one of last year, perhaps reborn but certainly dead. Though Omar Khayyam views with bleak sadness the inexorable rotation of the planets, enslaved like men, one might also be intoxicated by that monotonous universal necessity, as Hafez was intoxicated by the unfolding of flowers, by the emptied wine cups, and by the young girls and cupbearers who refilled them. Poetry, as a thirteenth century Persian treatise writer, Shams-i Qays, cautioned—as did the Greeks at one time—is also falsehood, fabrication, and immoderate hyperbole.

8. Francesca Toscano brings us to the Armenian Cathedral of Isfahan. The Armenian Christian community, which lives primarily in the adjacent neighborhood, has a seat in Parliament guaranteed by law. Documents and memorabilia recall the great extermination of the Armenians, in particular at the hand of the Young Turks, the first large-scale massacre of the twentieth century, about one-third of the entire population; the discomfiture over whether to call it genocide, characterizing international diplomatic discussions on the subject, is significant. Faced with the testimonies of atrocities, everyone is

left uneasy; I wonder if, among us, Nil Pope Cerrahoglu — a Turkish journalist in the forefront of her country's information channels who, along with her husband, has been our friend for many years — is perhaps especially so. I am well aware of the contradictory feelings that any individual, except those dehumanized by visceral nationalism, experiences in these or similar situations. Faced with a horrible page of the history of one's country, one can easily be seized by conflicting impulses; the urge to gloss over it and move on, but also to dwell on it with even greater obstinacy than that shown to crimes committed by others; the philological scruple of rectifying possibly exaggerated details is hindered by the fear, perhaps not unfounded, that such honest rectification may unconsciously arise from the desire to minimize the incident, as often happens with many revisionist historians. A guilt complex, which does not spring from clear moral awareness but from psychological twists, is a poor counselor.

Is it right and proper or is it wrong to feel responsible for what other people and other political forces in our country have done, which we perhaps opposed? When Mussolini's Italy attacked France, already prostrated by the Germans, Pietro Nenni, then an exile in France, felt the urge to apologize to his French neighbors, though perhaps they should have thanked him since he fought for their freedom as well. Yet it is also true, as Benedetto Croce said, speaking in 1947 to the Constituent Assembly against the peace treaty, that you cannot separate yourself from the good and evil of your homeland. And of all humanity, we might add. That said, it should always be remembered that wrongs and atrocities are not committed by Germans, Serbs, Muslims, or Italians as a whole but rather by particular, specific individuals and political forces. The testimonies of Armenian martyrdom are certainly not an authorization to attack today's Turks or Turkey in general or to underestimate the negative repercussions — as Giampaolo Pope observes, knowing the country in depth as a diplomat and political scholar — that a European stance that is disdainful of Turkey would have today when its moderate Islamist government is looking toward Europe to thereby curb dangerous fundamentalism.

9. In Iran, there are only thirty thousand followers of Zoroaster, but they are respected, and their religion, which has profoundly marked Persian civilization, is recognized; like the Christians and Jews—also fanatically despised by Islamic fundamentalists—they have a seat in Parliament guaranteed by law. Zoroaster (or Zarathustra) is one of the creators of monotheism; it is no accident that the Magi, Zoroastrian priests, traveled to Bethlehem to revere the newborn Jesus, almost as though to symbolize the encounter of the transcendent religions; for the same reason *Nathan the Wise*, Gotthold Lessing's masterpiece of the Enlightenment on the search for truth and religious tolerance, places a representative of Zoroastrianism side by side with those of Christianity, Judaism, and Islam.

Zoroaster was not the first to conceive the idea of one sole transcendent God, but he was the first to proclaim the survival of the individual soul after death and its salvation or perdition based upon good or evil actions. Nietzsche considered him first among those whom he regarded as the corrupters of humanity: Socrates, Plato, Jesus, and the other founders of religions who had sought to restrain the free, natural flow of a life unmindful of good and evil, imposing the chains of morality, faith, values, and all that purports to transcend and repress life. His Zarathustra is one who, released from those chains, liberates men and announces the advent of a new type of man and the death of God. *Thus Spoke Zarathustra*, Nietzsche's only unfortunate, shrill, and bombastic book among his many brilliant and poetic masterpieces, is less appealing than the *Zend Avesta*, the sacred book of Zoroastrianism. Some say that Zoroaster, venerated today in the Fire Temples, died a martyr, others that he died peacefully. One of the fundamental components of our civilization, monotheism, can also be traced back to Iran.

Baha'is are far more numerous than Zoroastrians, but their religion — a branch of Islam that evolved in the nineteenth century — is not recognized, and its worship is not permitted. In the end no one, regretfully, is surprised or shocked by that, maybe because its origin is so recent and we sense the sanctity of religions only when they are enveloped by an aura of antiquity, of remote times, and do not believe that new Revelations may occur in an epoch close to us — even if the temporal distance between Abraham and today, with respect to the age or even just the history of the world, is very brief, an instant as regards millennia.

10. Parched landscapes, cool, green oases, the faces of Afghan girls in Abyaneh, the enchanting, ancient village on the barren mountains near Kashan, with its houses facing East, toward the rising sun. Not far from Kashan, in an arid, sultry region, a ziggurat soars like a grim archaic divinity, the ancient Mesopotamian tower built in overlapping tiers whose width decreases as they get higher, like a pyramid. The ziggurat intrigues the Western imagination with its aura of remote millennia — dark primordial seduction, unfathomable power of myth, tower of Babel, assault on the heavens, altars of idols and ruthless gods. It is above all the assumed sacredness of origins that, even in garish forms at times, makes an impression on us postmodernists fearful or content to be wilted epigones far removed from the sources of life. *Sacred* is a word — and a dimension — that is ambiguous; it also means cursed, untouchable, ominously closed to the profane; modernists all feel, somehow, sacrilegious, whether they agree, with servile pleasure, to stay out of the inaccessible temple of the gods or whether, gripped by periodic iconoclastic rage, they destroy all the temples within reach.

Like any idolatrous superstition, the sacredness and halo of the origin are a mistake, often also a deception. True sanctity is a religious respect for all creation at all times, for all existence — for every home where human beings are born and live, for every grain of wheat that dies and is reborn. When it becomes an arcane cult reserved for privileged, falsely mysterious places, things, or images, it is trickery, deception or self-deception, a room kept in the dark to prevent anyone from realizing that there is nothing inside and that the supposed god is a fetish. Idolatry that relegates God and the divine to a carnival mystery is the enemy of religion. The origin—of an individual, of a nation, of a civilization—is not at all more sacred than any other phase of life. False sacredness is violence, it is the fear and obscurity that every brutal power requires to make men slaves. Climbing this tower of Babel brings to mind the hall in the Palace of Golestan (the imperial palace in Tehran) visited a few days ago, the room where in 1943 Roosevelt, Churchill, and Stalin met and determined—more fully than at the Yalta conference—the division and fate of the world for the next half a century. It is Stalin whom these arcane ruins remind me of. The Stalinist Kremlin—a shrine of power, obscurity, and terror—was in its way a ziggurat. Both distant in time yet with respect to world history very close, contemporary, last night's news.

11. *Teheran.* At the Artists House, to talk about border literature and the issues that such a discussion entails, each time, in new forms and new contexts: uprooting, exile, migrations, obsessive identity, ethnic, political, or religious purity and cleansing, crossbreeding. There are students, diplomats, professors, intellectuals, writers; many women, particularly rigorous in the demand for frank discussion. The conversation, when it touches upon topics that are directly political, clearly has some constraints. I realize that I am uncertain about the right tone to assume, on the fence between respect for truth and respect for individuals, conscientious concern not to put others in difficulty and conventional caution. It would be easy for me to hold forth on freedom, democracy, and the West, not worrying about making others uncomfortable and not having to pay the price, letting them, eventually, pay it. The ethics of responsibility, which takes into account not only the purity of ideals but also their consequences for

others, is a foundation of civic life and of democracy. Never as when traveling, however, does one sense how easily it can taper off into unintentional complicity or at least blameworthy neutrality. Denizens, those who reside there, are forced to fully come to terms with the reality in which they live, without slinking away like those of us who the following night will sleep under another sky. Traveling is immoral, said the uncompromising Otto Weininger. But he said it during a trip . . .

September 5–11, 2004

IS CHINA NEAR?

1. What is lost by writing? Posing the question, with a shy smile on her broad, cheerful face, is a Chinese student and aspiring writer in her first year of Italian studies at the university in Xi'an, the city known for its famous terracotta warriors and the tomb of the first emperor. Her Kafkaesque question comes unexpectedly in this campus classroom where we are discussing the Chinese translation of my *Microcosms*, and indirectly reveals the great distance traveled in recent years by China, which is perhaps nearer — as an old Bellocchio film said in another sense — than we realize.[1] It is Western literature that was questioned and is being passionately questioned with regard to the contradictions of writing, what it gives and what it takes away by pursuing life and standing outside it, grasping the meaning of love and opening to it, but also stepping back in a delirium of omnipotence or narcissistic obsession. Kafka, Mann, and Borges sense the absence that is in every expression; true life sought and lacking causes the compulsive searching that is at times misleading, art that to express existence loses it, the "I" who by writing gives meaning to the world's fluidity but finds himself to be someone else, an actor or substitute for himself.

The question sums up an issue that is exasperatingly Western; it was put to me many years ago in Paris by Maurice Nadeau, one of the greatest living critics, at the presentation of my *Danube*. And so, thanks in part to that query, the arc of years between that Parisian evening and this one in Xi'an seems like a circular journey, an odyssey that leads back home. We talk about it, and at this point the dialogue encounters some difficulty, because — as was the case a few

days earlier in Beijing—while the students display a fairly good literary foundation and excellent linguistic preparation with regard to the
Italian, many of them have only a vague idea of what the *Odyssey* is.
Globalization makes the establishment of a common cultural canon
more and more essential, the development of a core of knowledge
and fundamental values for everyone, beyond any borders of civilization. But the process of globalization encourages and at the same
time hinders the formation of a shared foundation, never more required than it is today; the dizzying over-proliferation of information,
stimuli, and changes constantly deletes itself, destroys the memory,
disintegrates the common cultural fabric. The universal mingling and
extraordinary technological innovations themselves would require,
in a form that is current and extended to new areas of knowledge, the
old universalistic secondary school, which the muddled reforms of recent years in Italy have hastened to dismantle. In a prestigious American college a year ago, only one of thirty-nine students knew who
Marshal Tito was, and that made it difficult to speak with them about
border literature, about Trieste, about central and Eastern Europe.

 With the students in Beijing or Xi'an, guided by first-class instructors, the difficulty is no greater and is virtually overcome by the
fervor of their interest in Italy, which prompts them to seek every
means possible to come study in our country. Today more than ever
living means traveling; the spiritual condition of man as traveler,
which theology speaks of, is also a real condition for ever larger masses
of people. In the dizzying transformations of living, the return—
material and emotional—to oneself appears increasingly uncertain;
today's Ulysses does not resemble Homer's or Joyce's, who eventually
returns home, but rather the one of Dante who is lost in the absolute
or of the *Li Sao* of Qu Yuan, a Chinese Ulyssian adventurer, who ultimately sees his village from above but cannot return to it.

 2. What does it mean to have been in China, to have seen two
cities of a country with 1.2 billion people, which is changing at a pace

so fast that it is hard to follow? It is ridiculous to claim to know it on the run or—as Yao Wenyuan, then Mao's ideological heir apparent, said, quoting a Chinese proverb to Alberto Cavallari, who recounts it in his splendid *Lettera da Pechino* (Letter from Beijing)—claim to contemplate the flowers without dismounting from your horse. Traveling is a school of humility; it lets you see for yourself the limits of your comprehension, the precariousness of the apparatus and methods by which a person or a culture presumes to understand or judge another. Excellent books written about China by noteworthy writers and journalists are surpassed by unpredictable events occurring shortly afterward and are soon no more adequate to those events than the photographs that Maddalena, J., Roberto, and I are taking on the Great Wall.

The gap between the urban reality that you have before you and that of the vast, remote countryside must be enormous, but even the urban reality was radically different a few years ago. The Party is both absent and omnipresent, though imperceptible. No one talks about it—I heard it mentioned only by my interpreter, when he told me about the time he spent working the land during the Cultural Revolution—and you get the impression that nobody or nearly no one is Communist, although the mindset on this point is elusive, perhaps inspired more by an ethics of duty than one of conviction. China's transformation into a capitalist country seems generally accepted and welcomed. But it is the Party that determinedly guides such transformation, namely, its own demise, perhaps without much opposition, managing it so that it occurs in an orderly manner, without the country falling to pieces, without its regressing like Russia or being torn apart—in its ethnic, cultural, and religious diversity—like Yugoslavia, with a bloody price that would be incalculable. So far the process seems to be succeeding; there is a growing middle class (which enjoys a modest but acceptable quality of life) comprised of 250 million inhabitants, I hear from Sergio Balbinot, CEO of Assicurazioni

Generali, which, active for some time in Hong Kong, is expanding in the Chinese market.

If China becomes a modern liberal country, it will happen in spite of communism—the mass exterminations of peasants who died of starvation during the Great Leap Forward, the ideological delusions and violence of the Cultural Revolution, the ruthless repressions—but also thanks to communism, without which the country would have remained in a state of backwardness, poverty, exploitation, and unnamed slavery. This does not justify the violence and the mistakes of yesterday or the human rights violations of today, because no success and no progress can justify any violence, though that applies to all countries, regimes, and organizations, not just to those that are Communist. Nor does economic development justify the current social strictures—similar to those of the initial phase of capitalism in Western countries—which deprive several vulnerable categories of social protection and abandon them to the jungle of savage competition. But Marshal Zhu De, the strategist of the Long March, recalls in his memoirs that his peasant mother did not even have a name, an indigent country woman in China at that time being of such little— or no—value that she did not deserve a name any more than a hen in a chicken coop. The revolution was born and triumphed in part to give a name to people like her. Women—now emerging—are leading figures in the literature. Zhang Jie, a prominent writer in today's China, gives me her latest book translated into German; it is dedicated to a great maternal figure.

3. Although relatively mitigated now, birth control, in its cruel forms—the suffocating restrictions of family life and that of couples, the desire for male children and the resulting harshness of the female condition, the high number of abortions, infanticides—remains one of the most searing scourges of today's China. Once again, it is great literature that, with a radical humanity removed from ideologies and

moralisms, allows us to fully understand a terrible reality. Abortion and abandoned newborns appear insistently in several extraordinary stories by Mo Yan, such as "Explosions." To understand what paternity, maternity, birth, infancy, abortion, abandonment mean—not just in China—just read the pages of this great writer, who does not preach but tells a story, inventing his own language of original and often violent imaginative power, which enabled him to write *Red Sorghum*, a great novel trivialized by the famous but reductionist eponymous film by Zhang Yimou, one of the greatest, most epic books of our time. Mo Yan lives in China. Deeply rooted in his world but in terms that are universal and far removed from those young writers, such as Mian Mian, whose Bukowski-like pages could just as well come from Los Angeles as from Shanghai, he is entirely free of the "chinoiseries" often found in exiled writers, perhaps unconsciously led to "act" Chinese because they fear they are no longer so or because they're trying to appeal to non-Chinese.

4. At the University of Beijing and at the Italian Institute of Culture, to discuss border literature. The ancient "Middle Kingdom" has experience with borders—with their protection and their menace, their obsession, their precariousness.[2] Internal and external borders; there are "one, ten, a thousand Chinas," wrote Francesco Sisci, a great authority on the country, who directs our Cultural Institute. In the second-century poem "Eighteen Songs of a Nomad Flute," the author, Cai Yan, tells her story as a Chinese woman forced to marry a leader of the enemy Huns who had kidnapped her and became the father of her children, flesh of her flesh and at the same time foreign to her. The laceration, the uprooting, the insurmountable walls between cultures divide her from herself, making her a foreigner both in the land of her forced exile and in that of her origins; she feels mutilated but also enriched by such a fate, which enables her to live life and its contradictions more fully.

It is therefore not too difficult to speak here of Scipio Slataper, who proclaimed himself "Slavic, German, and Italian" shortly before creating the literary landscape of Trieste with his "My Karst" and dying in the Great War for the Italian identity of Trieste. I am surprised not to notice any alienation, or almost none, in this city so distant and different, to feel much more at ease than I thought I would. I know quite well that this feeling may apply only to certain particularly Westernized corners, that in this vast country there are millions of square miles in which I would feel lost, and that at any moment an affable yet impenetrable barrier can arise between me and my fellow deliberators. But I did not expect to hear Chinese students recite several passages from my *La mostra* (The Exhibit), including the quips in Triestine dialect.

Among the teachers, of great intellectual vitality, is Lu Tongliu, the chair of the Chinese Italianists. Many years ago, he translated some poems by Biagio Marin. I remember when the elderly poet spoke to me about it in Grado, in the summer of 1984, a few months before he died. The "Daoist of Grado," as Anna Buiatti called him, had always been a great admirer of Tang Dynasty poetry and especially that of Li Bai, which he often read to me when I went to see him. In several letters to his Chinese translator, Marin spoke of their affinity despite the cultural distance: all diversities, he wrote to him, inform our circumstances differently, and it is this diversity that in every creature, in every age, and in every land shapes the eternal that is immanent in each of us. To breathe life into this eternal, he said, we must give it our face, from moment to moment, our intonation, our zest; that distant China, he added, is not foreign to me, it contains my own humanity.

5. War is the mother of all things, Heraclitus said. That is no reason to love it; there are unseemly or unnatural mothers whom it is best to keep away from. But to avoid war or at least contain it, one must understand its logic and mechanisms; oncology too is a distasteful science, though necessary. The great books about the syntax and

grammar of war—from Clausewitz's masterpiece to the writings of Sun Tzu or Mao to *The Edge of the Sword* by De Gaulle—are certainly not silly warmongering adulations, but impressive examinations of a phenomenon which at times assails all of life and which, to be understood and mastered, requires the power of systematic thinking, the intellectual capacity to place every single detail within the totality of the global reality. Of course there are fools in uniform as well, like the clichés portrayed in numerous stale jokes, but some of the most lucid thinkers, free of any bellicose rhetoric, are found in the military; General Powell, for instance, is the figure most untouched by any reckless warlike posturing in the entire current U.S. government.

Unrestricted Warfare, a work by two top-level Chinese colonels, Qiao Liang and Wang Xiangsui, with a preface by General Fabio Mini (himself the author of *La guerra dopo la guerra,* The War After the War, another excellent book recently released by Einaudi), is a masterful work, worthy of Clausewitz. Combining a straightforward, succinct logic and a sharp literary power, like certain science classics, and immune to ideological and propagandistic prejudices, the two authors analyze the global transformation of war, which has transferred it from the battlefield to all sectors of daily life, and offer a pressing and disturbing picture of globalization, in which everything is tied to everything else. At times it seems to read like some of Ernst Jünger's pages on new forms of organizational, workplace, and life conflicts. The two colonels do not love the subject of their science; it is no surprise that at the beginning they quote an ancient sage who recalled how many powerful states had invariably perished when they were scorched by the desire for war.

6. One of the possible reasons for affinity, despite the cultural distance, that I note in these dialogues and encounters is a sense of rapport between the landscape and human beings: the "I" inserted in the landscape not as arrogant protagonist but as a lateral or con-

cealed figure, as in many Chinese paintings. The "I" in the changing colors of things, in the emptiness. Sometimes the "I" itself as emptiness, filled by the landscape: as in the parable of Borges that I chose as the epigraph for my *Microcosms*, which tells of a painter who depicts landscapes—mountains, rivers, trees, Chinese *shan shui*—realizing in the end that he has painted his own self-portrait. Extreme discretion does not obliterate, it intensifies the feeling of passionate life, flowing like a river; *Six Records of a Floating Life* is the title of a novel written by Shen Fu in the late eighteenth century, one of the most beautiful stories about marital love and a shared life.

7. The march of history. Revolutions exacerbate an intolerable pressure exerted by all societies: the imperative to keep step with the times, to march in the direction of History and progress, to follow the day's agenda and what's more be ardent and passionate about it. The current ultra-liberal so-called "groupthink" also has a petulant intolerance typical of a Cultural Revolution, though fortunately less violent. Lao She, the amiable and profound Chinese writer who died— most likely a suicide—during the Cultural Revolution, claimed the right, alternatively, to sympathize with the Revolution but not be a part of it and therefore not write about it; we should not apologize for being old, he said. When he died, some reproached him, saying that suicide is a counterrevolutionary act.

8. It is often recalled with admiration that Mao, conscious of being close to death, told Edgar Snow that he was preparing to meet God. But why should death make God closer and more visible to us? Those who believe in Him, eternal and omnipresent at all times, cannot think that a heart attack or being overtaken on a curve makes Him more accessible, as if death were the threshold of a building whose hidden master will finally show himself once we cross it. Every rose, whether newly blossomed or rotted, is always and forever in the mind of God, wrote the baroque mystic poet and Catholic priest Angelus

Silesius; the poet also said that he was a stream flowing toward the sea of the divinity, though he was already that sea. Mao was more in his element when he said that every death should be observed as a celebration of the dialectic—which is a rush to become—of transformation and dissolution, of the flower—or, as Christians, the seed of wheat—that must die to become and bear fruit.

9. Departure for Vietnam, passing through Hong Kong. A border with China and itself, the Chinese metropolis—not (yet) Chinese—has been, as is every borderland, a place of exiles and refugees, such as those who came mainly from Vietnam. At first the welcome given to the immigrants was warm, but over time and with the growing influx it came to be less so. A terrible term was coined in Hong Kong, "compassion fatigue." Being fed up with compassion may be a fatal attitude bound to spread throughout the world like a virus.

December 12, 2003

THE BORDERS OF VIETNAM

1. *Hanoi.* In 1975 Huu Thinh was behind the wheel of a tank in the march on Saigon, which was ignominiously falling; today he is the president of the Vietnam Writers Association. He has returned from a recent trip to the United States—he tells us at dinner, in a colonial-style French restaurant—where he published a book of poems, *The Time Tree.* Though initially at the reading of his verses in New York there were virulent protests by exiles wearing old South Vietnamese military uniforms, his American tour was nonetheless a literary success as well as an occasion for discussion and encounter. One of his two translators, Nguyen Qui Dúc, was among those who left Vietnam as a child, and this translation is now a way for him to heal that severance, to overcome the borders of war and exile that divide him from his country and from himself. A poem by Huu Thinh speaks about a fragment of life left behind in the flow of years and events. Is it possible to recover the pieces of ourselves that the continual lacerations of living, individually and collectively, rip from us and hurl into the river's current? Peace signifies this as well: reconciliation with everything that is a part of us, one's own country and one's own history.

Peace is sometimes more difficult than war, and no one knows this better than the Communists, often heroic and brilliant victors when it comes to the latter and inept or despotic failures at the former. Vietnam has often successfully fought and prevailed over much more powerful invaders. The epic of the last gloriously victorious war against the French and then against the Americans, which made the Vietnamese successors to the heroes of Thermopylae, is part of a tradition of defeats inflicted, in past centuries or in recent years, on the

Mongols or the Chinese, as a famous play by Peter Weiss, *Discourse on Vietnam*, reminds us. Years ago, as the conflict with South Vietnam and the United States was raging, I happened to hear on television (I think it was a German or Austrian broadcast) an interview with a North Vietnamese leader who said that his people, involved for so long in a war that had occupied several generations, were in grave danger of identifying life with war, of being unable to conceive of life without war.

2. Now, however, I am the one thinking about the war of thirty years ago, about the Tet Offensive or the Ho Chi Minh Trail, more than my Vietnamese hosts and companions. The city—beautiful, not prosperous certainly but with an assured, graceful vitality, its streets jammed with people and motorcycles of all kinds, its pagodas on the lakes—suggests peace and a modest but productive life, not the bombs that rained down for so many years. For the ingenuous traveler, the spatial distance easily becomes a temporal distance that ferries him back to a long-gone past. After the epic victory there was reconstruction, but also violent repression, revenge disguised as reeducation, the persecution of the boat people, and the ruinous, iniquitous land reform—now openly and freely criticized—with its collectivization, which crushed numerous small landowners and created new profiteers and favoritisms. But there was also schooling, a new dignity attained in many sectors. Scant attention is paid to this postwar Vietnam, and this is a grave sin of omission toward a country which offers aspects of extraordinary interest. I am astounded to hear them tell me that I am the first Italian writer to come to Vietnam following the end of the war.

3. At the university, the students and instructors of an Italian language course introduced barely a year ago welcome their visitor with a warm, almost ceremonial hospitality reminiscent of earlier times. The female teachers and students wear the long garment appropriate

for distinguished occasions, which plays up a gentle, enigmatic love-liness. Their passion for Italy is fervent, thanks in part to the astute, enlightened efforts of our ambassador, Luigi Solari, and to their quite remarkable knowledge of Italian. The dialogue with them is intense and open-ended. The instructors—predominantly female—know the Italian university as well as I do and are able to kindle great inter-est in our country among their students. Professor Nguyen van Hoan, a Dante and Classics scholar, talks about the first Vietnamese trans-lation of the *Commedia*; the work of Le Tri Vien and Khuong Huu Dung, it was published in 1979 in a partial edition with a print run of ten thousand copies, exceptional in a country prostrated by war. The volume was enthusiastically received, despite the cultural distance between Italy and Vietnam, and the difficulty of translating from Italian, a polysyllabic language, into Vietnamese, essentially mono-syllabic; not to mention the challenge of devoting time and energy to the endeavor at a time when the war and later the postwar period absorbed all one's efforts.

The same scholar, though a fervent Vietnamese patriot, recalls how another literary academic, Professor Dang Thai Mai, whose essays on humanism and the Renaissance paved the way for the re-ception of Dante, had been criticized because his studies did not serve the country's immediate strategic needs. Reading Nguyen van Hoan's writings on Dante or on Ca Dao, South Vietnamese popu-lar poetry ("to love one another is also to love the path one travels together"), one gets a sense of the universality of poetry, of that humanity cherished by Goethe's writer friend Johann Gottfried von Herder: a sole immense tree made up of a diversity of leaves, roots, branches, and flowers.

What's striking, of course, is the gaps in information. The most recent Italian book to be translated here, they tell me, is Dino Buz-zati's *Il deserto dei tartari* (The Tartar Steppe); it's amazing that *The Name of the Rose* has not been translated and is so little known. Dur-ing the talk on border literature at the French Institute introduced by

Ha Minh Duc, a Vietnamese author declares himself a reader and an admirer of "the famous Italian writer Carlo Rossi," convinced that he is mentioning a name as renowned as Alberto Moravia's, and I don't have the heart to tell him that I have no idea who that is. These disparities say a lot about the diffusion of culture, its limits and its obstruction. And yet it is not at all difficult to talk to these individuals about my world. Perhaps it is not a world all that distant from theirs, since they too, having experienced it for themselves, know all too well what a border means, the laceration, the expatriation, the estrangement.

4. To some extent, for me, getting to know a country involves diving into its sea, experiencing the density of the water, its luminosity and clarity, its taste — naturally the criterion and reference point is always the Mediterranean, as it is for Raffaele La Capria: Naples' Tyrrhenian Sea for him, the Istrian and Dalmatian Adriatic for me. The water in Halong Bay is jade-green, dense without being opaque, and has a tropical warmth; a last taste of summer, a summer that does not seem like an ephemeral season but rather a way of being, a condition. Enchanting islands and cliffs frame the vast gulf; the boat skims by slimy caves, yielding and crumbly. Rather than the Vietnam of today, the landscape evokes the atmosphere found in the novels of Graham Greene or Marguerite Duras. The tropics is like sinking into deeper layers of reality, into a vital silt, soft and earthy like the smell of durian, which the guides warn you not to take into your room, and which in fact poor Emilio Salgari, who had probably never had occasion to taste one, pronounced acrid for European palates. Even tastes and smells, the most sensual details, can be discovered on the printed page, staying home and only "traveling," like Salgari, in the library. On the way back to Hanoi, the enchantment of evening falls damp and swift; in an undersea light, the countryside glides by, plowed and irrigated, buffalo in the fields, the houses curiously narrow since taxes are levied according to the width of the facade. Under a large conical hat, the beautiful face of a woman, eyes raised to glimpse the car

as it passes by; in an instant it's gone, outdistanced, one of the many things left behind.

5. The country, ruled by a single party, ideologically rejects Western democracy, even though the speech in which Ho Chi Minh proclaimed the independence of the Democratic Republic of Vietnam on September 2, 1945, was full of references to the American Declaration of Independence. Today a spirited, courageous dissident literature denounces state-party control, freedom violations, and an insinuating parasitism, often combining political commitment with linguistic experimentation and the pursuit of creative expression. These writers are almost always individuals who have fought for the liberation of their country, like Bao Ninh—a kind of Vietnamese Erich Maria Remarque—whose *Sorrow of War* portrays with laconic power the devastation of a conflict whose battlefront is everywhere, or like Duong Thu Huong, the leader of a youth brigade during the war, who later became committed to the defense of human rights, was expelled from the Party and briefly imprisoned, and who a few weeks ago left Vietnam for France. In her intense books—*Paradise of the Blind*, for example—a determined political and social criticism is accompanied by the evocation of a tragic but enchanting landscape. In Pham Thi Hoài's novel *The Crystal Messenger*, on the other hand, the condemnation becomes subtle and grotesque, describing a world of emptiness and absence; it also becomes a metaphor for an existential maladjustment, a refusal to grow up.

Criticism from within is perhaps more factual and effective than that of exiled writers, which is inevitably, though understandably, marked by a certain bitterness that often obscures or distorts one's gaze. Alongside the official association of dissident writers and authors, there are also informal associations such as the East-West Center, headed by Hoang Thuy Toan, an extremely dynamic circle of writers, translators, and literary figures, with whom discussion is immediately open, liberal, and frank, even regarding awkward subjects.

This cordiality seems to bring people together, beyond their political and cultural positions. At dinner they are all affably together, official (or at least sanctioned) authors along with rebels such as Nguyên Huy Thiêp, author of *The General Retires*, a novel that caused a stir for its harsh denunciation and linguistic creativity. Bao Ninh is not necessarily correct when he writes that the ardent determination which at one time saved the country no longer exists.

6. Trấn Quốc Pagoda, on Ho Tay (West Lake) in Hanoi (one of the many lakes which refine the city and render it more graceful) is one of the oldest in the country.[1] In its gardens are the tombs of various monks, including the burial site of the abbot who preceded the current one. In a few years his remains will be moved elsewhere, as is customary; death does not result in permanent possession, not even of a grave, but, like everything else, involves further passage and transition. There is a funeral. Several Buddhist monks are praying, family and friends of the deceased are consuming the funeral meal. Composed, kindly faces, hospitable gestures. An old woman offers J. some apples, for her and for me; and so, for a moment, we too take part in this communion for an unknown brother who has left us behind. Distant prayers, worlds apart; imitating them would be ridiculous. The Dalai Lama is so right when he advises us not to convert from one religion to another, not even to his. Like any dialogue, even the ecumenical one must maintain its distinctions, an encounter of diverse individuals. It is this that allows us to become closer, to feel united in a common pietas, over and above our own unique qualities.

7. A temple is dedicated to Literature. Unlike a pagoda, a temple does not necessarily have a religious purpose; it can be dedicated to institutions, values, and traditions, in a spirit that is religious in a broad sense, such as veneration of life, of history, of memories. This one — a university that dates back to 1079 — is devoted primarily to learned men and scholars who, starting in 1442, passed the doctoral

examinations. Numerous studies record the names of the candidates and the marks they achieved. Rarely have I felt such a profound sense of respect for learning, tradition, exams, and academic standing; this too plays a role in shaping a country's strength, its ability to grow and endure. Perhaps knowing more about grammar and syntax, even the Latin passive periphrastic, helps one to know men, to be less ingenuously unprepared amid the world's chaos. In the library inside this temple is a book, in English, by Robert McNamara, the U.S. secretary of defense at the time of the war: *In Retrospect: The Tragedy and Lessons of Vietnam.* Hindsight, as the saying goes . . .

8. A figure emblematic of the reality and of the literature is the person of mixed birth, the unwanted son or daughter of a Vietnamese woman and an American soldier; a soldier who more often than not, at the time of the defeat, left behind not only the country but also his family. Often these children of war, as small landowners after the agrarian reform, found themselves exposed to oppression, ostracism, and violence, divided within themselves as well, cut in two by a border of hatred that passed through their body. *The Unwanted,* in fact, is the title of a novel by Kien Nguyen, an autobiographical account of this cruel odyssey. It is a book written in English, like that of another Vietnamese-American writer, Le Ly Hayslip, who in her book *When Heaven and Earth Changed Places* (written with Jay Wurts) describes the atrocities committed on all sides, by the French, the Viet Cong, the Americans, the South Vietnamese, and the allies and accomplices of one or the other. In these pages, war and violence especially strike at the weakest moments and stages of life: childhood, old age, prenatal existence. Babies and those as yet unborn, at the mercy of ruthless brutality, are a recurring motif: tragic, touching figures of exposed, defenseless humanity.

These exiles do not idealize the pre-Communist reality; in his novel *The Tapestries,* Kien Nguyen re-evokes the barbarism of the feudal and colonial past. But as often happens with writers in exile—

all the more if they come from a country culturally set apart—they sometimes run the risk of writing "for others," in a kind of unintentional literature course for foreigners.

9. It is not always easy to determine where progress lies. At the time of French colonization in the nineteenth century, an intellectual like Tôn Tho Tüöng supported collaboration with the invaders, in part because he also saw them as bringing about a modernization that would loosen ancient shackles; another figure, Phan Thanh Gian, was a patriot who resisted compromise with the exploitative occupier, celebrating archaic values, reactionary traditions, and feudal hierarchies. One is reminded of the powerful passage where Cesare Cases recalls an ancestor of his, a rabbi from Reggio, who had confronted Napoleon, First Consul of France, accusing him of destroying Jewish identity with measures that made all citizens equal and abolished discrimination and racial ghettos.

10. The mausoleum of Ho Chi Minh is closed. At this time of year his mummy is being restored, to better preserve it. According to an urban legend, our escort tells us, the mummy is sent to Moscow for these "facelifts," a place that today seems unlikely for such operations. It is tempting to imagine this surreptitious transport, the mummy loaded on the train, the bodyguards, the possible accidents along the way. The small lake in front of us, with its large water lilies, is at odds with these bizarre fantasies, as are the poems written— even in prison—by the great revolutionary leader. Classical lyrics, evening skies with high clouds scudding above the prisoner, a flute and a solitary woman, the individual set in just the right place in nature—neither arrogantly in the center nor insignificant or secondary. Writing poetry, one of his poems says, helps while awaiting freedom.

11. Devotion to family, conjugal love, and hearth and home have a steadfast presence in Vietnamese tradition. This pure affection does

not discount sentimental complications, but resolves them in an intense clarity of attachments devoid of ambiguity. This is expressed in the legend of the woman who, remarried after leaving her perpetually drunk first husband, reencounters him as a beggar and comes to his aid. Seeing her new husband arrive, and fearing that he may have unfounded suspicions, she imprudently hides her former spouse in the fireplace, where he dies; she too will die there in the flames out of remorse, and her second husband will willingly die there as well, unable to live without her. A multifaceted, choral love — yet limpid and chaste, so as not to interfere with the love between a couple — is an age-old dream. Even Goethe longs for it in his play *Stella*, except that his drama is about a man and two women, whereas the Vietnamese legend — as though to redeem the dignity of women trampled by feudal, peasant tradition — concerns a woman and two men.

12. We return home. Many of my friends ask me how come I never get tired of traveling so much, often to such distant places. On the contrary, it's staying home that's tiring, in one's own city and one's own world, ground down by nagging thoughts and obligations, pricked by a thousand everyday arrows, inconsequentially poisonous, oppressed by the idols of one's own tribe. Furthermore, it's at home that one's life, one's joy and sorrow, one's passion and destiny are played out, for better or worse. Travel, even the most zealous kind, is always a hiatus, an escape, irresponsibility, a break from any real risk. So we go back home, to the adult, serious, intrusive world. Sometimes, like the protagonist in *Mua Oi* (The Guava House), Dang Nhat Minh's film, you really don't want to grow up, but would prefer to shrink, go into hiding, maybe — like the gnomes under the mushrooms in fairy tales — under one of those big conical Vietnamese hats that we dutifully take home as a souvenir.

December 14, 2003

THE GREAT SOUTH

1. On every journey, at every start, some senses are heightened and others dulled. Dozing off are the antennas of suspicious, anxious daily surveillance, usually prompt at registering the signals of anything that can threaten the order and rule of the little world within our power; starting out also means letting go, shedding the ballast, squinting your eyes as when looking at the sun, seizing whatever comes along. The perception of colors reawakens, along with that of scents, the smooth or rough touch of things, even insignificant details. A city is also revealed in the shimmer of its clouds, in the quality of its light, in its lingering sunsets or abrupt nightfalls. Going from the Sydney Airport to the downtown area you already instinctively notice the difference between the varieties of eucalyptus along the roads with a much more focused attention than that given to the shrubbery you happen to pass on your way to the office, which often remains just generic vegetation.

The journalists I meet at the Sydney Writers' Festival don't ask me what I think of Australia, and that breezy freedom suggests a great country of vast horizons, inner ones as well, very different from the oppressive insecurity that reigns in places—at times even in my Trieste—where people are too caught up with themselves and with the image of themselves that is projected to others. Besides, it would obviously be ridiculous to draw conclusions about a continent after a few days. Luckily a book by Guerrino Lorenzato, *La visione italiana dell'Australia* (The Italian View of Australia), an occasionally controversial survey of the impressions of visiting travelers, warns against hasty opinions. Perhaps Emilio Salgari, who naturally had never had the opportunity to go there, described Australia better than some who have seen it, in the adventures of the *Continente misterioso* (The Mysterious Continent) and the *Pescatori di Trepang* (Fishermen of Trepang). But then Salgari, in his own way and in his own dimension, was a genius . . .

One has the feeling of being in an open, vigorous country, during what is perhaps the most felicitous phase of capitalist development. Having overcome the tumultuous, barbarous period of initial growth, with its great expansion, its creative force, its brutality, and its injustices, Australia seems to be experiencing a time of orderly, civilized productive energy. One doesn't notice — or at least the traveler, perhaps not very discerning, doesn't notice — the frantic, overwhelming metastases of Western capitalism, incredibly vital and a source of benefit, but also, like a cancerous proliferation, which is also an expansion of life, destined and driven to grow unabatedly, to invade and engulf everything, to expand in all directions and into every material and spiritual sector of existence: a process that is unprecedented in the history of the world and that, if and when it comes to an end — and it is sure to end, though in a still far-off era, since eternity is not of this world — will bring about something that we cannot imagine, a radical transformation comparable only to the collapse of the ancient world but even more colossal, being of planetary proportions.

On this fifth continent there is the sensation of great spaces — not just physical — that are not yet occupied, of time marked by a more traditional rhythm; the future somehow appears more stable and the extreme multi-ethnic and multicultural diversity seems like a manifest, harmonious condition, not the apocalyptic chaos depicted in films such as *Blade Runner*. During these days, for example, only the intensity with which the Indonesian crisis is experienced, as a reality that touches people directly, makes you feel that you are not in Europe. Perhaps the scores of emigrants, besides finding work here, have also found breathing space. An elderly, chatty Chinese taxi driver takes me back to the city from a windy beach on Botany

Bay, the largest bay reached for the first time by Captain Cook in 1770, where I spent the morning amid thunderous waves and surf and numerous pelicans, and tells me about his flight, many years ago, from Manchuria. "From the Japanese invasion?" I ask him. "No, from the Communists," he replies, adding that there were, and are, always many occasions and reasons to escape. But he talks about it serenely, without acrimony.

At the Sydney Writers' Festival the recently released book *The Stolen Children* is presented. It is about the Aboriginal Australians. Their tragic stories, along with the infamous penal colonies whose convicts are for the most part the nation's forebears, constitute the fulcrum of Australian history, a topic long debated with impassioned controversy. The plight of the Aboriginal peoples is well known; they officially became extinct in 1876, in Tasmania (although there is talk now of descendants, at least from mixed marriages), with the death of a woman, Trucanini, who in her will took care to prohibit having her body exposed and studied by scientists like that of a prehistoric animal.

Now there is an effort to protect, albeit with contradictory measures, existing Aboriginal peoples, whose properties are being returned but to whom the government, unlike the American one, is reluctant to apologize. *The Stolen Children* concerns one of these measures, in this case with catastrophic outcomes. A few decades ago, many Aboriginal children were wrested from their families by force or deception—taken from normal parents who cared for them—and given to white families so that they would grow up to become white, apart from the color of their skin. The book brings together the stories—often intense, laconic poetry devoid of sentimental pathos—of these forced adoptions, of the search of parents and lost children, respectively, and often of the violence, humiliation, and various abuses which those uprooted children were exposed to in their new, imposed, and generally appalling families.

But the book, which focuses on these infamies, does not fully address the overall problem of this painful event, namely the good intention that had promoted those measures. Besides a racist contempt for the Aboriginals, viewed solely as semi-brutish savages to be civilized, others probably believed that their population was too small and weak to be able to truly maintain their identity with dignity, that they were inevitably destined for extinction, and before that to a degrading debasement. The only possible way to save those children therefore seemed to be to uproot them violently from their world and make them become white — though the concern must not have been very heartfelt, given the negligence with which the adoptive families, often brutal, were chosen. In any case the story, besides being one of many accounts of abused children, is also one of the tragedies of enlightenment, of projects meant to rescue people by force, against their will.

Perhaps only today, despite the long road still ahead, can the beginning of a real chance of survival for the Aboriginal people be seen, not in contrived isolation but in an integration that preserves the meaning of their origin and inclusion; the only salvation lies in a twofold, multiple identity, not frozen in legend. David Malouf, whom I see again at the festival after several years, wrote the sad, dramatic story, for example, of a dual, rejected identity in his *Remembering Babylon*, an intense narrative about a white boy raised by Aboriginal Australians in the previous century and spiritually lost in a no-man's-land.

2. Lizard Island is a northern island in the Great Barrier Reef, between the Tropic of Capricorn and the Equator. Lizards three feet long grudgingly yield to you on the trail, birds of every color flutter among the dense vegetation splashed with showy flowers; some of them, a dazzling white, gleam like stars when night falls abruptly, virtually dispensing with sunset. A group of seagulls — one in particular, with a more malevolent eye than the others — is preventing a weaker, limping gull from approaching the food. The air is filled with an in-

tense fragrance. It seems natural to hold a huge grasshopper in your hand, any aversion forgotten. At certain moments beauty is unbearable and ruthless, Apollo flaying Marsyas, at other times it is letting go, blissful sleep: "Sleep and long life" was a greeting meant to bode well in Samoa in Robert Louis Stevenson's time.

The sea, turquoise on the reef, is an absolute Gauguin-like blue in the distance. But Raffaele La Capria is not wrong when he acclaims the Mediterranean—its colors its allure its gods—over the oceans. This Pacific, with its dark, reddish rocks, lacks the white stone of the Dalmatian Sea, which together with the bora or the mistral gives the waters, as in Sardinia, a more breezy, affecting transparency. But here there are corals and fish with iridescent colors; one swims underwater among fantastic efflorescences, blue golden purple; it is like penetrating the convolutions of a brain. In aerial photographs the shoals and atolls look like enlargements of cells affected by pathological changes. In a fractal structure of the universe, in which every detail reproduces the articulation and disarticulation of the whole, there is perhaps no difference between illness and health—there is only, as Italo Svevo had staggeringly understood, a great, terrifying health, unsustainable for the consciousness and existence of the single individual.

In Sydney, thanks to Giovanna Jatropelli, who directs the Italian Cultural Institute with great sensitivity and enterprise, I meet some Italians, mainly from Trieste and Istria, immigrants for decades. I listen to stories of hardships, courage, difficulties overcome through hard work and an adventurous taste for life; compared to those people's odyssey, individuals who travel like me and my colleagues, to give a decent enough lecture and read some of their own writings, are merely extras on the world's stage, stand-ins for real life. These are people tied to their land of origin but open to the world and rooted in their new homeland, which they love as much as they do Italy and the region from which they came; they make you see that the only genuine identity is not the monolithically regressive one applauded by ethnic ravings, but one that is at once loyal and transportable, capable of being enriched by a new sense of belonging.

In the stories they tell me, work and family affections combine with a robust zest for life, without which any morals are fastidiously acidulous and any earnest hard work is a grim penance. One of them, an Istrian, tells me that on his first trip back to Italy to visit relatives — after a number of years, since it was necessary to save up for a house and send the children to the best schools — during a stopover in Messina they discovered that the ship's captain and a couple of officers were also from Trieste, from Istria, or from Losinj, and they celebrated the discovery with a lavish dinner and generous libations, until they realized, with dismay, that by that time the ship must already have left. Only when they were about to rush off to the port, alarmed, did it occur to the captain that they were the only ones who could sail the ship, so they treated themselves to another round of bottles.

In Port Arthur, Tasmania: a land of variable beauty, barely penetrable forests, steep coastal cliffs against which the ocean pounds furiously. Port Arthur is one of the dreadful prisons upon which Australia was born, thanks to England's deportation of convicts, in a horrific epic of suffering and barbarity narrated with unforgettable power by Robert Hughes in *The Fatal Shore*. Isolation cells in freezing, total darkness, unspeakable conditions. At Point Puer, on an island a few hundred yards off the coast, docents point out to tourists the high rocky cliffs from which children jumped to kill themselves when they could no longer stand it; children too were deported or sentenced to death for minor thefts, with unimaginable cruelty, in a primitive ignorance of the due proportion between crime and punishment that is a foundation of law and social order.

On the nearby Isle of the Dead there are prisoners' graves; the tombstones are abridged novels of incredible lives, villainous, violent, or just unfortunate, but almost all assisted by a fierce, untamed capacity to withstand unimaginable conditions.[1] A certain Dennis Collins, for example, not mentioned by Hughes, knowingly went to the gallows for not resisting the satisfaction of throwing a stone at the head of King William IV, who had denied him a pension to which he felt entitled for serving in the navy. Had he thought of evening the score by killing the king, his crime would have merely been a banal offense; braving the scaffold for the pleasure of giving the sovereign a lump on the head is a gesture whose grandness cannot be denied.

In the evening I return to Hobart Town, the capital of Tasmania; I wander through the streets and deserted docks in the rain, along the great estuary of the Derwent which already seems like the sea. When the Europeans arrived for the first time, in 1803, the mouth of the river was populated by whales. Beyond the empty expanse of sea lies nothing until Antarctica and the South Pole, and therefore nothing at all. It is the only time, on this journey to the antipodes, the great South, when I feel truly far away, at the end of the world. "How do you like it here?" I ask an Italian who has lived here for many years. "Well, I don't really care, you know," he replies, "so this is just the right place."

June 13–17, 1998

NOTE

With respect to the original edition, published in French in
Françoise Brun's translation in 2002, in the collection *Voyager avec*,
edited by Maurice Nadeau (Paris: La Quinzaine Littéraire Louis
Vuitton), the present volume contains additional chapters (on China,
Iran, and Vietnam) and has been modified or amply supplemented
in others; the Preface was also revised and expanded. I wish to especially thank Renata Colorni, who encouraged the Italian edition of
this book.

Preface

1. "Here, if one is willing and receptive, one can easily fill oneself to the brim like an open bottle plunged under water." Johann Wolfgang von Goethe, *Italian Journey, 1786–1788*, trans. Elizabeth Mayer (Harmondsworth, U.K.: Penguin, 1970), 373.

2. "There sat the man who had traced to their source the mighty ponds of Hampstead, and agitated the scientific world with his Theory of Tittlebats, as calm and unmoved as the deep waters of the one on a frosty day, or as a solitary specimen of the other in the inmost recesses of an earthen jar." Charles Dickens, *The Posthumous Papers of the Pickwick Club* (New York: Sheldon, 1867), 1:21.

3. Now Rijeka, Croatia.

4. The phrase is taken from the poem "In lieblicher Blaue," by Friedrich Hölderlin, which begins: "In lovely blue the steeple blossoms / With its metal roof." The verse referred to reads: "Well deserving, yet poetically / Man dwells on this earth." The second quotation is from "Patmos": "Yet where danger lies, / Grows that which saves." Friedrich Hölderlin, *Hymns and Fragments*, trans. Richard Sieburth (Princeton: Princeton University Press, 1984), 249, 89.

5. Don Quixote replies to the peasant Pedro Alonso, his neighbor, "I know who I am, and I know that I may be not only those I have named, but . . . even all the nine Worthies." Miguel de Cervantes, *Don Quixote*, trans. John Ormsby (1964), BompaCrazy.com, part 1, chap. 5.

6. "'Whither are we going?' 'Ever homewards.'" Novalis (Friedrich von Hardenberg), *Henry of Ofterdingen: A Romance* (Cambridge, Mass.: John Owen, 1842), 203.

7. "*True genesis is not at the beginning but at the end,* and it starts to begin only when society and existence become radical, i.e. grasp their roots . . . [then] there arises in the world something which shines into the childhood of all and in which no one has yet been: homeland." Ernst Bloch, *The Principle of Hope [Das Prinzip Hoffnung]*, trans. Neville Plaice (Cambridge: MIT Press, 1995), 1375–1376.

8. "Leave everything. Leave Dada. Leave your wife, leave your mistress. Leave your hopes and fears. Sow your children in the corner of a wood. Leave the substance for the shadow . . . Set out on the road." André Breton, "Lâchez tout," in *Littérature* n.s., no. 2 (April 1922), repr. and trans. in Dawn Ades, *Dada and Surrealism Reviewed*, exh. cat. (London: Arts Council of Great Britain, 1978), 166.

9. The quotation from Jorge Luis Borges is one of the epigraphs to Claudio Magris, *Microcosms*, trans. Iain Halliday (London: Harvill, 1999).

10. "Gather round, fishes, those of you to the right still in the River Douro and those of you to the left in the River Duero." José Saramago, "The Douro and the Duero: the Sermon of the Fishes," in *Journey to Portugal: In Pursuit of Portugal's History and Culture*, trans. Amanda Hopkinson and Nick Caister (New York: Houghton Mifflin Harcourt, 2002), 3.

11. Bernard Malamud, *The Fixer* (New York: Farrar, Straus and Giroux, 2004), 312. John Leonard writes in a review ("The Shaman and the Schlemiel," *New York Review of Books*, January 19, 1984): "According to Yakov Bok in *The Fixer*, 'Once you leave you're out in the open; it rains and snows. It snows history, which means what happens to somebody starts in a web of events outside the personal.' And the Malamudim, his victims, imaginary Jews in an imaginary ghetto, leave home for history surprisingly often, on quests, to Rome or Kiev or Chicago or Vermont . . . there to find another tenement and another prison, more bad weather and bad luck."

12. Cervantes, *Don Quixote*, chap. 23.

13. Cees Nooteboom, *The Following Story*, trans. Ina Rilke (San Diego: Harvest, 1996), 4.

14. "If there is a sense of reality, there must also be a sense of possibility. . . . To pass freely through open doors, it is necessary to respect the fact that they have solid frames. This principle, by which the old professor had lived, is simply a requisite of the sense of reality. But if there is a sense of reality,

and no one will doubt that it has its justifications for existing, then there must also be something we can call a sense of possibility." Robert Musil, *The Man Without Qualities*, trans. Sophie Wilkins (New York: Vintage, 1996), 1:10.

15. "And so it is that the traveller plunges deeper into his own allergies, his own imbalances, hoping that through those chinks slashed in the back-cloth of daily living, there might be at least a puff of wind or a draught coming from what is truly life, though concealed by the screen of reality." Claudio Magris, *Danube*, trans. Patrick Creagh (New York: Farrar, Straus and Giroux, 2011), 26.

16. "Travel is immoral, since it is supposed to be the annulment of space within space." Otto Weininger, *Collected Aphorisms, Notebook and Letters to a Friend*, trans. Martin Dudaniec and Kevin Solway (self-published, 2000– 2002), 50, available at http://www.huzheng.org/geniusreligion/aphlett.pdf.

17. "Travelling, one accepts everything; indignation stays at home. One looks, one listens, one is roused to enthusiasm by the most dreadful things because they are new. Good travellers are heartless." Elias Canetti, *The Voices of Marrakesh: A Record of a Visit*, trans. J. A. Underwood (London: Marion Boyars, 2002), 23–24.

18. "But Fear and Menace climb up to the same place / where the lord climbs up, and dark Care will not leave / the bronze-clad trireme, and even sits / behind the horseman when he's out riding." Horace, "Odi Profanum," in *The Odes*, book 3, ode 1, trans. A. S. Kline (2003), available at Poetry in Translation, http://www.poetryintranslation.com/PITBR/Latin/Horace OdesBkIII.htm.

19. Giorgio Bergamini, review of Magris's essay "Il mito absburgico," in the Trieste daily *Piccolo*, November 6, 1963.

20. Musil, *Man Without Qualities*, vol. 1, chap. 84: "Assertion That Ordinary Life, Too, Is Utopian."

21. "And safe to harbour, through the deep untried, / Let him, empower'd, their wand'ring vessels guide." Luís Vaz de Camoes, *The Lusiad; or, The Discovery of India*, trans. W. J. Mickle (London: George Bell and Sons, 1877), 13. "Haven't we, together and upon the immortal sea, wrung out a meaning from our sinful lives?" Joseph Conrad, *The Nigger of the "Narcissus*," ed. Robert Kimbrough (New York: Norton, 1979), 92.

22. Grigory Potemkin is said to have erected fake settlements along the

banks of the Dnieper River in order to fool Empress Catherine II during her visit to Crimea in 1787. The phrase is now used to describe a construction, literal or figurative, built to deceive others into thinking that a situation is better than it really is.

23. "What can a man not learn when he once ventures forth from hearth and home!" Joseph von Eichendorff, *The Life of a Good-For-Nothing*, trans. Michael Glenny (London: Blackie, n.d.), 44. Available at http://www.archive.org/stream/lifeofgoodfornotooeichuoft/lifeofgoodfornotooeichuoft_djvu.txt.

24. "Noi invece che abbiamo per patria il mondo, come i pesci il mare, noi, che pure prima di mettere i denti abbiamo bevuto l'acqua dell'Arno e amiamo Firenze tanto da subire ingiustamente l'esilio per averla amata, noi poggiamo le spalle del nostro giudizio sulla ragione piuttosto che sul senso." Dante Alighieri, *De vulgari eloquentia*, ed. Sergio Cecchin, in *Opere minori di Dante Alighieri*, vol. 2 (Turin: UTET, 1986), 1.6, available at http://www.classicitaliani.it/dante/prosa/vulgari_ita.htm.

25. An essay on Walter Benjamin by Beatrice Hanssen begins: "An anecdote in which Kant captures himself in pithy fashion: [Kant's] Famulus, a theologian who was unable to connect philosophy to theology, once asked Kant for advice as to what he should read on the subject. Kant: Read travel literature. Famulus: In dogmatic philosophy, there are things I do not understand. Kant: Read travel literature." Beatrice Hanssen, "Physiognomy of a Flâneur: Walter Benjamin's Peregrinations Through Paris in Search of a New Imaginary," in Hanssen, ed., *Walter Benjamin and the Arcades Project* (London: Continuum, 2006), 1.

26. "And again they are silent, until the German cries out, 'Then why the devil are you sitting here in the saddle, riding through this godforsaken country to meet the Turkish dogs?' The Marquis smiles. 'So that I can return.'" Rainer Maria Rilke, *The Lay of the Love and Death of Christoph Cornet Rilke* [*Die Weise von Liebe und Tod des Cornets Christoph Rilke*], trans. Stephen Mitchell (Minneapolis: Graywolf Press, 1985), 17. Rilke wrote the poem in 1899, when he was twenty-three; later republished in 1912, it inspired German soldiers on the front lines during World War I, who carried it in their knapsacks.

27. Palermo, a neighborhood in the Argentine capital, Buenos Aires, is

named after the capital of Sicily. It is "Borgesian" because Jorge Luis Borges once lived there, and it is where he wrote his first poetry. Borges's poem "Fundacion mitica de Buenos Aires" mentions a square adjacent to his childhood home in the barrio.

28. The reference is to Charles Baudelaire. In an essay written in 1935, Walter Benjamin discusses Baudelaire, a poet he considered emblematic of the modern city and its changes. *"Le voyage pour connaître ma géographie.* Record of a journey. (Paris 1907)" is one of the pieces found in Walter Benjamin, "Paris—Capital of the Nineteenth Century," sect. 5, "Baudelaire or the Streets of Paris," available at http://nowherelab.dreamhosters.com /paris%20capital.pdf, p. 85.

In Don Quixote's Footsteps

1. The Spanish title of Miguel de Cervantes Saavedra's work is *El ingenioso hidalgo don Quijote de la Mancha.*

2. Fyodor Dostoyevsky paid high tribute to Cervantes, and critics have noted the influence of *Don Quixote* on Dostoyevsky's *The Idiot* and *Crime and Punishment.* In *A Writer's Diary*, trans. K. A. Lantz (Evanston, Ill.: Northwestern University Press, 2009), 449, Dostoyevsky wrote: "Oh, this is a great book. . . . Man will not forget to take this *saddest* of all books with him to God's last judgment."

3. Antonio Muñoz Molina (b. 1956) is a Spanish writer whose first novel, *Beatus Ille*, appeared in Spain in 1986. The passage is found in Edith Grossman's translation, *A Manuscript of Ashes* (New York: Houghton Mifflin Harcourt, 2008), 4: "Once, when the boy went with him to visit someone, his father stopped next to the fountain and with the sad irony that was, as Minaya learned many years later, his only weapon against the tenacity of his failure, he said . . ."

4. In ancient times Lake Avernus, near Naples, was looked upon as a portal to the underworld, from whose waters vile-smelling vapors rose, supposedly killing birds that flew over it.

5. In John Ormsby's translation of *Don Quixote* (1964), part 2, chap. 17, the lion "turned about and presented his hind-quarters."

6. The verse "y la última hora, negra y fría, / se acerca, de temor y sombras llena" (and now the last hour, black, and cold, and drear / approaches,

full of shadows and of fear) is from the sonnet beginning "Ya formidable y espantoso suena." (The sonnet can be found online in Alix Ingber, "Thinking and Writing About Poetry," at http://sonnets.spanish.sbc.edu/analyses.html [accessed May 25, 2017].)

7. The lines are from the poem "Mientras por competir con tu cabello": Luis de Góngora y Argote, "While yet, in competition with your hair," in *Selected Sonnets*, trans. A. S. Kline, 2012, available at Poetry in Translation, http://www.poetryintranslation.com/PITBR/Spanish/Gongora.htm.

8. Félix Arturo Lope de Vega y Carpio (1562–1635) was a Spanish playwright and poet whose reputation in the sphere of Spanish literature is said to be second only to that of Cervantes. He was about to become a priest when he fell in love, and the church's loss was a gain to Spanish theater since Lope de Vega did some of his best writing when he was in love. His sonnet 78 contains these lines: "Dust now, but ever lovely, / that light that takes my life lives on serene. / [And what] was once my pleasure and my pain / wages war on me, but rests in peace." Quoted in Isabel Torres, "Outside In: The Subject(s) at Play in *Las rimas humanas y divinas de Tomé de Burguillos*," in *A Companion to Lope de Vega*, ed. Alexander Samson and Jonathan Thacker (Woodbridge, Suffolk: Boydell and Brewer, 2008), 106.

9. "Cuántos paisajes con tu mismo dolor se alejan de ti, / se sumergen en sí mismos, te exculpan. / Oh! Si supieran que tu existes y los amas." The lines are from "Para no ir a parte alguna," the title poem of César Antonio Molina, *Para no ir a parte alguna* (Valencia: Editorial Pre-Textos, 1994), 9. The poem is also found in the anthology *El rumor del tiempo* (Barcelona: Galaxia Gutemberg, 2006).

At the "Mentitoio"

1. "Nothing demands more caution than the truth: 'tis the lancet of the heart": Baltasar Gracián, *The Art of Worldly Wisdom*, trans. Joseph Jacobs (Mineola, N.Y.: Dover, 2005), 64, no. clxxxi.

A Father, a Son

1. The description of *Portrait of Antonio Anselmi* from the website of the Thyssen-Bornemisza Collection reads: "Titian focuses all his attention

on the face, which is highly finished and emerges from the background into which the clothing, hair and beard almost disappear. Only the white of the collar and the fur trim around it stand out and function to emphasise the features still further, particularly Anselmi's gaze." Museo Thyssen-Bornemisza, https://www.museothyssen.org/en/collection/artists/titian/portrait-antonio -anselmi (accessed May 26, 2017).

The Fortunate Isles

1. "Now I want / Spirits to enforce, art to enchant, / And my ending is despair, / Unless I be relieved by prayer." Spoken by Prospero in William Shakespeare, *The Tempest*, act 5, epilogue.

The Old Prussia Puts On a Show

1. "A hundred years later, in 1931, Hoffmann's name appeared on the 'List of Forbidden Authors' of the Paris bookseller José Corti—a centre of surrealism. So after having been condemned by Scott, Goethe and Hegel for his morbid, pathological, chaotic disorder, he was now rejected by the surrealists." Michael Haldane, *Little Ernest, Great Ernst: The Trials and Tribulations of E.T.A. Hoffmann in English, with Especial Reference to His "Klein Zaches, genannt Zinnober,"* rev. M.A. diss., available at http://www.michaelhaldane .com/HoffmannDissertation.htm#_edn31 (accessed August 21, 2017).

2. Wilhelm Voigt, an ex-convict and impostor, impersonated a Prussian Guards officer, the Captain of Köpenick.

3. In *Grand Illusion* (1937), Jean Renoir's antiwar masterpiece depicting French soldiers held in a World War I German prison camp, Erich von Stroheim plays Captain von Rauffenstein.

4. The reference is to the film *Nashville*, a 1975 American satirical musical comedy-drama directed by Robert Altman, which portrays people involved in the gospel and country-music businesses in Nashville, Tennessee.

The Wall

1. Alfred Döblin's *Berlin Alexanderplatz* (1929) is said to be the first German novel to adopt the technique of James Joyce.

In Freiburg the Day of German Unity Is Remote

1. The Federal Republic of Germany and the Democratic Republic of Germany united into a single, federal Germany on October 3, 1990. German Unity Day (Tag der Deutschen Einheit) is celebrated annually on October 3 to mark the anniversary of the nation's unification.

The Dying Forest

1. "Man is not the lord of beings. Man is the shepherd of Being." Martin Heidegger, "Letter on Humanism," in *Basic Writings: Martin Heidegger*, ed. David Farrell Krell (Abingdon, U.K.: Routledge, 1993), 167.

2. Cf. Heidegger's essay "The Question Concerning Technology," ibid.

Ludwig's Castles in the Air

1. Richard Wagner's *Kaisermarsch*, composed in 1871, is a patriotic march celebrating the formation of the German Empire following the victorious Franco-Prussian War and the proclamation of William I, king of Prussia, as the new nation's emperor.

Among the Sorbs of Lusatia

1. The reference is to the December 25, 1911, entry of Kafka's *Diaries* in which Kafka discusses minor literatures.

2. "Our land is small, my friend, / And our people, too, like a tiny islet / In the midst of the great sea. . . . A land which will remain eternally Sorbian. / The spirit of the people / Must swell with life / And bring together these scattered members / Into one mighty unit, with ardent love / For the Sorbian language and Sorbian soil. / May you, too, know this: we remain Sorbs!" From Jakub Bart-Ćišinski, "My Sorbian Confession" (1891), in *An Anthology of Sorbian Poetry: From the Sixteenth Century to the Present Day: A Rock Against These Alien Waves*, trans. and ed. Robert Elsie (Boston: UNESCO/Forest Books, 1990).

3. The tale "Beauty with the Gold Star" in *The Collected Sicilian Folk and Fairy Tales of Giuseppe Pitré*, ed. and trans. Jack Zipes and Joseph Russo (Abingdon, U.K.: Routledge, 2008), tells of seven rivers, seven mountains,

and seven forests that must be crossed to find the land of the Beauty with the Gold Star.

The Anonymous Viennese

1. The reference is to the story "A Friend of Kafka" in Isaac Bashevis Singer, *A Friend of Kafka and Other Stories* (New York: Farrar, Straus and Giroux, 1979).

2. Bertoldo, the title character in a work by Giulio Cesare Croce, is an ill-treated peasant who with incredible cunning always manages to reclaim his dignity. When forced to bow down, he refuses to do so, but when King Alboino has the top of the doorway into the throne room lowered so Bertoldo will be forced to bow when he enters, he goes in bowing, but walking backward, showing his buttocks.

3. The "constitutional arch" refers to the parties that formulated Italy's postwar constitution.

The Rabbi's Dance

1. "To me, however, the whole world is a homeland, like the sea to fish—though I drank from the Arno before cutting my teeth, and love Florence so much that, because I loved her, I suffer exile unjustly." Dante Alighieri, *De Vulgari eloquentia*, trans. Steven Botterill (Cambridge: Cambridge University Press, 2005), 13.

Musical Automatons in Zagreb

1. Legend has it that Saint Albert the Great, whose disciple was Saint Thomas Aquinas, constructed a robotic automaton in the form of a brass bust that answered questions.

Istrian Spring

1. "*Gò perso i me morti. / La povara Italia / xe tanto distrata.*" (I lost my deceased. / Poor Italy / is so distracted.) From Giacomo Noventa, "Mi vegno da Pola (lamento di un pescatore, profugo da Pola)," in *Versi e poesie*, ed. Franco Manfriani (Venice: Marsilio, 1986). The poem is dedicated to a

fisherman-refugee who lost everything—his house, his boat, his roots, his memories—in the exodus from Pola. Claudio Magris writes about it in the article "Oltre la nostalgia," *Corriere della Sera*, September 14, 1987.

Cici and *Ciribiri*

1. Sweet coal is a sugary, crunchy type of candy that resembles a lump of coal.

2. The primary task of the zvončari, or "bellmen," is scaring off winter's evil spirits and reawakening a new spring season; at Carnival time zvončari march from village to village throughout the region.

3. Torquato Accetto's *On Honest Dissimulation* was originally published in 1641; during the reign of fascism it was used to make the point that not all dissimulation is dishonest, a message meant to relieve the uneasy consciences of those too young to speak out openly against the regime.

In Bisiacaria

1. The nationalist poet Gabriele D'Annunzio was often referred to as Il Vate, the Poet, or Il Profeta, the Prophet, because of the inspirational notes in his work.

On the Charles Bridge

1. The slogan "All power to the imagination!" was popular with students during the late 1960s, who adapted it from Herbert Marcuse's *Eros and Civilization: A Philosophical Inquiry into Freud* (Boston: Beacon, 1955).

2. "By chance, I asked, 'You are from Prague, Doctor?' 'I *was* from Prague,' he answered." From Jorge Luis Borges, "Guayaquil," *Doctor Brodie's Report*, trans. Norman Thomas di Giovanni (New York: Dutton, 1972), 127.

The Tragedy and the Nightmare

1. Magris mentions Poldy Beck and his tract *Das Buch der Pfiffe* in a piece called "Of Central Europe: Myths and Reality," *Contemporary European Affairs* 3, no. 3 (1990), published as *European Immigration Policy* (Oxford: Pergamon, 1991), 181.

Poland Turns the Page

1. Czesław Miłosz, *Rodzinna Europa* (1959). The title of the English translation, *Native Realm: A Search for Self-Definition*, trans. Catherine S. Leach (New York: Farrar, Straus and Giroux, 2002), expresses Miłosz's desire to explain who he is as a representative of the part of Eastern Europe that he comes from.

The Woodland Cemetery

1. "Avevamo studiato per l'aldilà / un fischio, un segno di riconoscimento. / Mi provo a modularlo nella speranza / che tutti siamo già morti senza saperlo." (We had devised a whistle / as our signal of recognition in the afterlife. / I try to modulate it now in the hope / that we all are dead already without knowing it.) From Eugenio Montale's "Xenia," IV, in memory of the poet's wife. "Eleven Poems from *Xenia* of Eugenio Montale," trans. Helen Barolini, *Quarterly Review of Literature Poetry Retrospective*, 1974.

The Fjord

1. The reference is to the uprisings of 1848 (*Quarantotto*) and the war of 1859 (*Cinquantanove*).

Water and Desert

1. "A Letter for Tomorrow" (also referred to as "A Letter for the Future"), May 3, 2004, was an open letter from Mohammad Khatami, president of Iran at the time, addressed to the citizens of Iran, especially the youth.

2. In Brecht's *The Life of Galileo*, Andrea says, "Unhappy the land that has no heroes," and Galileo replies, "No, unhappy the land that needs heroes." Bertolt Brecht, *Life of Galileo* (Leben des Galilei), a play written in 1938 and first performed (in German) in 1943.

3. Friedrich Nietzsche, *Thus Spoke Zarathustra*, trans. Thomas Common (e-artnow, 2017). German: "Dem Reinen ist Alles rein—so spricht das Volk. Ich aber sage euch: den Schweinen wird Alles Schwein!"

Is China Near?

1. *China Is Near* (*La Cina è vicina*) is a 1967 Italian film written and directed by Marco Bellocchio. The title of the film, which portrays small-town provincial politics, was a Maoist slogan smeared on a wall near the headquarters of the Italian Socialist Party in those years; Bellocchio thought it was funny, provocative, and absurd, a way of saying that a revolutionary wind could actually sweep away the parasitic politicians of the time.

2. At one time the term "Middle Kingdom" designated the Zhou Empire in the north of China, whose people, unaware of civilizations in the West, believed their empire occupied the middle of the earth and was surrounded by barbarians.

The Borders of Vietnam

1. Situated between rivers, built from lowland, Hanoi has many scenic lakes and is sometimes called the "city of lakes." The Trấn Quốc Pagoda is a Buddhist temple located on the outskirts of the city, on a small island near the shore of Ho Tay (West Lake). It is the oldest pagoda in the city, originally constructed in the sixth century, and thus about fourteen hundred years old. A small causeway links it to the mainland.

The Great South

1. The Isle of the Dead was used as the graveyard for the penal settlement of Port Arthur from 1833 to 1877.

CLAUDIO MAGRIS is the author of the best-selling novels *Danube* and *Microcosms*, which have been translated into over twenty languages. He was awarded the Erasmus Prize in 2001, the Prince of Asturias Prize in 2004, the Premio Viareggio Tobino (writer of the year) in 2007, the 2009 Friedenspreis, and the FIL Prize in Hispanic Literature in 2014, and is a perennial contender for the Nobel Prize in Literature. Magris has also been a professor of Germanic studies at the University of Trieste since 1978 and is currently writer-in-residence at the University of Utrecht. In addition to being an author and a scholar, he has translated into Italian authors such as Ibsen, Kleist, Schnitzler, Buchner, and Grillparzer.

ANNE MILANO APPEL, Ph.D., was awarded the Italian Prose in Translation Award (2015), the John Florio Prize for Italian Translation (2013), and the Northern California Book Awards for Translation-Fiction (2013, 2014). She has translated works by Claudio Magris, Primo Levi, Giovanni Arpino, Paolo Giordano, Roberto Saviano, Giuseppe Catozzella, and numerous others.